SOMEWHERE IN AMERICA

SOMEWHERE IN AMERICA

☆ Under the Radar
with Chicken Warriors,
Left-Wing Patriots,
Angry Nudists, and Others

MARK SINGER

HOUGHTON MIFFLIN COMPANY

BOSTON • NEW YORK   2004

Copyright © 2004 by Mark Singer
All rights reserved

For information about permission to reproduce selections
from this book, write to Permissions, Houghton Mifflin Company,
215 Park Avenue South, New York, New York 10003.

Visit our Web site: www.houghtonmifflinbooks.com.

ISBN-13: 978-0-618-19724-9   ISBN-10: 0-618-19724-9

Library of Congress Cataloging-in-Publication Data
Singer, Mark.
Somewhere in America : under the radar with chicken warriors,
left-wing patriots, angry nudists, and others / Mark Singer.
p.   cm.
ISBN 0-618-19724-9
1. United States—Social life and customs—1971—Anecdotes.
2. United States—Social conditions—1980—Anecdotes.
3. United States—History, Local—Anecdotes. 4. City and
town life—United States—Anecdotes.   I. Title.
E169.04S625 2004
973.92'09732—dc22   2004040506

Printed in the United States of America

Book design by Victoria Hartman

MP 10 9 8 7 6 5 4 3 2 1

All of the essays in this book were previously published
in *The New Yorker,* two under different titles.

FOR MY PARENTS

CONTENTS

SOMEWHERE IN AMERICA

INTRODUCTION

GROWING UP, I made a lot of trips along the turn-pike between Oklahoma's two largest cities (by my demographic reckoning, its *only* two cities) — Tulsa, where I was born and raised, and Oklahoma City. My grandparents, both sets, lived in Oklahoma City, as did an abundance of cousins, with plenty more scattered about the state. Except for my maternal grandparents, this bumper crop of relatives all came from my father's side. His parents happened to be first cousins, and in their generation and the next there were, oddly, a few other instances of intramarriage. Never mind the genetic consequences; how did this tricky-to-diagram extended family fit together? I wasn't interested in genealogy but in something more textured: How were we connected? What was our common story? And given that each of us, individually, possessed a story, what were the fine points?

My mother's mother had a particular talent for keeping the players and the details straight, a skill she honed during her frequent exposure to her son-in-law's large clan. Neither shy nor gregarious, Grandma Rose would obligingly meet you halfway; if you wanted to talk she would listen, and vice versa. As to why people seemed so willing to open up to her — not just near and distant relations, but strangers who abruptly ceased being strangers — she was pleasantly mystified: "I don't know what it is. I say hello, and they start telling me about themselves." I'm confident it never crossed Grandma Rose's mind that she had the makings of a terrific reporter, though I believe she did. My father liked to say that on a trip to the ladies' room she could collect enough information to write a biography. For a number of reasons, I enjoy ruminating about her DNA and mine.

Early on I grasped that by local standards my people were somewhat exotic, and I felt ambivalent about that. By and large, Tulsa was a forward-looking little metropolis. But it was also home to a lot of reactionary ideologues and noisy evangelists who made it their business to define the narrow limits of what was politically and culturally tolerable. I recall riding in a car with a school chum and his mother around the time that Khrushchev was pounding his shoe on the table and feeling constrained to clarify that my grandparents, all Jewish immigrants, had started out in Russia "back before it was Communist."

Part of me was in a rush for our family to assimilate. At the same time, I couldn't help loving the harmonies of my grandparents' conversations in Yiddish or the inflections of their contemporaries who had also made the unlikely journey from Eastern Europe to the middle of America, to the purlieu that not long before had been Indian Territory. I was equally enamored of the twangy rhythms and idioms of my other kinsmen, my fellow native Oklahomans. Tulsa was surrounded by poetically named rural communities (Bixby, Jenks, Turley, Skiatook) where the elders, deep-dyed Okie folk, tended to be Depression survivors whose experiences, in many respects, must have felt no less perilous or uncertain than a boat ride in steerage across the ocean. Just hearing those people talk — about anything (a hailstorm, a ball game, a cat in a tree, and would you be wantin' to try the fried okra today) — made me as curious about their stories as I was about my own family members'. It hadn't yet occurred to me, however, that I could go around asking strangers questions about themselves and earn a living that way.

My sense is that I gave little or no thought to what my adult life might be like, only that I would almost certainly live it someplace other than Oklahoma. (I could always come home again, I figured, for a visit of whatever duration.) I didn't realize that my desire to put distance between myself and a place I trusted and where I felt secure — that mixture of resolve and regret — meant that I was on my way to becoming a writer. That possibility dawned in an indirect, unanticipated way. One summer during college, when I repatriated briefly to work as a reporter for the *Tulsa Tribune* — a job my father helped arrange; I'd never previously worked for a newspaper or studied journalism — I heard a friend of my parents' favorably mention a new book by Calvin Trillin. The title was *U.S. Journal,* and it was a collection of articles that had appeared in *The New Yorker* under that same rubric. My parents subscribed to the magazine, but I'd never bothered to look at it other than to skim the cartoons. So when I got my hands on a copy of the book and read it in a couple of sittings, it was a revelation.

Evidently, Trillin came from the same corner of the world I did (if you granted, accurately, that northeastern Oklahoma belongs to the Midwest rather than the Southwest); there were allusions to his hometown, Kansas City. (Before long, I would be gratified to learn that he had attended my college and that his mother, still in Kansas City, lived in the same building as my grandmother's sister, Aunt Sally.) Each year he spent many weeks on the road, reporting about uncelebrated people, and the stories he wrote seemed to me sui generis renderings of life in America during a decade, the sixties, when change was occurring so rapidly and unpredictably that the country could barely catch its breath. Trillin's dispatches, unhurried and dispassionate, revealed his lucid understanding of how little pictures connected to the bigger picture. They were leavened with a deadpan irony, so deftly applied that the writing never got in the way of the storytelling. ("In rural Alabama, people who belong to organizations like the Ku Klux Klan often have a strong notion of general philosophy but get mixed up on the details.") The dialogue reflected an affection, wherever he traveled, for the American vernacular. ("'In them times . . . a man fightin' the Klan around here had about as much chance as a one-legged man at a tail-kickin'.'") Trillin avoided sociological cant or pre-scriptive pronouncements. He made no bloviating attempts to Tie Everything Together. I suppose the fact that he came from Missouri, the Show Me State, accounted for his congenial blend of openness and bemused skepticism. Above all, what excited me about his writing was its implicit notion that a lone reporter could arrive in an unfamiliar locale where some event resonating beyond that specific place had occurred (or was still unfolding), and within a few days, by getting just the right people to open up, could unravel what had happened and how lives had been affected. The revelation was that I had stumbled upon a plausible vocation.

Within a few years, I'd been hired as a reporter for *The New Yorker*. My first day on the premises, I met Trillin, and we quickly became friends (eventually, close friends; he and his wife, Alice, became the godparents of one of my sons). I had a lot of catch-up reading to do. *The New Yorker* had by then been around for almost fifty years, and the received wisdom was that the publica-tion of certain book-length articles — John Hersey's *Hiroshima*, Hannah Arendt's *Eichmann in Jerusalem*, Rachel Carson's *Silent Spring*, Truman Capote's *In Cold Blood*, Jonathan Schell's *The Vil-lage of Ben Suc* — had forged the magazine's role in the culture and its reputation as a paragon of serious, worthy, *literary* journal-ism. I got busy reading (or rereading) those books, then segued to Liebling, Mitchell, Thurber, White, McKelway, Gibbs, Rovere, Tynan, and Arlen, among others. New additions to the core canon were being hatched — John McPhee's *Coming Into the Country*, Schell's *The Fate of the Earth*, Jane Kramer's *The Last Cowboy*, Susan Sheehan's *A Welfare Mother*, Janet Malcolm's *The Impossi-ble Profession* — and Trillin, meanwhile, continued to file "U.S. Journal" pieces. In all, he kept it up for sixteen years — a new in-stallment every three weeks, with time off every summer — from

1966 to 1982. In my mind, this was not merely a feat emblematic of what *The New Yorker*, at its best, represented; it was the journalistic equivalent of Gehrig's consecutive-games-played record (Cal Ripken Jr. was yet to come), with highlights from DiMaggio's fifty-six-game hitting streak thrown in.

In the summer of 2000, David Remnick, the editor of *The New Yorker*, and I agreed that I would begin writing, on a regular basis, "U.S. Journal"–like stories. What would this series be called? The "U.S. Journal" rubric had been retired since 1982 — and, I felt, deserved to stay retired, but Remnick proposed that we revive it. He checked with Trillin, who didn't object, and almost three decades after I'd fantasized about being a reporter with such a beat, it was mine. Remnick's only specific advice was to urge me to find my own rhythm — none of that every-three-weeks stuff.

A reporter cold-calling someone, explaining that he's working on such-and-such a story and would like to ask a few questions, often hears "Before I talk to you, I want to know what your angle's going to be." My reply is always some variation of "I'm a blank slate — I don't have an angle." What I don't add, though it's true, is that all my stories are really "about" one thing: my curiosity. Whatever the facts might be, I'm trying to get a fix on how this connects to that — in pursuit of my lifelong preoccupation with how we're all connected. When someone agrees to an interview, once we start talking I'm doing my best to channel Grandma Rose.

Choosing subjects, my ambition has been to stick with what some editors refer to as "under-the-radar stuff" — one complication being that, with the advent of 24/7 cable news, *USA Today*, the national edition of the *New York Times*, the Internet, the anywhere, anytime satellite link and simultaneous cyber-feed, and the Weblog, the radar has progressively gotten lower. With the exception of three consecutive post–September 11 stories and an attempt (foiled by the FBI!) to cover the first scheduled execution of Timothy McVeigh, my meanderings have rarely been dictated by what seemed to be the news of the day. During the months leading up to the war in Iraq I was on a leave of absence and so filed no reports from the home front; by the time I was ready to travel again, the story that grabbed my attention, because, under the radar, it had upset the lives of people all over the country, involved a worm-farming Ponzi scheme.

THE AMERICA THAT I encountered in Trillin's early "U.S. Journal" stories was, in its physical particulars (as well as by many sociological measures), manifestly different from the one that awaited me. Most conspicuously, regional boundaries and characteristics have blurred. On a reporting trip a couple years back, I awoke from a deep afternoon nap in my hotel room and, unable to remember where I was, looked out the window but still couldn't come up with the answer and finally had to consult the phone directory. It turned out I was in Cincinnati. (The story I'd gone there to research — the aftermath of the fatal shooting of a young black man by a white policeman — shares a theme with several pieces in this book: our perpetual national wound, the racial divide.) When I'm not feeling sleep-deprived, I can usually get a reasonably quick fix on the difference between, say, western Montana and coastal New Jersey, but the sprawl in North Carolina is disturbingly indistinguishable from the sprawl in northern California or southern Ohio or you name it.

One thing I'm not on the lookout for is the proverbial "colorful" or "weird" character or narrative, especially now that exotic behavior of the spurious, ready-for-reality-T.V. variety has become ubiquitous. What does strike me as authentic is the degree to which America, in this new century, has become a land of deep unease. Increasingly, I'm drawn to stories about how people, one way or another, are earnestly trying to hold on to something — whether it's the "right" to pray at a high school football game or skinny-dip on someone else's property or promote cockfighting or wave the Confederate flag or refuse to pledge allegiance to the American flag. Snowmobilers colonize a remote outpost in Montana, and anyone who objects to their presence becomes a pariah. Three brothers, orphaned by a suicide terrorist, manage to enrage their New England neighbors by proposing to turn the family farm into a luxury golf course. A café proprietor in western Massachusetts decides it's time to retire and an entire town fears that its soul is imperiled. A Texas community loses its weekly newspaper and the social fabric begins to fray. In eastern Oklahoma, an early-retirement couple watch the stock market swallow their savings, then mortgage their house to finance a dubious earthworm-breeding operation. Trying not to appear desperate, we seek security in unlikely places, with uncertain results.

The notion that we necessarily have a common story now strikes me as naive, but that hasn't stopped me from looking for, and hoping to find, whatever it is that does connect us. I am a pathologically optimistic person: not that I believe everything's going to turn out just swell, but that hope doesn't hurt. Americans are notorious for their ravenous appetites, and I can't help, reflexively, wanting/hoping for more. So, perhaps quaintly, I still want to go to a place, somewhere on the map, where someone has a story to tell. That a tale matters to its teller usually means that it also matters to me. There's been an uneven geographic distribution to my datelines — a matter of happenstance rather than design. Typically, I plan my travel schedule weeks in advance but with rarely a clue as to where I'll wind up. Often there's a last-minute scramble, involving scattershot readings of on-line editions of newspapers, that dictates my destination. I've checked out story possibilities in all fifty states and, inevitably, I believe, will get to all of them — just as, inevitably, each time I board a plane at LaGuardia I believe I'm heading home.

THE CHICKEN WARRIORS

Kingston, Oklahoma
JANUARY 2001

IT'S TRUE that I hadn't absolutely made up my mind to join the Oklahoma Gamefowl Breeders Association. Still, I felt let down when, preemptively, I was deprived of the opportunity. Ever since last winter, after I was nominated but failed to get elected to the Oklahoma Journalism Hall of Fame, I've been looking for ways to pad my résumé in my native state. Which explains, in part, how one Friday morning in mid-December, in the wake of a sleet storm, I wound up driving from Oklahoma City toward Kingston, on the Texas border. Specifically, I was on my way to a two-day cockfighting derby at the members-only Texoma Game Club, where, as I understood the protocols, I'd be expected to pay twenty dollars and pledge allegiance to the Gamefowl Breeders before being allowed inside — never mind that the sum of my avian holdings is a couple of faint-hearted parakeets. As I pondered what sorts of friendship I might forge, I weighed some conflicting information I'd received from two reliable sources, both attentive students of the cockfighting subculture.

Janet Halliburton, the chairman of the Oklahoma Coalition

Against Cockfighting — a political-action committee pushing for an initiative that, in all likelihood, would result in Oklahoma's becoming the forty-eighth state to outlaw this quaint pastime (Louisiana and New Mexico are the other holdouts) — had suggested, "While you're down there with the cockfighters, make sure you keep an eye out for the guy who showed up to harass me at the state fair in Oklahoma City when I was trying to gather petition signatures. He had the tattoo of a headless nude female torso running from his shoulder to his elbow."

On the other hand, Gregory Albert, an Oklahoma Supreme Court referee who had recently spent a month listening to the sworn testimony of cockfighters determined to defend and preserve their way of life, had told me, "People who engage in cockfighting look just like everybody else. Cockfighters are like the couple next door, or the Waltons. They're just people."

After stopping for a maximum-cholesterol late breakfast — buttered hotcakes and sunny-side-ups — at a place called Hobo Joe's, in the blink-and-you-miss-it town of Madill, I traveled ten more miles until I came upon a gymnasium-size building with a cream-colored metal exterior, set back about a hundred yards from the highway. No signs identified it as the Texoma Game Club, but I knew from the fence postings that said "Private Property" and "No Trespassing" — the unwelcoming scrutiny of a beady-eyed gatekeeper was another tip-off — that this was the place. Among the curious allurements of the Texoma Game Club is that it's a strictly-within-the-law establishment whose operators have cultivated the coy ambience of a speakeasy.

While I waited, the sentry went to find James Tally, the president of the Gamefowl Breeders. He materialized five minutes later, a sallow blond-going-gray fellow in his mid-fifties with a mustache and the slightly mournful demeanor of someone burdened by unwieldy responsibilities. We stepped into a narrow hallway lined with snapshots of cockfighters posing with tournament trophies, and before I realized what was happening — that is, before I had a chance to compromise my professional integrity or even to equivocate — he escorted me past a ticket booth. No one demanded to see proof of my membership in the Gamefowl Breeders Association or the Texoma Game Club. Just like that, dang, I'd been granted journalistic immunity.

Tally, a Union Pacific freight-train conductor who lives not far from Kingston with his wife, two stepchildren, two dogs, three hundred roosters, and seventy-five hens, introduced me to the Texoma owners, a slender white-haired Alabama native named Roy and a straight-talking, compactly built brunette named Judy, who made it clear that they weren't eager to see their last names in print. Then we settled in the stands, where steeply raked rows of cushiony yellow theater chairs surrounded a dirt-floored, wire-enclosed, eighteen-by-twenty-six-foot fight pit. Occasions arise during the cockfighting season, which runs from November through July, when the Texoma crowds reach capacity — a little over seven hundred — but at the moment the place was less than half filled. Red and silver tinsel and Christmas lights had been strung along the top of the wire cage, a homey touch that went nicely, I thought, with the disingenuous "No Gambling" signs that had been affixed to each of its four sides.

Inside the cage, a couple of black roosters equipped with two-inch stainless steel weapons on both legs were trying to perform surgery on each other. This was one of seventy or so bouts during what Tally described as "a prelim-type deal," a warm-up for the next day's Christmas Derby — a four-cock tournament followed by a seven-cock tournament. The way the scoring worked, not all the livestock would see action; cockfighters who fared poorly in the early rounds would be eliminated, and their remaining birds would, for the time being, be spared. The entry fee was a hundred dollars on Friday and three hundred on Saturday, and the triumphant handlers stood to take home a few thousand dollars, plus or minus their ancillary winnings or losses if, like virtually everyone else on the premises, they neglected to obey the "No Gambling" injunction.

Not that cockfighting is mainly about, or really is in any way about, money, I was repeatedly informed; it's about freedom — nowadays, especially, the freedom not to get pushed around by the anticockfighting lobby. "We don't solicit people to come to rooster fighting," Roy, the proprietor, said. "People who come, ninety percent been doin' it all their lives. It's part of our national heritage. I'm gonna bet you there's never been a rooster fighter asked an animal rights activist to come to a rooster fight, and I'll bet you an animal rights activist never invited a rooster fighter to one of their events. And that's all right with me. All we want to do is break even: they leave us alone, we leave them alone" — "they" being the Oklahoma Coalition Against Cockfighting and its fellow-travelers, the sinister forces arrayed to try to put out of business Roy and Judy and the forty-one other cockfight-pit operators in Oklahoma, along with countless game-fowl breeders scattered around the state, many of whom had emigrated from jurisdictions where the lawmakers took a dim view of people who amuse themselves by watching animals battle to the death.

I STUCK AROUND both days and did witness quite a few cockfights. At one point, with a red Hatch Roundhead and a Hatch Grey cross and their handlers standing poised for battle, and the cacophonous gentlemanly wagering that precedes each fight getting under way ("Bet fifty on the red! . . . Lay a hunnerd to your eighty! . . . Call eighty!"), I felt like an agnostic trying to ignore a gospel choir as I resisted the temptation to do a little gentlemanly wagering myself. But it was mainly the particulars of the fight over cockfighting, rather than cockfighting itself, that interested me.

When Oklahoma joined the union in 1907, its criminal code, a vestige from territorial days, was generally understood to outlaw cockfighting. Anyone "who maliciously, or for any bet, stake, or reward, instigates or encourages any fight between animals, or instigates or encourages any animal to attack, bite, wound or worry another" was guilty of a misdemeanor. (I recall, from an eighth grade course in Oklahoma history, that the brave pioneers also made it illegal to get a fish drunk.) The cockfighting ban survived until 1963, when a decision by the Oklahoma Court of Criminal Appeals prevented a county judge from proceeding with the trial of a half-dozen citizens who had been caught in flagrante. The defendants argued, among other things, that the law was insufficiently explicit, and the appellate panel unanimously agreed, establishing the foundation upon which the local cockfighting industry thrives to this day. The opinion, written by the chief judge, Kirksey Nix, remains noteworthy as a novel theological treatise. After quoting Genesis and its delineation of the distinctions between the "fish of the sea" and "the fowl of the air" and "every beast of the field," Judge Nix asked rhetorically, "Is a 'gamecock' an animal?" Though stopping short of a flat-out declaration that it wasn't, he nevertheless found that "persons of ordinary intelligence" could read the law and not necessarily grasp that it covered chickens. What the authors really intended to prohibit, he surmised, was organized dogfighting.

Nix concluded his opinion with the tongue-in-cheek observation "The Legislature is now in session and if it so desires, it can make a direct approach to the act complained of by making cockfighting an offense against the state." Judge Nix knew the tenor of the legislature, an institution in the grip of rural logic, and he understood that a law against cockfighting was as likely to get adopted as a law making Russian the official language. In the decades since, not much has changed. During one memorable debate several years ago, a noble statesman from Muskogee named John Monks declared, "In every country the Communists have taken over, the first thing they do is outlaw cockfighting." The last time the question arose in the legislature, two years ago, it was dead on arrival: an anticockfighting bill proposed by a representative from Oklahoma City also would have outlawed such sacrosanct diversions as rodeos, coon hunts, and rattlesnake roundups, and might as well have included football games and church suppers.

Lately, however, the cockfighters have come up against formidable opposition. Oklahoma is one of many states that allow citizen initiatives, a cumbersome constitutional provision that makes it possible to circumvent a recalcitrant legislature. In the fall of 1999, anticockfighting canvassers, concentrating their efforts in Oklahoma City and Tulsa, collected signatures endorsing a vote on a proposed new law that would define as felonious behavior just about everything I witnessed at the Texoma Game Club — except for the act of merely being a spectator, which would be a misdemeanor.

When the petition drive ended, the secretary of state certified that the canvassers had gathered thirty thousand more signatures than were needed to place the question on the ballot in the next statewide general election. (Public-opinion surveys, meanwhile, indicated that two out of three voters favored outlawing cockfighting.) The Gamefowl Breeders Association responded by challenging the validity of tens of thousands of signatures. That the proposed law wasn't voted on in last November's general election — and may not be in the foreseeable future — is, if you ask most cockfighters, a consequence of their tenacity and organizational skills and the adroitness of their lawyers. The cockfighting opponents are more inclined to attribute the delay to the boorish behavior of certain cockfighters and, above all, foot-dragging by the Oklahoma Supreme Court. This past fall, after a month of hearings, the Supreme Court referee Albert — he of the belief that cockfighters are just like the folks next door — upheld enough of the cockfighters' objections so that, in the end, the petition proponents came up almost eleven thousand short. The anticockfighters have formally challenged the referee's decision and are awaiting a hearing by the full Supreme Court. The cockfighters, naturally, don't see any reason to rush.

WHEN JANET HALLIBURTON agreed to become the chairman of the anticockfighting campaign, it had nothing to do with the fact that as a child she owned a pet rooster named Ichabod, which died a semi-natural death after "a varmint, most likely a skunk or a badger," invaded the henhouse. Halliburton is somewhere in her forties and has streaked blond hair and a seeming disinclination to smile. For twenty years — until last spring, when she opted for early retirement — she was the chief counsel of the Oklahoma State Bureau of Investigation, which probably accounts for her clipped, coplike diction. In our first conversation, she made a point of telling me, "I used to ride in rodeo barrel races. I love animals, but I regard them as property." She elaborated: "My father's side of the family is from southeastern Oklahoma. We have land there and we run cattle on it . . . steers that are going to be slaughtered. My brother-in-law hunts deer and turkeys on that land. He fishes there, too. I'm not a vegetarian and I don't believe that animals have rights."

Such sentiments might not seem to qualify her as the cockfighters' nemesis, but she is that nevertheless. In the fall of 1998, during a seminar organized by the Oklahoma Humane Federation, an animal-welfare coalition, Halliburton delivered a presentation on the links between violence against animals and human violence. The following spring, the federation, encouraged by successful anticockfighting crusades in Missouri and Arizona, decided to mobilize a similar effort in Oklahoma. Precisely because Halliburton didn't fit anyone's stereotype of an animal rights activist, she was drafted to be chairman. Recently, when I asked whether she regretted having gotten involved, she said, "It seemed like a sensible thing to do. I thought the cockfighters just had the issue buttonholed in the legislature, and if you give the people a chance to vote they'll solve the problem. But I didn't realize that from A to B was so far."

The moments during the campaign that Halliburton least enjoyed, she says, occurred when petition gatherers were verbally menaced, threatened with physical harm, and spat on. More than once, her car was followed. One morning, she found a dead rooster in her backyard. She received so many harassing phone calls at home that she had to get an unlisted number. Harassing phone calls at work, including some to her superiors, contributed to her premature retirement. Early in the campaign, she gave an interview to a public television station in which she alluded to reports that prostitution, illegal gambling, and illicit drugs proliferated in the vicinity of cockfighting pits. These comments prompted two game-fowl breeders to sue her for slander, which she says came as a surprise: "None of the cockfighters I met impressed me as being public television watchers." When the anti-cockfighters tried to gather petition signatures at a crafts festival in a suburb of Oklahoma City, a group of cockfighters who didn't resemble the Waltons showed up and the festival manager asked them to leave. "They went away and came back carrying signs that said, 'Don't Ban Cockfighting. Don't Ban Christmas in Schools,'" Halliburton said. "They told people about me, 'She's an atheist and head of the atheist movement in Oklahoma.' At the time, I was a deacon in my church. And my dad's a minister."

Much of this mischief was the handiwork of the Oklahoma Animal Coalition, a splinter faction of rather more militant cockfighters organized by a gung-ho breeder named Chuck Berry, whose general estimation of the Gamefowl Breeders leadership was that it was "unprepared and unmotivated to deal with the problem." The Berry shock troops' standard tactic was to appear at anticockfighting rallying spots and intercept potential petition signers, urging them to read carefully what they were about to endorse. The coalition also paid for newspaper ads stating that if the cockfighting opponents succeeded their next endeavor would be to make pet ownership illegal. At Texoma, I met Anthony Villalobos Jr., one of Berry's cohorts. During an Oktoberfest event at a park in Tulsa, Villalobos recalled, he and a few fellow tricksters mingled with petition gatherers, some of whom carried "Ban Cockfighting" signs, and held up signs of their own that said "Ban Hunting" and "Ban Fishing."

"They called me the Tulsa Area Harassment Coordinator," he said. "If you want someone harassed in the Tulsa area in a coordinated fashion, I'm the man to see. Just before Thanksgiving, the *Tulsa World* ran an editorial asking both sides to call their troops off, to cool the rhetoric. But then the other side went out and started collecting signatures on Thanksgiving Day. When we found out about it, we had just enough time to finish our turkey and get back out in the streets."

Such stratagems wouldn't have been necessary, the cockfighters say, if their adversaries hadn't stooped to various forms of carpetbagging, including soliciting assistance from subversive organizations like the Humane Society of the United States, raising money from out-of-state animal-protection groups, and employing so-called petition gypsies — itinerant professional canvassers who weren't necessarily legal residents of Oklahoma. In his final report, the Supreme Court referee Albert more or less agreed, invoking the phrase "outside agitators." Despite such xenophobic flourishes, Albert appeared to be evenhanded. He disqualified more than four thousand signatures collected by a petition gypsy who gave as his legal address what turned out to be a vacant lot. But Albert agreed to accept more than seventy-five hundred gathered by a hermit who gave as *his* address an abandoned house. In the end, the majority of the disqualified signatures were tossed out on technical grounds, because the signers' addresses, when compared with those listed in voter-registration records, didn't precisely match.

*   *   *

GAME-FOWL BREEDERS seem to derive perverse enjoyment from being accused, usually by animal rights activists, of "training" otherwise pacifist birds to fight. The scientific explanation for combative rooster behavior, they're happy to point out, is rooted in Darwinism and DNA, an inbred male desire to control sexual territory — literally, an uncontrollable urge to impress chicks. And it's not only because humans, when they engage in approximately the same activity, tend not to have sharp weapons strapped to their limbs that their mortality rate is much lower. "A rooster's testosterone level, per body weight, is seventeen times greater than a male *Homo sapiens*'," a breeder named Jimmy Tyler told me. "So they can't help themselves. They're gonna kill one another." Or, as another breeder, Kurt Oleksuk, said as he was on his way to collect his trophy and prize money after winning the four-cock preliminary tournament at Texoma, "Very rarely, you'll get a rooster that won't face, that won't show courage. And if you do an autopsy you'll find that he'll have only one nut or a deformed testicle, in almost every case."

The crowd-stirring action in a cockfight typically occurs in the first thirty seconds. That's when the birds, though aerodynamically ill-equipped for sustained flight, actually do levitate, generally about as high as an average small-college Caucasian basketball player can jump. Most cockfighting pits offer combat with a variety of metal weapons — gaff (sharp point, no cutting edge, worn in pairs), short knife (one inch), and long knife (two inches). The knives are sickle-shaped, are worn on only one leg, and usually have only one edge sharpened: knife duels usually end in swift death for the loser and, quite often, permanent disability for the ostensible winner.

At Texoma, whenever a fight lasted longer than about five minutes, the birds, their handlers, and the referee would shift from the central pit to one of three contiguous combat areas, or drag pits, beneath the grandstand, trailed by spectators with financial interests in the outcome. Some fights went on for almost an hour, adhering to specific and complicated endgame rules. As often as not, the denouement was the equivalent of a technical knockout: one bird, through injury, fatigue, testosterone deficiency, or perhaps existential despair, couldn't or wouldn't respond to his opponent, who was deemed to possess superior "gameness."

Shortly after nine o'clock the morning of the Christmas Derby, I found James Tally standing in one of the drag pits, looking more preoccupied than usual. He hadn't gotten much sleep the night before, he said; he had a lot of details on his mind, and at the moment he was struggling with a friend's lively Hatch Grey rooster. The cock wouldn't stop sexually harassing a couple of hens with which it had been sharing a cage, and Tally, wearing a crimson Oklahoma Gamefowl Breeders Association warm-up jacket, had the bird under one arm while someone hunted for an extra cage. Hens normally don't make appearances at cockfighting pits, but these were on hand because a brood-stock auction was scheduled for that morning. Several breeders had donated trios, a rooster and two hens, and the proceeds — the trios would bring prices ranging from five hundred to twelve hundred and fifty dollars — would go to the Gamefowl Breeders legal fund.

Before the auction, two attorneys who represented the cock-fighters in the initiative-petition challenge, Larry Oliver and Lee Slater, entered the fighting pit and addressed the crowd. Oliver, a broad-shouldered, gray-haired former police officer and the current vice chief justice of the supreme court of the Creek Nation, wore black jeans, black boots, a red turtleneck, a black ski vest, and a broad-brimmed black cowboy hat with a turquoise hatband, and did most of the talking. "Let me tell you somethin' about my good friend James Tally," he began. "He got me a hotel room last night. I told him this morning I wasn't gonna complain about the water being cold. I wasn't gonna complain about the light that wouldn't turn off, so I had to fish around under the bed to unplug it. But I was gonna complain that there's no girls come with it. . . . Hey, what about those Sooners?" — a reference to the University of Oklahoma's undefeated, Orange Bowl–bound football team — "Tell me about 'em, huh? Aren't they great? Lemme ask you another question: What about those cockfighters? Aren't they great? When the Sooners started their season, nobody thought they'd get anywhere, did they? When y'all started this process, did anybody think you'd get anywhere with it? Both of you are world champions. I think the referee's decision will stand. I've often said, and it's no truer ever before than it is now, there ain't no lawyer any better'n his clients. And you people united and brought yourselves together, and you're the best clients a lawyer could ever expect to have."

In this upbeat and optimistic spirit, Oliver declined to dwell on a suggestion he'd floated several months earlier — that, in the event cockfighting was outlawed, the breeders should be compensated for their lost property, and the funds could come from a twenty-five-million-dollar payment due Oklahoma as its share of a multistate tobacco litigation settlement. On his way out, Oliver stopped by a table that was selling veterinary supplies — vitamins, hormones, antibiotics, appetite stimulants, parasite treatments — and picked up a jar of something called Cock Booster and another product called Pecker Wrecker. As he paid for them, he told me they were for "friends."

A scoreboard above the bleachers listed the Christmas Derby entries, which were identifiable by their fighting handles — Porkchop, Gunrunner, Showtime, Skeeter, Pinky & The Brain, Cold Blue Steel, Bad Company. There were a hundred and fifteen entries, which I gathered meant that something like fourteen hours of continuous cockfighting lay ahead. I had no illusions that I was game enough to go the distance.

I spent most of the day camped out in a seat in the top row, entertaining the fantasy that there was less cigarette smoke up there. From that vantage point, I could see the feathers fly but couldn't really detect the moment when a spur pierced flesh. And I could avoid the glassy, opaque expression of a bird in extremis. (One breeder assured me that "a rooster doesn't have a fully formed brain, and he doesn't have a pain center." Another cockfighting bromide is that any bird battling for its life in a pit has, up to that point, led a far cushier existence, and possesses the potential for far greater glory, than a factory-raised supermarket-bound Perdue oven stuffer.)

Every ten or so fights, someone would enter the pit, rake the feathers, sprinkle the dirt with a watering can, and draw fresh boundary lines with cornmeal. Somewhat less frequently, Judy would pick up a handheld microphone and threaten to put the hurt to whoever's truck was blocking someone else's out in the parking lot.

In the early evening, I decided to visit the drag pits, and as I passed the veterinary-supply table I heard a woman in lavender stretch pants and a matching sweater and curly red hair that originally belonged to someone else say, "I got me some Viagra. He better come home tonight." It felt like time to hit the road again. I thanked Judy and Roy and James Tally for their hospitality. On my way to my car, I came across an old Buick with the wordiest bumper sticker I'd seen in a long time: "If They Take Our Game Cocks, Next Time They Will Take Our Rodeos, Race Horses, Our Hunting Guns and Shotguns, and Maybe Even Our Fishing Poles!" For a variety of reasons, I doubted that.

Cockfighting persists in Oklahoma, though it is no longer, strictly speaking, legal. On the other hand, it isn't absolutely illegal.

After a protracted court battle over the validity of petition signatures, the underlying question was put to a statewide vote in November 2002. By a 54 to 46 percent margin, the electorate approved a statute that outlawed cockfighting and made all cockfighting paraphernalia subject to confiscation. The immediate response of the Oklahoma Gamefowl Breeders Association was to file lawsuits in several district courts around the state, seeking to enjoin enforcement on the grounds that the statute amounted to an unconstitutional seizure of private property. Inevitably, these petitions received sympathetic hearings from judges in rural counties where game-fowl breeders and cockfighting pits proliferated. The practical effect has been that breeders and pit operators have managed, for the time being, to stay in business, albeit more warily than ever.

Jurisdiction over the law's constitutionality resides with the Oklahoma Supreme Court, which, for obscure reasons, has adopted a leisurely approach to resolving the matter. One cockfighting partisan in the Oklahoma Senate, Frank Shurdin, promises to introduce, as often as necessary, a bill that would repeal the new statute and thereby relegalize cockfighting. Senator Shurdin's avowal, however, is generally regarded as more symbolic than realpolitik — in the same spirit as his perennial attempts to legislate the castration of rapists. Most cockfighters recognize that the supreme court is unlikely to rule in their favor, and that when, eventually, their fears are realized they will be bereft of desirable alternatives. Louisiana is now the only state with no legal impediments to cockfighting (New Mexico having adopted a county-option approach). Meanwhile, a federal law enacted in 2003 makes the transporting of animals across state lines for pugilistic purposes a misdemeanor. If the Humane Society gets its wish, this crime will someday be a felony. Thus would a law-abiding Oklahoma-bred rooster with a hankering for la guerre a mort in, say, Assumption Parish, Louisiana, confront the burden of a considerably longer flight than he's accustomed to.

GOD AND FOOTBALL

Asheville, North Carolina

SEPTEMBER 2000

Given the inordinate number of houses of worship in Buncombe County, North Carolina (pop. 200,000), and its county seat, Asheville (pop. 68,000), disagreements inevitably arise — even over such nondoctrinal matters as, say, how many houses of worship there are in Buncombe County. "Well, I'm sure we have as many churches as we do restaurants," the Reverend Buddy Corbin of the Calvary Baptist Church estimated when I put the question to him not long ago. A couple of days later, hoping for a bit more precision, I queried Rabbi Robert Ratner of Congregation Beth HaTephila, who refrained from the Talmudic option of answering my question with a question but still wasn't very specific. "Bazillions," he said. I mentioned Reverend Corbin's yardstick, and Rabbi Ratner shook his head. "There are a *lot* more churches in Asheville than restaurants," he assured me. "And that includes the fast food places."

One recent afternoon in Asheville, where I'd gone to explore the debate over the relative merits of "spontaneous prayer" before high school football games, I was waiting in my motel room for a return phone call from Leni Sitnick, the mayor — a call that I'd correctly begun to suspect was never going to materialize — when I became engrossed in the phone book, my only bedside reading other than a Gideon Bible. As I surveyed the church listings in the Yellow Pages, I briefly considered compiling a list of denominational subgroups, then decided this was a pointless exercise. It wasn't just a matter of sorting through the various Baptists. Where would a downtown establishment like The Body of Christ in Asheville: A House of Prayer, A Center for Worship (two doors from Instant Karma Body Piercing) fit in? And how could I arrive at an accurate census if there was no phone listing for the Radical Faeries, a collective of homosexual pagans, or for the local adherents of Meher Baba or Sufism or for the dozen or so Wiccan covens whose members have erected sanctuaries amid the timbered slopes of the Blue Ridge and Great Smoky Mountains that surround Asheville?

From a chamber of commerce point of view, Asheville has evolved during the past decade in progressive and desirable ways, a fact that's reflected in the regularity with which publications as diverse as *Outside* and *Modern Maturity* and *Kiplinger's Personal Finance* extol its attractiveness as a recreation, retirement, and overall quality-of-life destination. The chamber of commerce people don't necessarily brag when *Rolling Stone* and certain alternative media anoint Asheville "America's New Freak Capital" or "the San Francisco of the East." Nevertheless, it's obvious that the downtown mix of New Age herbalist shops, organic bakeries, and tattoo parlors, along with a gentrified array of coffeehouses, wine bars, art galleries, antique shops, and restaurants, has enhanced the general business climate. A topic the boosters prefer to avoid is the chronic ozone that clouds the viewscape, making it a challenge to imagine how, a century ago, tuberculosis sufferers flocked to the mountains of western North Carolina.

Beyond the Asheville city limits, Buncombe County gets rural very quickly, and a substantial portion of its populace consists of people who draw comfort from the notion that they reside, as the apt cliché goes, in the buckle of the Bible Belt — a designation that still applies to any number of enclaves where the Old South resists efforts to reconstitute it as the New South. For these citizens, the smog is a handy metaphor for that New South and for the pestilence of secular culture in general, a visual reminder of the hazard to one's well-being posed by the noxious influences of "pluralism" and "diversity." A lot of Asheville preachers have been delivering sermons lately in which the metaphors have grown more urgent, reflecting a siege mentality, the only proper response, as they see it, when powerful external forces pose a threat to personal freedom — specifically, the freedom of Christian evangelicals to pray whenever, wherever, and however they please.

THE REVEREND EMILE WOLFAARDT, a South African émigré who a couple of years ago found his way to Asheville and the pulpit of the Bent Creek Baptist Church — guided, he says, by a crystal-clear divine directive — awoke one day in June of this year with what he recalls as "an incredible burden, a heaviness in my heart." When he arrived at his office after an early-morning prayer meeting and realized he still didn't feel better, he sat at his desk and asked God what to do. There wasn't an audible response, but the next thing Reverend Wolfaardt knew he had written "We Still Pray" on a piece of paper: "because God visited that phrase in my heart." Evidently, God was as disturbed as Reverend Wolfaardt by news that the United States Supreme Court, in a Texas case called *Santa Fe Independent School District v. Doe*, had found that student-led prayers before high school football games violated the principle of church–state separation.

The landmark opinion that outlawed officially organized prayer in public schools was rendered in 1962, and in the years since the Supreme Court has been regularly petitioned to hear cases seeking reinterpretations. Until *Santa Fe v. Doe* came along, the most recent significant precedent was a 1992 ruling that barred clergymen from leading benedictions at public school graduation cere-monies. Meanwhile, somehow — perhaps owing to the sacrosanct nature of high school football — the widespread ritual of having "student chaplains" deliver pregame prayers over public-address systems has flourished beneath the radar.

The day after the announcement of the *Santa Fe v. Doe* deci-sion, the Buncombe County superintendent of schools dispatched a memo apprising employees of the need to follow the law. A report in the *Asheville Citizen-Times* headlined "STUDENT-LED PRAYER WON'T BE TOLERATED" was followed two days later by an editorial applauding the high court ruling. Evangelicals and fundamentalists, however, had a different reaction: if organized prayer wouldn't be tolerated, that amounted to religious intoler-ance, which in turn implied a grave threat to religious freedom. It was thoughts along those lines that weighed upon Reverend Wolfaardt, and as he started talking with like-minded members of the cloth, he discovered that several were prepared to take action.

One such activist was the Reverend Ralph Sexton Jr., the pastor of Trinity Baptist Church and a high-profile figure locally. "We're arguing this as a liberties issue," Reverend Sexton told me when I went to see him one morning in mid-August. By then, a lot had happened in Asheville. Most notably, the phrase "We Still Pray" had been taken up as a call to arms. It had found its way into an op-ed essay, "The Myth of Separation," that Reverend Sexton published in the *Citizen-Times;* it was the name of a newly char-tered nonprofit corporation with its own office and Web site; and it had become the theme of an upcoming rally at a high school football stadium, the primary purpose of which was to instruct the devoted in Supreme Court–subverting techniques for spontane-ous prayer.

This was something I was eager to witness. With the rally only two days away, Reverend Sexton, a youthful-looking fifty-three-year-old who wore braided brown leather suspenders and a suit, shirt, tie, socks, and shoes in matching tones of cream and beige, was in a state of acute readiness. Before he became a Baptist preacher, he ran a vending machine business. He had a salesman's affability and wanted to introduce me to an innovative product the "We Still Pray" folks were promoting: a constitutional amendment — one that had already been referred to the House Judiciary Committee — to the effect that "neither the United States nor any state shall establish any official religion, but the people's right to pray and to recognize their religious beliefs, heritage, or traditions on public property, including schools, shall not be infringed." When Reverend Sexton spoke of organized prayer before football games as a liberties issue, he meant that it should be protected by the First Amendment. That this line of reasoning had already been rejected by the Supreme Court in *Santa Fe v. Doe* didn't daunt him a bit. A new constitutional amendment could handle that problem.

It was inconvenient, of course, that an amendment would be needed to accomplish what, according to Reverend Sexton's reading of constitutional history, the framers had intended in the first place: "that the church would be a moral influence; the Founding Fathers really intended for God to be in the government, but they didn't intend for the government to be in the church." It was also inconvenient that a constitutional amendment couldn't be ratified in time for the start of football season, which was less than two weeks away. The mechanism Reverend Sexton had in mind as a short-term solution — spontaneous prayer, most likely in the form of an unannounced segue from the national anthem to the Lord's Prayer — hinged on the assumption that no fair-minded person would regard it as an unwelcome imposition.

"Bible believers — I'm almost hesitant to use the word 'Christians,' because in the Jewish community it's so often misunderstood — are tolerant people," he said. "Because if I love God with all my heart then I'm going to love you as a human being and I'm going to allow you to be what you feel you need to be. Because I have morality. I have knowledge of right and wrong. I'm not going to pass a law to make you be me. If people in the crowd at a football game want to say a prayer, we're not advocating that everyone has to say the prayer. We're talking about spontaneous prayer. If it's not in your heart, it's meaningless, anyway.

"I'll give you a hypothetical situation. We're at a football game, you and I, and we happen to be seated on either side of Joe and Mary" — a couple of names he pulled out of the air — "and we don't go to church. I'm a Muslim and you're a Buddhist. We're going to listen to them say a prayer but not say it ourselves. In my opinion, Joe and Mary are not going to be intolerant of us for not praying. Is their prayer not a gentle reminder that there are people of faith and this is a community that is kind and God-conscious?"

Well, maybe, though Reverend Sexton himself told me, "There are some people who aren't behind us, and I look forward to dialoguing with them." For instance, Reverend Joe Yelton of the Hominy Baptist Church told me he viewed a prayer gathering in a football stadium as "a Rambo style of theology in which what I believe I'm going to work hard to make you believe, which is antithetical to everything Christ represented, who told us to speak with quiet voices."

I WENT to do a little dialoguing of my own with another contrarian, Reverend Buddy Corbin, whose congregation, Calvary Baptist, occupies a large white-columned red-brick building in a working-class neighborhood on the west side of Asheville. At the outset, Reverend Corbin — imagine Andy Griffith as a cerebral preacher — emphasized that he didn't wish to be depicted as engaged in a running dispute with Reverend Sexton and Reverend Wolfaardt. "Ralph, Emile, and I met here the other day," he said. "We couldn't have had a better love fest in terms of the fundamental mission of Jesus. And they asked me to join in the rally. And my heart was breaking because I couldn't take that next step with them. Because we know how hard it is to get the word out. You can't ask for better enemies. We have the same aim, which is to bring a spiritual renewal to our communities in the name of Christ. But I want to do it under the rubric of freedom. And what they're going about is a form of cultural coercion. My biggest concern is the lack of prayer in church, not in school. What we don't do in church we seem to want to make happen in school, where there's no premise other than that you've got a bunch of kids there."

At one point, Reverend Corbin alluded to an episode last year that polarized the Christian clergy. By Asheville standards, this one began typically enough. With Halloween approaching, a woman named Byron Ballard, the high priestess (a.k.a. head witch) of a Wiccan coven called Notre Dame de l'Herbe Mouillée (Our Lady of the Wet Grass), submitted to the office of Mayor Leni Sitnick a request for an official proclamation of Earth Religions Awareness Week. The mayor, a hospitable woman who has a reputation for being open-minded to a fault, not only agreed to sign it but welcomed the coven members and their children's group, the Blessed Bees, to the city council chambers. There the Blessed Bees sang a traditional pagan song and had their picture taken presenting the mayor with a basket of organic apples, an event reported in the next day's *Citizen-Times* under the headline "AREA WITCHES GET A BOOST FROM THE CITY." Soon enough — it was the sort of reaction that could have been timed with a stopwatch — an alliance of fundamentalist and evangelical pastors and laypeople called the Community Council for Biblical Values (which has a significant membership overlap with the "We Still Pray" organizers) presented Mayor Sitnick with a request for a Lordship of Jesus Christ Awareness Week proclamation. The mayor, who happens to be Jewish, was on the verge of signing this as well when Reverend Corbin and four other ministers, including the Episcopal bishop of the western North Carolina diocese, intervened and implored her not to. "That strained every Baptist bone in my body," Reverend Corbin recalled. "I went to her and said,

'Leni, God love you, we would like for you not to do this. It trivializes everything we're trying to accomplish in our ministries.' She thought she would be making us happy by declaring Lordship of Jesus Christ Awareness Week, but right after signing a proclamation for the Wiccans, that made us mad. Then the Evangelicals said, 'There goes a bunch of liberals who don't care about the Lordship of Jesus.'" In the end, the Wiccans decided to return their proclamation, which gave Mayor Sitnick the leeway to decline to proclaim Lordship of Jesus Christ Awareness Week and to announce a self-imposed moratorium on mayoral proclamations.

A few hours before the "We Still Pray" rally, I visited with Reverend Jimmy Dykes of North Asheville Baptist Church, who was then the chairman of the Community Council for Biblical Values. "There was never any question in the Christian community that the Wiccans have the same right to organize and worship that my church does," Reverend Dykes assured me. "We just wanted to set the record straight concerning our heritage. We simply were declaring that Jehovah God and Lord Jesus Christ were sovereign over Asheville."

THE RALLY, which was scheduled to begin at seven P.M., got started about half an hour late because of congestion on the roads leading to A. C. Reynolds High School. Newspaper advertisements and flyers — sent along with "Dear Pastor" cover letters to area clergymen, including Rabbi Ratner, who gave me his copy — had urged "Bible believing Christians" to "stand up and be counted." In the end, ten thousand disciples filled the stadium bleachers or milled on the oval track surrounding the football field, and the police, after blocking the highway exits, estimated that they turned away as many more. Idling motorists had the consolation of being able to tune in to a couple of Christian radio stations that broadcast the proceedings. (Later, when I asked Reverend Sexton about the phrase "Bible believing Christians," he said he "would have preferred different wording" but hadn't been consulted. No matter. Given the phenomenon known as Jewish Standard Time — the tendency of about eighty percent of any given synagogue or temple congregation to show up at least forty-five minutes after a service begins — it's unlikely that many Hebrews would have ever made it off the interstate.) I left my motel extra early and arrived just in time for the delayed opening prayer. I parked and was trudging up a long incline, past rows of chartered buses, when I heard a voice say over the public-address system, "Whether you eat or drink or sit in traffic, do it all in the glory of God!"

That seeming non sequitur established a fitting tone, given that the premise of the entire event was the straw man proposition that the Supreme Court opposes prayer, period. Reverend Sexton worked that angle effectively when he quoted from William Rehnquist's fierce dissent in *Santa Fe v. Doe*, in which the chief justice contended that the majority opinion "bristles with hostility to all things religious in public life." Reverend Wolfaardt added a bit of ironic commentary when, during his turn at the microphone, he asked all Board of Education employees and police officers to stand and be recognized, explaining, "We want to honor those people who carry the gospel light into places that you and I are not allowed to go."

A parade of preachers with variegated homiletic styles provided the main entertainment: old-style mountain gibbering, tearful warbling, take-no-prisoners fear-mongering. One crowd pleaser was a lapel-grabbing missionary named Wendell Runion, who said, "Someone asked me today, 'Is this gonna be an in-your-face rally?' And here's my answer — Yes, *this is in your face!* And why is that? Because we need to remember what happens when people fail to understand what a document says. Whether it's the Constitution or the Bible, it says what it means and it means what it says. When we start interpreting, then we're in trouble. We started out as a nation under God. Then came the pluralistic society. Everybody says, 'Give me my rights.' So we're living in an age of rights and we've forgotten that *God* is what is right. It's a *sin* to deny the privilege to pray in this ballpark. We're still a Christian nation because we were founded as a Christian nation and we're letting *them*, the Supreme Court, take our liberties away from us. They, the opposition, ask, 'When will you speak out?' We will speak now. We will speak loudly."

Reverend Runion was followed by Donnie Parks, the police chief of the town of Hendersonville and one of four African Americans in the VIP section (more than in the entire rest of the stadium, as near as I could tell). "The Supreme Court says that when we pray at football games we're imposing our will upon others with those prayers," said Chief Parks. "Well, that's what opposing teams do at football games, isn't it? They try to impose their will on each other. Perhaps our Supreme Court justices should come to a few ball games."

When the faithful weren't boisterously expressing their enthusiasm for that sort of logic, they behaved with a poignant docility. At twilight, a scrim of gray mist descended beyond the silhouette of the mountains, and a blanket of shirt-soaking humidity settled in. For an outdoor gathering, the ambience felt remarkably claustrophobic. People fanned themselves with American flags, empty pizza boxes, and pasteboard signs that said "Luke 11:1 — Lord, Teach Us to Pray."

Finally came the much-anticipated spontaneous prayer portion of the program. "We Still Pray" business cards with the Lord's Prayer printed on the back had been circulated, but, of course, everyone present already knew the words and knew what to do. Describing a scenario he hoped would take place subsequently at football games, Ralph Sexton explained, "Miss Yolanda Miller is going to sing the national anthem, we're going to applaud, and after the applause we're going to pause for a moment of reflection — and in that moment of reflection there just might be some *spontaneous prayer!*"

During the anthem itself, a lot of people had their hands on their hearts, but the singing was the usual low-decibel, mumbling stadium crowd fare. Not so, however, the recitation of the Lord's Prayer. It rang out loud and clear.

"Thank you, God bless you," Reverend Sexton said at its conclusion. "Thank you on the visitors' side. Thank you in the end zones. Thank you on the outside. Thank you, Lord Jesus."

EIGHT DAYS LATER, Reverend Sexton returned to the stadium for the season opener of the A. C. Reynolds Rockets, who had won the state championship a year ago but lost twenty-six players to graduation and therefore were perhaps in the market for some divine intervention. During the pregame, everything went according to plan. At the conclusion of the national anthem, Reverend Sexton bowed his head for a minute and, he said later, "Spontaneous prayers broke out all around where I was. And the proof that it was spontaneous was that there was no orchestration." Reverend Sexton decided to attend the A. C. Reynolds game not only because the stadium had been the site of the "We Still Pray" rally but because Josh Meadows, the Rockets' star running back, is a member of his congregation. Josh scored twice and knelt in the end zone with his head bowed after both touchdowns. He was praying, but it wasn't quite enough; the Rockets lost to the Tuscola Mountaineers, 27–26.

Meanwhile, "We Still Pray" tremors were spreading throughout the Bible Belt, with reports filtering in from Texas, Mississippi, and South Carolina of similar local initiatives in the wake of *Santa Fe v. Doe*. Asheville, naturally, had its homegrown response. Three groups of pagans — Coven Oldenwilde, the Appalachian Pagan Alliance, and the Earth Religions Awareness Week committee — have filed requests for permission to use football stadiums for rallies. The Appalachian Pagan Alliance hopes to hold its rally to coincide with the autumn equinox, under the banner "We Still Work Magic." The Earth Religions Awareness Week committee, Byron Ballard said the other day, is applying for a date in late October.

"We're calling this 'a candlelight vigil to honor the ancestors' rather than mentioning witches," she told me. "It's the same language we used last year, when we kicked off Earth Religions Awareness Week with a 'prayer breakfast.' We try to be very careful with how we phrase things. If you say, 'We meditate and cast spells,' that sounds scary. So what we're saying is 'We are praying, and our prayer may take a little different form than yours. But it's still prayer.' We're saying, 'What we do is what you do. We pray.'"

THE WIDOWER'S TALE

Cape May Courthouse, New Jersey
JANUARY 2001

For a long while, no one seriously challenged the underlying explanation for the sudden death of Tracy Rose Thomas — that is, the version in which the perpetrator was a deer. Very early on a slushy Sunday morning in February 1997, a motorist on a rural road in Cape May Court House, New Jersey, came upon an automobile mishap. A Ford Explorer sport-utility vehicle had struck a telephone pole and continued another fifty feet before coming to rest in a shallow grassy ditch. The left headlight was smashed, but the right one was still lit, the taillights were lit, the engine was running. Inside, the air-bag system had deployed, and the driver, a woman, and her front-seat passenger, a man, appeared to be unconscious or worse. A well-bundled toddler, strapped into a car seat in the back, was alert and evidently unharmed. On a cell phone, the passerby summoned help.

The call was answered by the police department of Middle Township, a municipality comprising sixteen towns and villages, the largest of which is the quaintly named Cape May Court House, the seat of Cape May County, the southernmost in New Jersey. A detective named William Scott Webster was home at that hour, two A.M., awake and monitoring his portable police scanner. When Webster reached the accident site, he'd been preceded by a couple of paramedics, three other police officers, and an investigator from the county medical examiner's office. The driver, displaying no vital signs, had been removed from the car, a somber task made more difficult by the presence of the air bag but mainly by the inordinate tightness of her shoulder-harness seat belt. Tracy Thomas was a small woman, five feet four inches and slightly built, a fact that was somewhat difficult to discern because she was six months pregnant. By the time she was extricated, placed on a backboard on the snow-covered pavement, and draped with a sheet, she'd been dead for at least an hour and a half, and her fetus, a girl, was also dead. The uninjured child in the back seat was Tracy's eighteen-month-old daughter Alix, and the front-seat passenger was her husband, Eric Thomas, a dentist and a respected citizen of Cape May Court House.

Webster spent about an hour at the scene and then went to the emergency room of the local hospital, where Dr. Thomas, who turned out not to have been seriously hurt, and Alix had been delivered by ambulance. Ironically, this had been, according to Dr. Thomas, the family's intended destination. The previous day, he said, Alix had been bothered by a fever, and as the evening progressed it spiked high enough that the Thomases decided she needed to be seen by a doctor.

At the hospital, Dr. Thomas gave Webster and the investigator from the medical examiner's office an account of what had happened. Many more details emerged during an interview that Webster conducted two days later, after Dr. Thomas, having complained of neck pain, had been transferred to and discharged from the trauma unit of a hospital in Atlantic City. The snow that fell the night of the accident was the first significant accumulation of the winter — three inches — but, Dr. Thomas told Webster, neither the road conditions nor the late hour had deterred Tracy.

She'd spent most of her life in New England and had plenty of winter-driving experience there and in Germany, where Dr. Thomas had been stationed with the army for more than three years before the family settled in Cape May Court House.

Preparing for the trip to the hospital, Dr. Thomas warmed up the Ford Explorer, which was parked in the driveway of the new four-bedroom colonial they'd moved into two months earlier. Walking to the car, Tracy slipped and fell face down in the snow, quickly recovered, brushed herself off, and got behind the wheel. They'd traveled a little more than a mile when they encountered a deer on the road, a common occurrence in that heavily wooded area. Though Dr. Thomas was wearing glasses, he didn't get a good look at the deer. Still, he felt certain one had been there because he recalled his wife mentioning it — the last thing he heard her say. Tracy was proceeding at a cautious speed, about twenty-five miles per hour, but instead of braking to avoid the deer she veered off the road and into the wooden telephone pole, shearing it. Dr. Thomas's next memory was of a rescuer's flashlight shining in his eyes.

While Dr. Thomas was hospitalized, members of his family arrived, from South Carolina, as did Tracy's parents, Donald and Doris Rose, who lived in Hyannis, Massachusetts, on Cape Cod, and a sister, Wendy Rose Mahdi, who lived in northern New Jersey. Together the relatives looked after Alix, who, remarkably, was in perfect health; any fever she'd been running had vanished by the time she was examined at the emergency room. In accordance with state law, the Cape May County medical examiner, Dr. Elliot Gross, conducted an autopsy. Two days later, at Dr. Thomas's request — obeying, he said, his wife's wishes — the body was cremated. The death certificate, when it was filed two months later, listed the cause of death as "blunt force trauma with asphyxia . . . motor vehicle accident" — attributable, apparently, to the explosive force and pressure of the air-bag apparatus. The deer in the road didn't merit a mention in the medical examiner's report. Nor, at the time, did any investigator, or for that matter anyone else, suggest that Tracy Thomas had actually been strangled by her husband.

AMONG THE MOURNERS at Tracy's memorial service — a standing-room-only event that the mayor of Middle Township recently recalled as "one of the saddest funerals I've ever attended" — was James Callaway, a dentist whose practice Dr. Thomas had bought in 1995. (An aunt of Dr. Thomas's lived in Cape May Court House, and as he neared the end of his army tour she had introduced him to Dr. Callaway, who was ready to retire.) When Dr. Callaway set up shop in the mid-fifties, an African-American professional was an anomaly in that part of southern New Jersey, which lay below the Mason-Dixon Line and had an ambience and social texture markedly different from cosmopolitan, industrial northern New Jersey. Then, as now, blacks constituted about twelve percent of the population in Cape May Court House, and Dr. Callaway's considerable achievement was to build a thriving practice that catered equally to blacks and whites. "People in this area were just very close-mouthed about race," a white woman in rural Cape May County who was one of his patients told me. "That was typical of the fifties, before things erupted in the sixties. Even when everyplace else started having racial unrest, around here we all just pretended to get along. It was very confusing. Back then, it was just hush-hush, like sex — nobody talked about it."

Cape May County attracts hordes of beachgoers, sailors, and recreational fishermen in the summer but has fewer than 110,000 year-round residents, including almost 5,000 in Cape May Court House. In a more populous locale, a dentist wouldn't necessarily enjoy the stature that Dr. Callaway did — school board member, Sunday school superintendent, ubiquitous figure in various civic organizations. Patients who had trouble paying their bills learned that he possessed a forgiving nature. That charitable spirit, along with a reputation for integrity and plainspokenness, accounted for the esteem in which he was held. When Eric Thomas took over the dental practice, he seemed to acquire, along with the business's equity and goodwill, an implicit entitlement to Dr. Callaway's role in the community.

Tracy and Eric Thomas, born in 1959 and 1964, respectively, belonged to the first generation of middle-class African Americans who regarded upward mobility as an expected reward for hard work. There were, naturally, strings attached — for instance, the peculiar burden of being the sort of well-educated, "clean-cut" black people that a lot of mildly confused white people like to congratulate themselves for befriending — but they had no difficulty adapting to and becoming integrated into the life of Cape May Court House. Eric was personable, outgoing, handsome. The mayor appointed him to the township planning board. A golfer, he was invited to join a country club where he became only the second black member. During the annual career day at the regional high school, he proved to be the most popular speaker — a charismatic young man whose success story encouraged students to believe that by setting goals and persevering they could achieve whatever they wished.

If Tracy hadn't put her own ambitions on hold in deference to her husband's, she too would have qualified as a career-day speaker. According to her sister, she was organized, successful in school, and particularly adept at getting along with other people. "She had the type of personality," Wendy Mahdi told me, "that if her car broke down, the next thing you know the mechanic's fixing it for free." After graduating from Skidmore College (where she received ample financial aid; on Cape Cod, her father was a bus driver and her mother was a hotel housekeeper), she moved to Boston. There she worked for a consulting company, earned a graduate business degree from Northeastern University, and met her future husband, who attended dental school at Tufts. They married in 1991 and almost immediately he began to repay the

U.S. Army for underwriting his education, a debt that obligated him to four and a half years of military service. Alix was born while they were still in Germany. During Tracy's second pregnancy, she told her sister that once Alix reached school age she intended to go back to school herself, to pursue a law degree. Until then, she had a full-time but unsalaried job as receptionist and business manager in her husband's dental office.

ONE MONTH BEFORE Tracy died — an innocent coincidence, perhaps, or the sort of fact a cynic might dismiss as a film noir cliché, but a fact nonetheless — Dr. Thomas had increased the death benefit of her life insurance policy. With the $400,000 proceeds, he reduced his mortgage and repaid a $12,000 loan from Tracy's parents, money they'd provided when he was setting up his dental practice. Before long, the thought occurred to Dr. Thomas that his wife's recent demise might yield a substantially greater financial return, and he raised the subject when the Roses came to Cape May Court House to spend time with Alix in October of 1997. Since the early nineties, air bags had been a widely available option in American automobiles. They had saved lives and mitigated injuries, but instances of air bags inflicting injuries and causing deaths had resulted in a number of highly publicized product-liability claims. Dr. Thomas announced to the Roses that he was contemplating filing a lawsuit against Ford Motor Company, and he asked whether they would care to join as co-plaintiffs. "No, my daughter's dead," Mrs. Rose recalls telling him. "I don't want a cent from that."

During that visit, a tangible unease began to cloud the Roses' dealings with their son-in-law. They were doting grandparents who longed for any opportunity to be with Alix. Mrs. Rose said she hoped the child could join them for Christmas on Cape Cod, but Dr. Thomas said he would be taking her instead to see his family in South Carolina. In general, his behavior seemed odd; at one point he alluded to the possibility that the grandparents might try to kidnap Alix. This and other comments so upset Mrs. Rose that she called a lawyer upon her return home. The lawyer said that Dr. Thomas was still grieving or suffering from survivor guilt and cautioned her not to take his remarks at face value. Her husband, who was eager to avoid any conflict that might jeopardize access to their granddaughter, also urged her not to overreact.

The strains worsened over the next several months, complicated, in part, by the fact that Dr. Thomas had a new romantic interest — or, rather, an old romantic interest that had been rekindled. (Eventually, the timing of the rekindling would become a matter of dispute with important legal ramifications.) The woman's name, when Dr. Thomas first knew her, was Stephanie Arrington, and they had been high school sweethearts in South Carolina. At the time of Tracy's death, Stephanie was living in Texas and married to a man named Sean Haley, a marriage that was coming undone. By the summer of 1998, she had divorced, was living with Dr. Thomas in Cape May Court House, and was pregnant. They married in July. Six months later, Stephanie Thomas gave birth to a son and within a week signed legal papers that formalized her adoption of Alix.

In the context of this domestic shuffle, Dr. Thomas insisted on ground rules for the Rose family's visits with Alix which disturbed them deeply. Before he would allow her into their home, they had to remove from view any photographs of Tracy. Nor were they even to mention her name in the child's presence. "He warned us that when Alix got home he was going to question her about whether there had been any pictures on the walls," Mrs. Rose told me. "I wasn't going to go along with Eric's demands, but my husband said, 'I'll do anything to see Alix.' So he did take down the pictures."

A line had been crossed, and the Roses and their daughter Wendy began asking themselves questions about Dr. Thomas's demeanor in the immediate aftermath of the car crash and about elements of his account that seemed not to make sense. In late October 1998, Mrs. Rose and Wendy went to police headquarters in Cape May Court House and, not really certain what they were looking for, requested a copy of the official reports relating to Tracy's death. At first, Mrs. Rose couldn't bring herself to read this material, so she delegated that task to Wendy. The most telling document, in Wendy's mind, was a transcript of Detective Webster's second interview with Dr. Thomas. "As soon as I read that police report, I knew it," she told me. "I said, 'Something's very wrong here.'"

The transcript was filled with hesitations and elliptical phrases that struck the family as evidence of dissembling. The description of Tracy's fall in the snow sounded dubious: "So uh . . . she's clumsy anyway, kinda dropsy, so sure enough she fell outside . . . just slipped on the snow and I think she was reaching for the car." Tracy, her parents and sister knew, was anything but clumsy; she'd studied ballet from an early age and at fourteen had been recruited by the Boston Ballet school, a commitment that required twice-weekly roundtrips from Hyannis.

Webster asked, "Was she injured during that fall?" and Dr. Thomas replied, "To my knowledge, I don't know."

"Did she hit her face on the ground?"

"I think she did. I think she did. From what I . . . I know I probably . . . looking back, I probably should [have] looked at her a little closer, but, I didn't. So, I . . . I don't know . . . uh."

Dr. Thomas told Webster that Tracy had experienced pregnancy-related dizzy spells, or "blackout" episodes, a revelation that provoked more skeptical questions: Why would a man whose vertigo-prone, pregnant wife had just taken a frontal tumble allow her to drive on a snowy night? But never mind that. Tracy, they felt, would never have ridden in the front seat and left her feverish baby alone in the back; she would have been seated next to Alix or cradling her in her arms.

About a month later, Wendy and her parents, having concluded that they needed a court ruling to protect their visitation rights with Alix, made a trip to Cape May County to talk with a lawyer. That same day, they also met with Webster and forthrightly stated their belief that Tracy's death hadn't been an accident. Webster was courteous and attentive but explained that there wasn't much he could do. In the light of the medical examiner's report, the case had been closed and the prerogative to reopen it rested with the county prosecutor. Without solid evidence, that wasn't about to happen. (Tracy's ashes had been scattered on a pond on Cape Cod.) They *could* try to hire an independent medical examiner, Webster said, but for starters they would need a lawyer. Could they afford one? No, they explained, they planned to spend that money on an attorney who would represent them in family court. Dr. Thomas had not yet filed his tort claim against Ford, but one was obviously in the works; a few months earlier, a photograph of him and Tracy had appeared in *USA Today*, illustrating a story about air-bag fatalities, and the caption said he was suing the carmaker. Wendy and Mrs. Rose both recall Webster's advising that, under the circumstances, they might consider getting in touch with the right people at Ford.

IN EARLY FEBRUARY 1999, almost exactly two years after Tracy's death, a lawsuit was filed in federal court in Camden, New Jersey, naming as defendants Ford Motor Company and two firms that manufactured crash sensors and air-bag modules used in Ford products. Formally, the plaintiffs were Dr. Thomas, his daughter, and the Estate of Tracy Rose Thomas, and they sought unspecified damages — potentially, it was understood, many millions of dollars. Dr. Thomas's attorneys, a suburban Philadelphia firm that had taken the case on a contingent-fee basis, orchestrated a skillful public relations campaign, and the litigation immediately attracted media attention that featured him in the role of grieving widower (rather than as a contented newlywed). Statistics compiled by the National Highway Traffic Safety Administration showed that children, especially, were dying or being seriously injured in air bag–triggering crashes, and that small women were also disproportionately at risk — though nowhere in the air bag–mortality database was asphyxia mentioned. In any event, according to one attorney involved in the case, "Tracy became a poster woman for short women dying in air bag–related accidents."

For several months, as the parties to the suit began taking depositions and plotting tactics, Tracy's family attempted, fruitlessly, to arouse Ford's interest in their suspicions. Routinely, Wendy and Mrs. Rose would call Ford headquarters in Dearborn, Michigan, and ask for the customer service or legal departments, and, with dismaying consistency, they would wind up talking to functionaries who didn't bother to listen carefully to what they had to say. When finally someone did pay attention, Mrs. Rose got a swift follow-up call from William Conroy, a lawyer in Philadelphia whose firm had been retained by Ford.

Last summer, the public relations momentum — it would be premature to say the overall advantage — clearly shifted from Dr. Thomas to Ford. With the Cape May County prosecutor watching from the bleachers, Ford, pursuing a best-defense-is-a-good-offense strategy, managed to divert the focus away from questions about air-bag safety and toward the question of why the plaintiff hadn't yet been charged with murder. Early in the litigation, Ford deposed Dr. Thomas. Recently, citing discrepancies between that sworn testimony and statements he'd made to investigators, as well as inconsistencies with other records that Ford has subpoenaed, the company petitioned to depose him again, a move his lawyers have resisted. The goal, of course, is to shred Dr. Thomas's credibility.

Even more problematic for Dr. Thomas is the deposition testimony of the medical examiner, Elliot Gross. Without altering his bottom-line assessment of the cause of death, Dr. Gross conceded that the evidence was ambiguous: "I considered, based on my findings, the death initially as suspicious. I conveyed this to the police." (Detective Webster, who has also been deposed, doesn't recall having such a colloquy with Dr. Gross. Instead, he told Conroy that, in effect, neither he nor the medical examiner had sufficient experience to evaluate certain aspects of the investigation: "I don't think [Dr. Gross] knew what the injuries would be specific to an air bag.") Yes, Dr. Gross testified, he did discover what are called petechial hemorrhages in Tracy's eyes, as well as hemorrhages in the area of the larynx — both of which, taken together, are typically seen with manual strangulation — but his inquiry was framed by the understanding that the victim had died in a car crash.

Dr. Gross: "If this body, not as Mrs. Thomas, not as February ninth, not as an automobile accident, is brought in and I do this autopsy and I see the hemorrhages in the neck . . . and I see the petechial hemorrhages and that's all I have, I would be very suspicious of the death as a strangulation."

Meanwhile, Ford enlisted its own medical experts, including Michael Baden, a well-known forensic pathologist. (As it happens, a longtime professional rivalry exists between Dr. Baden and Dr. Gross, dating to the seventies and eighties, when both served controversial tenures as chief medical examiner of New York City.) Both Baden and a physician and biomechanical engineer named James Benedict, whose specialty is "injury causation and crashworthiness," filed reports that made the same basic points: when an air bag deploys, it stays inflated for less than a second and therefore, by itself, cannot cause asphyxia, which requires compression of the neck for many seconds; asphyxiation could result from a spinal cord injury, but Dr. Gross's autopsy disclosed no such injury. Dr. Baden's conclusion: "In my opinion, Mrs. Thomas died of compression of the neck by the hands of another."

Dr. Thomas responded to the suggestion that he had killed his wife by amending his legal complaint to include allegations of defamation and intentional infliction of emotional distress. Ford's "Oh yeah?" rejoinder was to take a sworn statement from Sean

Haley, Stephanie's former husband, who testified that in early 1997 he reviewed his phone bills and became aware of "consistent calls on a daily basis" to numbers registered to Dr. Thomas. When Haley questioned his wife about out-of-town trips that were ostensibly business related, she acknowledged meeting Dr. Thomas "on occasions in various locations throughout the country." Ford's next move was to obtain copies of the telephone records for the months preceding Tracy's death. In October, after Ford had documented 140 phone calls from Stephanie to Dr. Thomas in the three months before the car crash, including seven the day of the accident (Dr. Thomas's phone records have yet to come to light), the Cape May County prosecutor's office announced that it had officially reopened the investigation of Tracy Thomas's death.

LAST SPRING, Eric Thomas submitted to — and, according to his attorneys, passed — two polygraph examinations. Ford has announced its intention to depose the polygraph examiners, even while acknowledging the universal evidentiary inadmissibility of polygraph results.

If, at some future point, Dr. Thomas finds himself confronting a jury of his peers, he could do worse than to draw a panel from among his fellow residents of Cape May Court House. During four days I spent there last month, almost no one I spoke with was willing to comment on the record. A couple of Dr. Thomas's friends volunteered that his dental practice was prospering, that shortly after Thanksgiving Stephanie had given birth to a baby girl, and that nothing they've read or heard had diminished their lofty opinion of him. I gleaned these comments during telephone interviews; considering how few folks were willing to sit down face to face, I might as well have stayed home.

In small communities, where the prevailing assumption is that everyone knows everyone else's secrets, most of us tend to sympathize with the spectacle of a life conspicuously unraveling, even if that life turns out to be burdened by secrets far darker than the bedeviling knowledge we harbor about ourselves. In Cape May Court House — a tidy red-brick-and-white-clapboard village on the road to nowhere but the beach, a place where the fact that nothing much happens is regarded as a prime virtue — the most common sentiment about Eric Thomas's predicament is that he had the misfortune to pick a fight with the wrong Goliath.

"I think the Ford Motor Company is trying to save themselves money, and I don't like it," I was told by one woman who sounded angry that I had even broached the question. "They'll say anything to make a point. I just think it's so cruel."

The phone calls from Texas? The testimony of Stephanie's ex-husband? Was Dr. Thomas or was he not engaged in an adulterous affair at the time his first wife died? "It's possible he was having an affair, but that doesn't make him a murderer."

And if he did do it, *how?* Just the sheer logistics — how did he manage it in such a way that, had he not sued Ford, no one would ever have publicly questioned his story? Seated in her dining room one day not long ago, Wendy Rose Mahdi told me, "I don't know if it was premeditated by him and Stephanie, I don't know if it was the money . . . I just don't know. I don't think Tracy left the house alive. I don't know how he did it. But I know he did it."

One person who I thought might offer useful commentary — or, at the very least, might provide some insight into the pervasive silence in Cape May Court House — was Dr. Callaway, but I showed up too late; he had died the previous month. Then I learned that even if I'd approached him I would have been knocking at the wrong door. His best friend, a retired schoolteacher named John Roberson, told me that Dr. Callaway had played golf with him three or four times a week and "never discussed" Dr. Thomas's travails. I called Dr. Callaway's widow, Barbara, and she delivered the same message.

"If there was something on my husband's mind, he'd let you

know what it was," she said. "But this, he just didn't comment on it at all. We expressed our sympathy with Dr. Thomas after the first wife died. We were just in sympathy with him. I had no reason to believe anything else was amiss. When I read about the murder allegation on the front page of the newspaper, I just went right over to his house and told him I didn't believe a word of it and I was angry at Ford and I thought it was cruel and they shouldn't do that. I said, 'It's not fair.' He said, 'It gives me sleepless nights, and this craziness has to be over sometime.' And that was the end of that conversation."

★

Eric Thomas's lawsuit against the Ford Motor Company became, in the end, a parable of unintended consequences. During a deposition by Ford's attorneys, Dr. Thomas was forced to acknowledge: (a) that he had been carrying on an extramarital affair at the time of Tracy Rose Thomas's death and (b) that he had, in a previous deposition, lied under oath about the affair. Which is to say that, evidently, he had also lied to his own attorneys. In July 2001 he withdrew the suit and Ford agreed not to seek compensation for its litigation costs. Ford subsequently shared with the Cape May County prosecutor the circumstantial evidence it had gathered supporting the allegation that Thomas was criminally responsible for his wife's death, but no charges have been filed.

In the summer of 2003, Dr. Elliot Gross, the medical examiner who determined that Tracy Thomas had been asphyxiated by an air bag, was, as a result of his actions in an unrelated case, declared incompetent by the state of New Jersey to conduct autopsies.

Tracy Thomas's parents, Doris and Donald Rose, attempted, unsuccessfully, to gain legal custody of their granddaughter, Alix. The Roses also filed a wrongful death claim against Dr. Thomas, which is still pending.

Eric and Stephanie Thomas and their children — including Alix, whom Stephanie legally adopted — continue to live in Cape May Court House, where Dr. Thomas still maintains a dental practice.

THE HIGH MARK

Cooke City, Montana

MARCH 2002

For RESIDENTS of Cooke City, Montana, where winter customarily announces itself before Halloween and sticks around well into May, occasionally into June, the official arrival of spring is an incidental fact. Not counting dogs and cats, Cooke City has a winter population of a hundred self-selected souls — all of whom, it seems, are wedded to the proposition that the climate is ideal. Cooke City (elevation: 7,600 feet) sits just north of the Wyoming state line in a narrow valley of the Absaroka Range. Although precipitation has been a bit below normal this season, at Daisy Pass, five miles away and two thousand feet higher, four hundred inches of snow have fallen. As a rule, the snow is the dry-as-dust variety — stuff that, if you dive into a fresh pile of it, gives you the sensation of tumbling into a bowl of flour. By the time it settles and gets compacted by snowmobiles, which are ubiquitous in Daisy Pass, it's down to a mere eight or ten feet.

Seven months a year, Cooke City is literally at the end of the road, cut off from its nearest neighbor to the east, Red Lodge, by snowdrifts in the spectacular Beartooth Pass so deep that Highway 212 disappears. It's a fifty-five-mile trip to the supermarket, another seventy to the county seat, Livingston, and thirty more to Bozeman, where there's a Costco. The only automobile access is by way of a two-lane meander through Yellowstone National Park. Once the road leaves the park, it runs another four miles until it becomes Cooke City's four-block-long main street. At the far end of town, just past a café and rental cabins called the Grizzly Pad, the snowplow stops and the snowmobile trail-grooming machine takes over.

The Grizzly Pad was my destination when I drove into Cooke City one Friday afternoon last month. I'd reserved what a travel agent assured me was the last available room in town on a busy weekend when visitors would outnumber the locals three or four to one. During the ride through Yellowstone, I found plenty to keep me occupied: agoraphobia-inducing mountains, valleys, and gorges; herds of elk and bison foraging in the pines or rooting in the snowy meadows or planting themselves stolidly in the roadway; pronghorn antelope; ravens; the occasional eagle. In the broad, glazed valley of the Lamar River, I spent several minutes studying a silvery critter a hundred yards away, perched atop a boulder beneath a black spruce, before concluding that it was a coyote rather than, as I'd hoped, a lone wolf that had strayed from one of the *Canis lupus* families that were reintroduced to Yellowstone in 1995. There wasn't much traffic, but, three times while I was parked on the shoulder, pickup trucks with Idaho plates, towing snowmobile trailers, chugged past me.

When I reached Cooke City, I knew immediately that by virtue of my being trailerless and snowmobileless I was consigned to a tiny, pitiable minority. Outside the town's biggest hostelry, the no-vacancy thirty-two-room Soda Butte Lodge, dozens of Yamaha, Ski-Doo, Polaris, and Arctic Cat high-performance machines were lined up uniformly, like suburban commuters on a train platform. While I was checking in at the Grizzly Pad, snowmobilers were arriving from beyond the "Road Closed" sign, pulling plastic sleds laden with luggage. I saw a multitasking father riding with two pacifier-sucking toddlers balanced in front of him, then a family of four clad in Martian-green snowsuits and helmets, astride matching mom-and-pop and junior-size machines. These travelers and scores of others had made the last leg of their journey from a parking lot ten miles east of town, where Highway 212 intersected a plowed road bound for Cody, Wyoming. Most had started out from what I heard one Cooke City citizen refer to as "back East" — Minnesota, Iowa, Wisconsin, Nebraska, North Dakota, South Dakota, and other places where flatness is the norm and unfenced snowmobiling terrain is an elusive commodity — and they had arrived with the breathless reverence of pilgrims at a shrine. They were buoyed by an absolute confidence that, no matter how noisy or smelly or generally obnoxious their vehicles might strike narrow-minded folk elsewhere, there wasn't a mortal in Cooke City who would utter a discouraging word.

MOST AVID SNOWMOBILERS believe that where the trail ends the real fun begins. One dubious but popular local activity is high-marking, an amusement that thrives in inverse proportion to good sense. High-markers seek steep slopes covered by fresh powder, and there they play chicken with the laws of gravity, full-throttling uphill until the moment when either they turn back down the slope or their sleds topple. While high-marking obviously involves a certain quotient of brawn and athleticism — demanding more finesse than, say, competitive peeing for distance — it was most aptly characterized, for me anyway, as "a perfect example of what happens to people's brains when they get a big machine between their legs." A successful day of high-marking is one in which the rider spends no time underneath his sled, the snowmobile itself emerges undamaged, and no one has triggered an avalanche.

The adult male who people in Cooke City agree is the least likely to devote his leisure hours to high-marking — or, for that matter, to driving a snowmobile — is a fifty-one-year-old environmental activist and iconoclast named Jim Barrett, who had distinguished himself among the locals in the aftermath of a Fourth of July 1998 mountain-bike ride that he took in an area adjacent to Cooke City known as the New World Mining District. To get there, Barrett pedaled east on Highway 212 and then onto a gravel road that steadily climbed toward Daisy Pass. During the winter, this is the main path to the backcountry playground that draws the snowmobiling masses to Cooke City. The New World Mining District — where gold was extracted from the late 1860s until the turn of the century — comprises ten miles of groomed trails and approximately twenty-five square miles where snowmobilers, depending on the topography and the trees, are free to roam. (Beyond its boundaries lie national forest and designated wilderness lands where motorized vehicles are prohibited — which is not to say that this prohibition is rigorously obeyed.)

Even though the high-marking season was, of course, long over by the Fourth of July, Barrett discovered ample testosterone flowing in the mountains. He was accustomed to seeing four-wheel all-terrain vehicles both on and off the trail, but he was startled to discover that the high-pitched internal-combustion whine he heard in the distance was coming not from an ATV but from a snowmobile. A descending snowmobile passed him on the gravel road, and when he reached Daisy Pass he was greeted by the sight of a dozen more snowmobilers hopscotching across the alpine meadows between the lingering patches of snow.

Barrett's subsequent sworn declaration of what he saw became evidence in a lawsuit against the U.S. Forest Service, the Fish and Wildlife Service, and the Department of the Interior. (The suit was brought by several conservation organizations, including the Sierra Club and the Park County Environmental Council, of which Barrett was the executive director.) There were already prohibitions about motorized vehicles in the wilderness areas; the suit arose because they clearly weren't being enforced. By neglecting to monitor snowmobilers adequately, the lawsuit alleged, the government was abetting the disruption of the habitat of grizzly bears, a protected species. As the litigation evolved, the plaintiffs argued that until the impact of snowmobiling was assessed, it should be banned from mid-April to mid-December, when the bears aren't hibernating.

What the lawsuit really amounted to, businesspeople in Cooke City will tell you, was an unconscionable attempt to deprive them of their livelihood. The Montana Snowmobile Association formally joined the action, volunteering itself as a defendant, and, even today, its legal defense fund is spoken of reverentially, in last-best-hope-for-mankind terms, by the owners of Cooke City's motels, restaurants, and snowmobile franchises and service shops. The suit is unresolved — last year a federal judge in Billings ruled that the snowmobiling season could be kept intact for now pending further evidence (leaving the bears, as ever, to fend for themselves) — and an atmosphere of pious vigilance remains in Cooke City. The consensus, in any case, is that it's only a matter of time before another bunch of environmental activists come along and try to ruin a good thing.

THERE'S no official municipal government in Cooke City, and no flesh-and-blood law enforcement personnel. During warm-weather months, a junked patrol car with a dummy behind the wheel is stationed at each end of town to discourage speeders. One implication would seem to be: what is there to steal? Indeed, for most of Cooke City's history prosperity was elsewhere. Hunting and fishing provided seasonal work for outfitters and guides, there was some small-scale logging, and the motels, bars, and retail shops got busy during the abbreviated summers and autumns, catering to Yellowstone visitors. Otherwise, as I was told by Bill Sommers, a forty-year resident now in the employ of Cooke City Exxon, a service station and snowmobile dealership owned by his son, Rick, "You couldn't make a dime from the middle of November to Memorial Day weekend."

In the late eighties, two significant events — one of which actually turned out to be a nonevent — took place. During the summer of 1988, lightning ignited a series of forest fires in the Yellowstone region that were allowed to burn freely for several days. After one fire spread north and east of the park, into the Gallatin National Forest, the Forest Service decided to combat it with a back-burn, which, when the wind shifted inauspiciously, very nearly incinerated Cooke City. One of the fire's legacies is a scarred, deforested mountainside that dominates the view to the north. Another, odder consequence was the snowmobiling boom. The trails in the New World Mining District had been opened almost ten years earlier and were attracting riders mainly from Montana and Wyoming. Suddenly, Cooke City was in the news and flatlanders in the Midwest began hearing about this off-the-grid place in the mountains where — check it out, dude — you could run your machine up, down, around, and sideways for miles and miles. The crowds have been showing up, in increasing numbers, ever since.

The year after the fire, a fight began over whether the Canadian conglomerate that owned the claims in the New World Mining District would be allowed to resume active digging for gold. Predictably, various environmental groups mobilized, describing scenarios of potential devastation to the Yellowstone ecosystem. By the time the federal government settled the issue in 1996 by buying out the conglomerate — after seven years of legal skirmishes and propaganda — the pro and anti factions in Cooke City had discussed the topic far beyond the point where civil discourse ceased. There were good reasons to oppose the resumption of mining, because it posed a genuine risk to a beautiful, sacrosanct national treasure. But for many people, opposition to the mines' reopening became irrationally bound up with the future of snowmobiling. The logic went: if you allow the government in now (to stop people from digging for gold), then you're setting yourself up to let the government in again later (to do something really evil, like stopping snowmobiling). The mine question is now a dead issue, but the urge to demonize continues as strong as ever. The prejudices of those most offended by the government's high hand during the mine fight were reinforced by the fact that, locally, the opposition was led by the town's willing pariah, Jim Barrett, and his wife, Heidi. Last year, a sign was posted on the cash register at Cooke City Exxon that said "We Reserve the Right to Refuse Service to Anyone" — anyone, in this case, specifically meaning the Barretts. Though they still own a cabin on Soda Butte Creek, where they spend occasional weekends, the Barretts now reside in Livingston.

MY FIRST NIGHT at the Grizzly Pad, I was serenaded, more or less, by a black Labrador retriever chained outside the quarters of a neighbor of mine, a long-term tenant whose name, I gathered, was Steve. Earlier, as John Gurbach, the Grizzly Pad's owner, showed me to my cabin, he said, by way of apologizing as we side-stepped a carpet of dog turds, "I told Steve, 'Clean up or the dog goes.' He's hoping for snow." Unlocking the door, Gurbach said, "Like I told 'em, it's not the lap of luxury." I liked it anyway, even the lethal icicles depending from the roof. I didn't mind that four of the five windows were covered with plywood and fiberglass insulation. No television, no telephone, and no room service, but on a coffee table I found a Grizzly Pad Café menu promising milkshakes "big enough to swim a moose — a very small moose." There was also a kitchenette, a propane heater, and brown-every-thing Wally the Woodchopper decor. In Manhattan, it would easily have fetched $2,500 a month, with or without the antler door handles.

I awoke at five-fifteen the next morning, jolted by the thought that someone had broken in with a chainsaw. Of course, it was just the snowmobile traffic outside my door. It kept coming intermittently, but somehow I fell back to sleep. By the time I stirred, ate breakfast, and wandered down the street for some fact gathering, I'd been overtaken by events. At around ten o'clock, three men, part of a group of five who had been high-marking on Mt. Abundance, a couple of miles northwest of Daisy Pass, had gotten caught in an avalanche. I heard about it when I dropped by the local Yamaha dealership, where I'd hoped to learn about the new four-stroke engine, high-performance model that will be available late next summer, a technology that will supposedly reduce hydrocarbon emissions substantially. The owner wasn't there, because, along with about half the adult population, he belonged to the search-and-rescue squad. I hung around long enough to listen to an employee give a safety drill to a party of eight from South Dakota who were renting snowmobiles and, wisely, strap-on safety beacons — radio transmitter-receivers that, it was later reported, none of the high-markers on Mt. Abundance had been wearing. One woman asked, hopefully, "So, if you're caught in an avalanche, you put your hands in front of your face to create an airspace, right?" "Yeah" was the reply. "And kiss your ass goodbye."

My next stop was Cooke City Exxon, where I had reserved a snowmobile for the next day. I also had to rent boots, gloves, coveralls, and a helmet, and I might have tried to rent a riding companion if I hadn't got lucky at the Elk Horn Lodge, an eight-unit motel owned by Suzy Schmitt and her fiancé, Jason Hahn. I'd heard Suzy described as a characteristic Cooke City jackette-of-all-trades. In 1994, on her way home to Virginia from Yellowstone, she had stopped in Cooke City, planning to stay for a couple of weeks, and never left. She'd tended bar, waitressed, owned another motel, substitute-taught at the Cooke City School (kindergarten through eighth grade; enrollment, six), and been the backup postmaster. She also played second base for the Cooke City Cream, which, when it isn't on probation because of rowdy behavior by its fans, competes in the Yellowstone Park Softball

League. Jason, who was the left fielder ("Jason pretty much had to share left field with an elk last season"), spends his winters working in Washington State and had just arrived for a long weekend. He volunteered to be my guide.

By nine o'clock the next morning, we were zipping up the denuded, lunar-looking trail to Daisy Pass. I rode a Polaris Rocky Mountain King 600, a machine that, I'd been assured, could do ninety miles per hour on a straightaway. An inch of fresh powder had fallen, and the morning light was dull and flat. Very few other riders were out and about — possibly because it was Sunday, or perhaps because there had been a minor exodus in the wake of the avalanche. At a spot called Lulu Pass, Jason pointed out an upright rod with a loop at the top, a storage device for the aluminum probe poles used in postavalanche searches.

Mountain snowmobiles have uncomplicated drive mechanisms — throttle, brake, no gearshift, no reverse — and, as I learned after we crested an abrupt declivity, almost no traction when the sled is moving steeply downhill on its runners. At such moments, there isn't much to do except steer and hope that you won't get turned sideways to the slope. We dipsy-doodled in woods of spruce and white-bark pine and then headed through a benign bowl-like valley until we came upon a far less benign vista — a perilous-looking cornice on Mt. Abundance. This was, we realized, very near the avalanche site. One of the victims had managed to dig himself out and escaped with a broken nose, but the other two had died. What, I wondered, could they have been thinking as they imprinted their high-marking tracks?

"I would stay off that slope for sure," Jason said. "Or, if I went on it, it would just be one sled at a time."

WE RODE for an hour and a half. The most rewarding aspect was the Imax scenery, and the least fun part was ingesting the rubbery exhaust from Jason's machine. Once we were back in town, a combination of, I assume, vertigo and carbon monoxide put me to sleep for an hour, a nap interrupted by a knock at the door from another Grizzly Pad lodger — and another Jason, this one named Flug — who invited me to go for another ride. We revisited some of the same groomed trails I'd covered that morning, and got considerably more adventurous off the trail. By three o'clock, I was ready to head back to Cooke City Exxon and return my sled, a couple of hours ahead of schedule.

The Upper Yellowstone Snowmobile Club was holding a weenie roast and raffle that afternoon at the Exxon station, a fundraiser for the Montana Snowmobile Association's legal defense fund. The emcee was Jerry Dye, a peripatetic civic booster who holds court at six o'clock every evening in the bar of the Soda Butte Lodge. His right-hand man was Mark Linthacum, a neighbor just down the road from Cooke City, in Silver Gate, where, depending on whom you ask, the winter population is either four or six or eight. Raffle tickets cost five dollars, and another five entitled you to all the chili dogs you could eat. For no extra charge, Dye was offering straight-from-the-bottle bumps of Doctor McGillicuddy's peppermint schnapps. This was a warmup for an attempt to get Cooke City listed in the *Guinness World Records* (category: largest number of people simultaneously participating in a toast). "We're gonna line people up on both sides of the street and pour everybody a shot of the Doctor," he told me. "We need a hundred and ninety to break the record." (Actually, according to the Guinness people the existing record is 462,572.)

I had noticed that snowmobilers — maybe their helmets got in the way, or maybe it was the Cooke City demographics — tend not to be sparkling conversationalists. This seemed especially true of the crowd that had gathered for the raffle drawing, buff and beefy guys with jock-and-cop haircuts, wraparound shades, and bright-colored, logo-emblazoned baseball caps and jackets that made them look like NASCAR-driver wannabes. Dye worked hard to get them animated. "Come on, people," he pleaded into a megaphone. "This is your last chance. Get your tickets. Now's the best time to buy 'em." But they were a taciturn, sullen bunch, except for the ticket-holder who won the first of many merchandise prizes — something called a hot-dogger, a doohickey that attaches to a snowmobile's muffler (a component I was surprised to learn existed) and cooks lunch while you drive — and the cash-prize winner, who walked away with half the kitty, just over a thousand dollars.

Later, at Dye's house, west of town, I sat down with him and Mark Linthacum for what I thought would be a lighthearted conversation about Cooke City's social rituals, and it did begin that way. Dye, who looks like Popeye with a trimmed white beard and a bulbous nose, started off talking about the annual hog roast and auction that he and his wife, Mary, organize to benefit the fire department and the search-and-rescue and emergency medical crews. Then, somehow, our discussion segued to a diatribe against the common enemy: any interventionist who would interfere with the rights of snowmobilers, or any other law-abiding citizens, to go where they pleased and do as they pleased on public lands. (There is, of course, a proposal being considered by the secretary of the interior, Gale Norton, to ban snowmobiles from Yellowstone and the Grand Teton National Parks.)

"Our community will fight multi-million-dollar organizations, the Sierra Club and these other groups, to keep what we have," Linthacum said. "A guy from the Montana Wilderness Association came to one of our Snowmobile Association meetings and told us that our trails are too close to the boundary of the wilderness area. He said we're guilty of all these incursions into the wilderness. But, you know, all the reports they come up with for incursions are double. Because, if they see forty tracks, they don't count that as half the tracks going in and half coming out. The math is obvious — you've got to divide by two — but that doesn't work with the Sierra Club, or with Congress, or with your tree-huggers, bunny-kissers, or whatever."

Linthacum had spent the previous day on the avalanche search and, after a border collie located the bodies, had dug one victim from the snow. I asked whether killer avalanches weren't as bad for business as environmentalists. He gave me a quizzical look.

"Hey, we're not discriminatory," he said. "We'd pull out snow-shoers, cross-country skiers. We'd even pull out Jim Barrett."

"I wouldn't pull the sonofabitch out," Dye said. "I'd let him lay there forever."

"But, Jerry," Linthacum said, "you wouldn't know who was in there until you pulled him out."

"Well, I'd stuff him back in."

EACH EVENING I had dinner at the Soda Butte Lodge — something long on cholesterol, washed down by a couple of Moose Drool beers. One night I wound up at a table adjacent to five Germans, devoted members of the Gesellschaft zum Schutz der Wölfe (Society for the Protection of Wolves), who were on their fourth annual visit to Yellowstone. They were ecstatic about what they'd been seeing in the park — mating time had arrived, or, as one of them described it, "high wolf-fucking season" — and diplomatic about the human species they'd encountered. ("We had some problems with snowmobilers who told us they were chasing foxes and coyotes with their machines. This is a point we have to oppose, of course. But we hope these are the exceptions.")

My last night in Cooke City, aware that I'd negligently failed to explore its after-hours charms, I went into the bar at the Soda Butte. John Gurbach was there, and he introduced me to an acquaintance named Wayne, a carpenter who had built the bar, as well as the one down the block, at the Miner's Saloon.

"Let me ask you this question," Wayne said. "I just want to ask you this. Who's the last person to ride a snowmobile from one end of the bar to the other at the Miner's?"

"I give up."

"You're looking at him. We had two skinny-track Ski-Doos, two snow machines, inside that bar. I finally said, 'Fuck it. I'll ride it.' I even jumped the goddamn waitress station. Next guy that tried, he fell into the cooler."

This was confirmed, with a slight demurral, by another patron, a fellow who said his name was Chips. "Wayne did not gracefully leap the waitress station," he said. "He took it out with him."

John Gurbach invited me to the Miner's Saloon, and when we got there he encouraged me to check out the men's room, where the urinal was full of loose change. I ordered a Moose Drool, and Gurbach asked for a shot of peppermint schnapps. The Miner's had video poker machines and pool tables and a beautiful stained-oak bar that Wayne evidently had not only built but rebuilt. Above my head, pinned to the rafters, was a T-shirt commemorating something called Butt Darts, a popular pastime that, according to the bartender, had lapsed "ever since the lady in charge moved to Red Lodge." The clock said eleven, well past my bedtime. As I walked back to the Grizzly Pad, it was snowing and utterly quiet, until I passed the Soda Butte just as Chips and Jason Flug were coming out. They jumped on their snowmobiles.

"Where you headed?" I asked.

"We're going to the Miner's," Jason said. The night was young, but as they embarked on their fifty-yard journey they seemed to be in a hurry.

NEVER SURRENDER

Shreveport, Louisiana
MAY 2001

ONCE LYNDA ESTES and Paul Gramling Jr. decided to get married, it naturally followed that the wedding would take place in April, because that's Confederate History Month. When they met, four years ago in Nashville during the national convention of the Sons of Confederate Veterans, Paul Gramling was a member of a contingent from Louisiana and Lynda Estes was with a guest delegation from the United Daughters of the Confederacy. At the time, she lived in a small northeast Texas town a couple of hours from Gramling's home, in Shreveport. They had each been married twice before, to people who lacked, as Estes puts it, "the interest and the love that Paul and I have for our history and our heritage." Neither of Gramling's ex-wives, for instance, had a closet full of crinolines, lace-up boots, frilly pantaloons, corsets, and long-sleeved dresses with hoopskirts and brocade-trimmed bodices, or a passion for refurbishing Confederate monuments, manicuring Confederate cemeteries, and baking cakes to raise money to restore antique Confederate flags. And Estes's ex-husbands had shown no propensity for attiring themselves in rigor-

ously authentic Confederate officer's garb and making proselytizing visits to schools to "teach the truth" about all that fussing and
fighting between the North and the South in the middle of the
nineteenth century.

Estes and Gramling next saw each other several months later,
in Merryville, Louisiana, the site of a mock Civil War battle. An
affinity for battle reenactments was what had originally attracted
Gramling to the Sons of Confederate Veterans. During the summer of 1990, a couple of co-workers had invited him to accom-
pany them to Mississippi for the Battle of Vicksburg, because, he
says plausibly, "I looked the part." Gramling, who is forty-four, is
tall and has swept-back auburn hair that reaches his broad shoulders; a drooping mustache; and an exhibitionist predilection that
wouldn't necessarily be evident to someone who had observed
him only in his day job, as a mailman. The Vicksburg reenactment
took place on a sweltering weekend, during which he "wore a
wool uniform, got dirty, sweaty, thirsty, and hungry, and loved
every minute of it." Soon, he began attending Sons of Confederate Veterans meetings as a visitor, and then he did the genealogical
spadework that enabled him to become an official member. On his
mother's side, he turned up a great-great-grandfather who served
as a second lieutenant in the Confederate States army, survived
the Battle of Gettysburg, and spent the last year and a half of the
Civil War in a prison camp.

Though Estes, who is fifty-two, waited until she was in her
mid-thirties to enlist in the United Daughters of the Confederacy, she would probably have done so as a teenager if there had
been a chapter in her hometown. Not that she received any en-
couragement from her family. "My mother could care less about
her heritage," she told me. "She says I live in the past. Which is
totally false." Indeed, when Estes gets going about the Confederate veteran in whose name she signed up — her great-grandfather
Benjamin Thomas Smith, who was wounded in three different
battles, fought at Gettysburg on the same bloody ground as

Gramling's Confederate ancestor, and, likewise, was captured and imprisoned by the Union army — she uses the present tense. "I almost feel that part of his spirit is in me," she says. "He just seems to have a fighting spirit. He gets knocked down and gets up and keeps going."

During their second encounter, Estes and Gramling spoke candidly about their pride as Southerners, a conversation that she recalls as "very long and deep . . . about how we have these feelings deep down inside and we can't put them into words to explain to anyone." The way he expressed himself, with a missionary fervor about the rightness of the Southern cause and the wrongness of the way most historians have portrayed the conflict, made her think he'd be an ideal candidate for the Jefferson Davis Historical Medal, which the United Daughters of the Confederacy gives to men and women for "excellence in history, essay writing, or declamation." So she nominated him, and he received the award a few months later, during a ceremony that coincided with his swearing-in as commander of the Louisiana division of the Sons of Confederate Veterans.

A couple of years passed before Estes and Gramling's friendship blossomed into romance. Along the way, he continued what had been a steady rise through the hierarchy of the organization. At the national convention last year, he was elected commander of the Army of the Trans-Mississippi. Among the thirty thousand members, two others hold the title of army commander, and only the commander in chief and the lieutenant commander in chief rank higher. These days, Gramling's official responsibilities are so demanding that he rarely finds the time to participate in battle reenactments. But he welcomes any opportunity to be in uniform, and whenever a situation arises that calls for him to uphold the sacred honor of the Confederacy — the Battle of Pierre Bossier Mall being the most recent noteworthy episode — he feels duty-bound to put his body on the line.

*   *   *

CERTAIN DETAILS of what happened on the first Sunday in April at the Pierre Bossier Mall in Bossier City — Shreveport's suburban neighbor, on the opposite bank of the Red River — are in dispute. What's not debatable is that a convivial get-together of members of the Northwest Louisiana Brigade of the Sons of Confederate Veterans ended with a substantial number, very much against their will, being evicted from the mall.

The brigade had arranged to inaugurate Confederate History Month with a luncheon at Bennigan's, a chain restaurant inside the enclosed mall. This was preceded by a low-key, informal procession — fifty or so people, members of the Sons of Confederate Veterans and their families, the majority in uniform, sauntering with Confederate flags for about a mile along the Red River. When the entourage arrived at Bennigan's, they retired to a private room decorated with more flags. (Between 1861 and 1865, the Confederate national flag evolved through three incarnations. The flag of the Confederacy most familiar nowadays — the one that incites the hostility of people who consider it a racist emblem — is the battle flag: a blue St. Andrew's cross with white stars on a red field.) As the revelry inside Bennigan's wound down, one member — whose compatriots think of him as a likable fellow despite his insistence on bringing his bagpipes to their gatherings — stepped outside the restaurant into one of the mall's corridors and began playing. He was soon joined by a couple of flag-toting allies.

Either the bagpipes or the flags, or both, got the attention of a couple of mall security guards. This, in turn, got the attention of Gramling and Chuck McMichael, a Shreveport high school teacher, who is the national chief of staff of the Sons of Confederate Veterans. The bagpiping would have to stop, the security guards said, a request that Gramling and McMichael deemed reasonable. Also, according to the guards, the flags weren't allowed in the mall, an edict that struck them as less reasonable. "Chuck and I asked them why," Gramling told me. "They never would give us a reason. They just pointed us to a sign near the door and said all the rules for the mall were there." By the time Gramling and McMichael read the rules — and discovered no mention of a prohibition against flags — the security guards had moved on. "We went ahead anyway and put the flags in our cars," Gramling said. "While we were doing that, a lady from Massachusetts asked us to pose for a photograph. She said we were the first real southerners she'd seen. Then we went back inside to walk around. No flags, no bagpipes. Just citizens dressed in Confederate uniforms walking through a mall."

One of the mall's posted rules banned gatherings of more than five people, a policy presumably written with loitering teenagers in mind. As Gramling, McMichael, Lynda Estes, and about a dozen other stragglers from the luncheon set out on a window-shopping stroll, they were careful to divide into groups of five or fewer. Estes and Gramling stopped by a jewelry store where they'd bought their wedding rings — hers in white gold, his in yellow gold, each with a central diamond flanked by a pair of diamond-studded battle flags. A few minutes later, they were again approached by the same security guards, who ordered them off the premises.

As the incident played out over the next few days in the *Shreveport Times*, it seemed that the mall personnel hadn't gotten their stories straight about what had happened. Or, more likely, they knew what had happened and why but saw no advantage in saying so explicitly. One spokesperson floated the explanation that the Sons of Confederate Veterans had been banished because they didn't have a permit to hold an organized event inside the mall, for which liability insurance was required. Estes, Gramling, and McMichael insisted, however, that the security guards — a white female and an African-American male who happened to be an off-duty Bossier City police officer — had never raised that subject. "We were asked to leave the mall because of the way we dressed," Estes told a reporter. "We asked why, and [the female guard] said because of the uniforms. She called them 'gray suits.'" Evidently, it was the men's clothing, rather than Estes's hoopskirted tea dress, that offended. Somehow, the Sons of Confederate Veterans had done something wrong. But it was hard to say just what that was, because, technically, they hadn't really done anything wrong.

In Gramling's estimation, he and his friends had been treated like "common criminals" by "rude, obnoxious, and condescending" security guards: "They did not *ask* us to leave; they *told* us to leave." As the retinue exited, they were greeted by three Bossier City police cars. The experience, Gramling said, made him feel "humiliated."

What was it, exactly, about a motley collection of mainly overweight men dressed in heavy gray nineteenth-century suits — a gaggle of still-pissed-off-about-the-war-but-otherwise-minding-their-own-business white guys — that was so objectionable? Presumably, it was the assumption that the uniforms connoted an allegiance to a cause that only a bigoted redneck provocateur could embrace. But, in fact, one doesn't have to spend a lot of time in the presence of Sons of Confederate Veterans members, as I did in the days following their ejection from the Pierre Bossier Mall, to recognize the fallacy of writing them off as proslavery racists. Many harbor political opinions that qualify as reactionary, and there's plenty of Lincoln-bashing. For the most part, however, the group is preoccupied with "heritage violations" that have little to do with contemporary political debates of consequence. The humiliation that Gramling spoke of — along with its companion emotions, the mantle of martyrdom and the hope of resurrection — has, since Appomattox, constituted the bedrock of Southern devotion to the "Lost Cause." A moonlight-and-magnolias romanticism, coupled with a strangely comforting sense of being dispossessed, runs through all this, but it doesn't add up to a calculated effort to distort history.

Southern history, the story of a region steeped in storytelling, has a habit of doubling back on itself. How was it possible for the

Sons of Confederate Veterans, reflecting upon their bum's rush out of a shopping mall — the sort of affront that southern black people, even beyond the Jim Crow era, had to put up with every day (along with unspeakably worse indignities) — not to appreciate the historical paradox? It was during my second day in Shreveport, while I was attending a meeting of the General Richard Taylor Camp No. 1308 — Gramling's chapter of the Sons of Confederate Veterans, the largest in Louisiana — that the thought occurred to me that one of the prerequisites for membership might actually be, in addition to a soldier in the family tree, a congenital immunity to irony.

THE GENERAL RICHARD TAYLOR CAMP convenes for dinner and camaraderie on the first Thursday of every month, at an El Chico Mexican restaurant in southeast Shreveport. The April meeting agenda was already crowded — thanks to Confederate History Month — when the Pierre Bossier Mall imbroglio crowded it some more. Many logistical details pertaining to the Sons of Confederate Veterans Ball — which was two days away, and which, for the sake of convenience and economy, would double as the Estes-Gramling wedding reception — had to be dealt with. Another pressing matter was a potential heritage-violation situation involving the Bossier City Fire Department. At seven o'clock, the camp commander gave the call to order. Sixty stalwarts, dressed in casual civilian clothes and ranging from their twenties to their early seventies, some with wives and children in tow, rose for the presentation of the colors, which was followed by a spirited rendition of "Dixie," with musical accompaniment generated by a boom box.

The commander made a few announcements — including an exhortation to attend an upcoming rally in Jackson, Mississippi, where a referendum on that state's flag design was imminent — and then called on Chuck McMichael to give a status report on the Bossier City Fire Department. Several African-American firefighters, it seemed, had complained about racially offensive work-place conditions, and in response the fire chief had forbidden employees to display Confederate insignia on their clothing or personal vehicles. One white firefighter, feeling that his constitutional rights were being infringed on, had gotten in touch with McMichael, who was happy to intervene. After McMichael and the Bossier City fire chief had a conversation, the insignia ban on vehicles was rescinded.

"Several good things came out of this," McMichael said. "One, I told the chief I appreciated him letting us be part of the process. And he said, 'Oh, thank you for the education. I've learned a lot.' I've also offered to have the Sons of Confederate Veterans come and do a little multicultural diversity training for his firefighters on the meaning of Confederate symbols. He sounds interested. What this shows is that when you have truth you have the mightiest weapon of all."

A hearty round of applause ensued, a burst of enthusiasm surpassed a few minutes later when Paul Gramling, after offering a chronology of the events that took place earlier that week at the mall, concluded with a bold peroration: "And now I'm going to get up on my soapbox. I, personally — because of my heritage, because of my ancestors, because of where I live — I am tired of being treated like a second-class citizen. You take any other nationality, creed, race, ethnic group, special-interest group, you name it — you say one bad word about them and you're marked. Except for the southerner. We're the only class of people that it's politically correct to ridicule and bash and demonize. And I am tired of it." This was greeted with a standing ovation.

"I, for one, will never again darken the hallways of that mall," said one of the older members.

"I was in the mall before Christmas, and you couldn't even get into the stores because of the roving groups of black teenagers," his wife interjected.

McMichael had a novel suggestion: "What you might do, if

you decide to buy something out there, is pay cash and stamp a battle flag on each bill. And if it's a five-dollar bill" — time for some Lincoln-bashing — "you might want to make some other alterations. A hole puncher works nice."

The most peculiar moment of the evening, serendipitously, was saved for last. The camp commander announced that a "special guest" would lead a final chorus of "Dixie." With this, a restaurant employee named Lessie Taylor, a middle-aged African-American woman wearing blue jeans and a red El Chico T-shirt, stepped to the front of the room. A man standing next to me recognized her and said, "You're the one who told me a few weeks ago how much you love this song." "It's true," replied Taylor. "I do." And then, as she posed with a battle flag on a long pole and smiled opaquely, the music played and the faithful crooned. Afterward, John Andrew Prime, a *Shreveport Times* reporter who happened to be present, took Taylor's photograph.

When I headed to my car, Vernon Love, the bagpiper who had gotten things rolling at the mall, stood on the sidewalk, shouldering his instrument, getting ready to play again. I drove half a block to a convenience store, where signs posted outside said "Pants Below the Waist Not Allowed — Shoes and Shirt Required" And "No Playing of Loud Music in Parking Lot." From a hundred yards away, I could hear Vernon Love all too clearly. As loud as any boom box, he rendered the evening's final iteration of "Dixie," clotting the moist spring air like glue.

THE WEDDING of Lynda Estes and Paul Gramling had been scheduled for four o'clock on Saturday afternoon at Caspiana House, a restored plantation cottage that is one of a half dozen antebellum and turn-of-the-century buildings gathered in a corner of the sprawling campus of Louisiana State University–Shreveport. I arrived around one o'clock — Gramling had told me that, in the hours before the ceremony, he'd be participating in a living-history exhibit — and was impressed to find the parking lots packed.

The cars, it turned out, belonged to spectators at an all-day soccer tournament, and I drove around for several minutes until I came upon a small concentration of vehicles with bumper stickers imprinted with battle flags and slogans like "Pride Not Prejudice" and "Heritage Not Hate" and "I Have a Dream" (illustrated with a battle flag flying above the U.S. Capitol). I found Gramling smoking a cigarette under the canvas roof of a field office that had been set up by the West Battery, an artillery-ordnance reenactment unit. Every hour, the troops fired a cannon as clusters of soccer moms and dads and kids looked on.

As the guests arrived — there were about a hundred, a majority in period attire — I began to feel out of place in my beige summer suit, white shirt, and red necktie. Then I got over it. I certainly didn't suffer from Confederate-uniform envy. Nor did I think the women, many of whom were not especially svelte, seemed all that comfortable in their corsets. Gramling wore a pearl gray wool general's coat, a charcoal gabardine vest with black buttons, a white formal shirt with a ruffled front, gray wool trousers, cavalry officer black boots, and about a dozen beribboned medals. Estes had on a Confederate gray satin hoopskirt with a white rose and seed pearl bodice, and lace mitts, and carried a bouquet of silk flowers. In one of my early conversations with the couple, I committed the faux pas of referring to "costumes" instead of period attire. As I surveyed the guests, it wasn't clear to me what difference the nomenclature made. The fact was that this was a crowd of middle-middle-class folk who had chosen to devote their discretionary spending to cultivate the illusion that they were the rekindled embodiment of the plantation aristocracy. I wondered what they did for Halloween.

We gathered at the veranda of the Caspiana House to witness the ceremony. Keenan Williams, the chaplain of the Army of the Trans-Mississippi and a minister in real life, recited the vows from a Civil War–vintage Methodist prayer book. At the end of the service, the cannon fired one more time, the bride and groom kissed, and, as they descended from the veranda, two rows of men in variegated uniforms, all armed with sabers, faced each other and raised their weapons to form an arch for the wedding party. This final bit of pageantry was choreographed by Chuck McMichael, who told me afterward, "Considering how little we rehearsed, we count ourselves lucky that no one lost an eye."

A FEATURE ARTICLE about the wedding appeared prominently in the next day's *Shreveport Times*, along with a photograph of Lessie Taylor holding the flag and singing "Dixie" at the General Richard Taylor Camp meeting. According to the most recent census, Shreveport's population is now slightly more than fifty percent African American, which would suggest that the photograph had at least half the readers scratching their heads. Or maybe not. Perhaps there was just a collective shrugging of shoulders.

Shreveport is a place with a long history of boom and bust (cotton, lumber, oil, and gas). The latest boom got under way seven years ago, with the advent of casino gambling. Oddly, though the casinos have kept unemployment low, the population hasn't budged significantly in the last twenty years. One's net impression is of a middling city of finite charm and an ingrained reluctance to press its luck.

Six weeks before the Sons of Confederate Veterans became newsworthy, the least charming side of Shreveport showed its face during a Mardi Gras parade. African-American members of two high school marching bands were subjected to racist taunts and allegedly pelted with beer cans and other objects by groups of young men waving Rebel flags. An African-American member of the city council proposed a resolution, which was unanimously adopted, calling for a police investigation, and an African-American law firm pledged five thousand dollars to any reward fund that might be set up to help apprehend the malefactors. But no such fund ever materialized, and the police haven't made any arrests. Nor, according to the assistant police chief in charge of the investigation, are they likely to.

I also spoke with a lot of black people in Shreveport. I heard considerable speculation that the black security guard at the mall, when he encountered the Sons of Confederate Veterans, probably had the Mardi Gras ugliness in mind. What I didn't hear in those conversations was any sympathy for the Sons of Confederate Veterans. A clergyman and newspaper columnist named Gregory Hudson said, "Do you realize how angry, how bitter, and how sorry you have to be as a white man not to be successful in the South? Everything is designed in your favor. Ninety percent of the businesses are owned by southern white men. So how can you feel discriminated against? What part of southern heritage do these guys want remembered, anyway?" In any event, the Pierre Bossier Mall owners are not apologizing. Two days after the wedding, the general manager issued a statement to the effect that the security guards had "acted appropriately . . . in the best interests of the tenants, customers, and children in the mall."

Contrary to popular understanding, Robert E. Lee's capitulation at Appomattox Court House on April 9, 1865, did not mark the official end of the war. From Richmond, Jefferson Davis fled southwest, bound for Shreveport, possessed of the idea that if he could reach that destination — the headquarters of the Trans-Mississippi Department — he might be able to broker better terms for a conditional surrender. He got as far as Georgia before being captured. Shreveport itself, the last Confederate command to surrender, held out until May 26. In *The Rise and Fall of the Confederate Government*, Davis wrote, "It was at Shreveport that the Confederate flag ceased forever to float over land." The Louisiana Sons of Confederate Veterans would say that Davis was in far too pessimistic a frame of mind. They can freshly recall the Battle of Pierre Bossier Mall. And, at last report, they were still weighing their options, as if it mattered.

LAST NIGHT AT THE DINER

Lee, Massachusetts
FEBRUARY 2001

O<small>N THE SURFACE</small>, there was nothing mysterious about Joe's Diner. It was a diner owned by a guy named Joe Sorrentino. All day long, people came in and sat down — at the counter or, if the stools were occupied, at one of four tables. You ordered, the food was delivered, while you ate you chatted with Joe or his sons or the grill cook or the waitresses or the dishwasher or your neighbors (or, if you didn't feel like talking, no one bothered you), the jukebox played, you asked for the check, you paid — never very much, no credit cards — and you vacated your seat knowing that it would soon be filled. If you'd come in happy, you tended to leave happier. If you'd come in unhappy, you might very well leave unhappy, but that wouldn't be Joe's fault. Nobody left hungry.

It was Joe's fault, though that seems an odd way of putting it, that everyone in Lee, Massachusetts, took him for granted. Starting in 1955, he stayed open round the clock, except for major holidays and a sixteen-hour interval every Sunday, from three A.M. to seven P.M. After thirty-three years of that, he cut back, closing all day Sunday and at six-thirty Saturday evening. Still, six mornings a week the place opened at five-thirty, and Monday through Friday closing time was midnight. Workers at the paper mills — Lee had six in 1955, and five continue to operate — could get breakfast before the seven A.M. to three P.M. shift or dinner after the three to eleven. Actually, you could order breakfast any time of day, and, if you felt like Salisbury steak, potatoes, gravy, and cauliflower at sunrise, that was okay, too. The litany of Joe's daily specials — Monday (roast beef), Tuesday (meat loaf, roast turkey, chicken breasts), Wednesday (roast pork, spareribs, stuffed peppers), Thursday (corned beef and cabbage), Friday (fish, fried chicken, veal cutlets), Saturday (baked ham) — was as familiar as a rosary.

Presumably, people in Lee, if pressed, would have conceded the possibility that Joe might someday decide he'd had enough, but what was the advantage of dwelling on a thought like that? You could say that the whole town was in a state of denial. Or perhaps they'd all been lulled into a blissful tortellini soup–induced inertia. Who could blame them? At the margins of plausibility, yes, one could contemplate a modified, Joeless Joe's Diner, but it was a soft-landing scenario in which Joe's sons Mike and Frank took over, Paul and Alice still worked at the grill, Jackie and Evelyn and Margaret still waitressed, Dottie washed dishes, the menu and the prices didn't change, and a couple of times a day Joe, in his emeritus capacity, would drop by for a bite or a cup of coffee. It was when you tried conjuring a Lee that was Joe's Diner–less, period, that you strayed into the realm of the truly unthinkable.

Residents of the postcard-perfect towns and villages of New England have had to defend their landscapes not only against the garden-variety American strip mall virus but also against the risk of getting strangled by their own quaint charms. At some point — broadly speaking, this would have been after the industrial revolution and before the invention of the Walkman — the Berkshire hills of western Massachusetts became a fair-weather destination for urban and suburban New Yorkers whose collective urge to get away from it all spawned, in towns like Stockbridge and Lenox, and especially on the roads leading to Tanglewood and Jacob's Pillow, the chronic traffic jams that give cultural uplift a bad name. Somehow, Lee, a blue-collar heart-of-the-Berkshires town without pretensions, was less afflicted with these annoyances. One thing Lee had going for it was Joe's Diner, and in a sense Joe's Diner *was* Lee. Without too much of a stretch, you could even say that the diner was America.

In 1958, what became a famous Norman Rockwell image — a friendly cop and a would-be runaway boy, a hobo's bindle at his feet, eyeing each other from adjacent stools at the counter of a diner, with the counterman looking on — illustrated the cover of the *Saturday Evening Post*. Rockwell, who lived in Stockbridge and was an occasional customer, had composed the drawing with Joe's Diner in mind. Ever since, first-time visitors had been coming in, arranging themselves on those same stools, and asking Joe to pose for photographs. There were citizens of Lee, diner regulars, who adjusted their eating schedules (or ordered takeout meals) during the summer, when a line on the sidewalk outside Joe's was a common sight. But, inside, a foamy egalitarianism prevailed, the tourists and the locals mixing as smoothly as a banana shake. Everyone felt legitimately entitled to feel proprietary about Joe's. Which is to say that if the cloud of calamity that hovered over the diner early last month — when the rarely deployed "Sorry, We're Closed" sign was hung in the front window and stayed there — had materialized in July instead of January, the sense of desolation that pervaded Lee might very well have triggered a mental health crisis as far away as the Upper West Side of Manhattan.

NOBODY FELT WORSE about this turn of events than Joe did. He'd spent his entire life in Lee, and he had an unblinking sense of civic duty. Since 1939, when he was seven years old, a diner had anchored the two-story clapboard building at the end of Main

Street, where Lee's central commercial district tapered and the road curved, crossing the railroad tracks and continuing north toward Lenox and Pittsfield. It was a strategic location, situated next door to the Schweitzer paper mill. Joe's father worked at the mill, and the family lived three blocks away. As kids, Joe and his friends would go to the diner, which was owned by Happy Navin, and play pinball until Happy shooed them out. Before the Massachusetts Turnpike opened, the diner was on the truck route to and from Boston, so Happy stayed open twenty-four hours. In 1950, he sold the business to Leo Gatewood, and five years later, at the age of twenty-two, Joe bought it from Leo.

Joe's business cards, like Joe himself, were good-humored and matter-of-fact. "Where the Elite Meet to Shoot the Sheet," they said. Also, "Best Food in Town." Partly because of the diner's provenance as a truck stop, and also because the mill workers could trade their meal tickets there, in the early years it had a reputation as a man's place. A housewife who didn't feel like cooking would send her husband or her son to pick up dinner, but women didn't really feel at home at Joe's until the mid-sixties. The exceptions were the waitresses, including Joe's Aunt Angelina and his wife, Theresa, who, when she wasn't busy looking after their kids — eventually, there were seven — toiled at the grill and was as distinctive a presence as Joe. At one time or another, every member of the family worked in the diner, all guided by a simple precept. "My father made it very clear," Joe Jr., the eldest son, said recently. "When you came to work you didn't come to play. You didn't come to talk on the phone or eat lunch or have breakfast. You came to work. Because if you didn't work he had to work even harder."

The children attended parochial school at St. Mary's, the same parish where they went to Mass every Sunday, and finished up at Lee High School. Senior year, the Sorrentino children confronted a choice: Joe would foot the bill for college or they could have the cash. The oldest, and the only girl, Debbie, opted for college, as did the three youngest boys, Robert, Sam, and Pete. In 1977, Joe Jr. and Mike graduated from Lee High and began putting in eighty-hour weeks at the diner, and three years later Frank joined them. (In time, Joe Jr. began moonlighting at a hobby shop he'd opened a hundred yards from the diner, and ten years ago he decided to make that his sole occupation.)

During the mid-nineties, a publicly subsidized, smartly unyuppified face-lift of downtown Lee took place — new street lights, sidewalks with brick borders, storefront upgrades. While Joe happily accepted a grant that helped pay for new clapboards on one side of the building and new windows on the second floor, everyone knew better than to tamper with the diner's cedar and red-brick façade or the illuminated Pepsi sign above the entrance. And the interior, of course, was absolutely untouchable: the gray and black checkerboard linoleum-tile floor; Masonite walls (including one festooned with snapshots of happy eaters, many wearing Joe's Diner sweatshirts and T-shirts in faraway places — Indonesia, Australia, China, Russia, Bulgaria, Antarctica); brown plastic-laminated tables; orange and yellow molded-plastic chairs; red vinyl-capped swivel stools; counter with creamy swirl-patterned Formica veneer; crucifix hanging over the thermostat, beneath the menu board ("Hamburger — $1, Cheeseburger — $1.25, Sausage Grinder — $2.50"); Tums, Juicy Fruit, LifeSavers, RoiTan cigars, and Red Man chewing tobacco on the shelves next to the cash register; photograph of Joe with Mitzi Gaynor and Johnny Ray, taken in his pre-diner days, when he was an army cook stationed in California and a Hollywood-cameraman uncle invited him on the set of *There's No Business Like Show Business*; shots of Joe posing with homage-paying politicians (Michael Dukakis, John Kerry, William Weld); photograph of Father Gary from St. Mary's, taken at the Vatican with the Holy Father, which inevitably prompted the question "Joe, you mean even the Pope eats here?" No right-minded person would have dreamed of altering a molecule of it.

So one can charitably assume a certain sheepishness on the part of inspectors from the Tri-Town Health Department who, three months ago, informed Joe that he would have to make some changes. Forty-five years in business, and he'd never been cited for a health code violation, but new rules were new rules. The code said you needed a sink reserved exclusively for employees to wash their hands, you needed grease traps in the basins where pots and pans were cleaned, an automatic dishwasher would have to be installed. Joe had faith in his own exacting standards; grease traps or not, no restaurant in Berkshire County could boast a more hygienic kitchen. His position on a dishwasher had always been why buy one when you can hire one. Obeying the Health Department edict would necessitate tearing apart a workplace where space was extremely tight and everything functioned according to a precise choreography.

The inspectors were willing to give Joe six months to comply, but he didn't need that long to plot his next move. A few weeks before their visit, he'd been hospitalized with pneumonia, emerging just in time to arrange the funeral of his only sibling, an older sister. He no longer had the stamina to be on his feet fourteen hours a day. His knees were killing him, and his blood-sugar level wasn't where it belonged. He recalled his honeymoon, in 1956, when he and Theresa drove to New York City in a fire-engine red Chevy convertible, spent three nights at the Taft Hotel and another three in Atlantic City, and returned to Lee at six o'clock on a Saturday evening, an hour before he went back to work at the diner. They took their next vacation, a weeklong Caribbean cruise, twenty-nine years later. The time had arrived for yet another, of the permanent variety.

JOE OFFERED THE BUSINESS to Mike and Frank, but they too had had enough. The idea of a fresh start appealed to Mike; he was forty-one, with a wife and four children of whom he saw too little, and he wanted to get into real estate. For years, Frank, who was also married, had done maintenance work on the diner building, which had four commercial tenants, and he'd acquired several other customers around town. Now he could turn that into a full-fledged enterprise and make his own hours.

The news that Joe's Diner was for sale appeared in the *Berkshire Eagle*, a daily paper published in Pittsfield, in early November. Television and radio stations in Boston and Albany picked it up, and the phone started ringing. Considering the value of the name alone, Joe's $100,000 asking price seemed as cheap as his menu prices. ("We make friends, not money," he liked to say whenever customers marveled that he charged only six or seven bucks for a full dinner.) The first serious buyer to show up was a nurse from Pittsfield named Ramona Hamilton. Though she had no experience running a restaurant — much less running a diner à la Joe — she had a sister and a brother who planned to get involved, plus lots of friends who wanted to help out, so he agreed to sell it to her. For five weeks, Ramona observed Joe and the staff in action. During that time, she didn't do much cooking, but Joe described his preparation methods step by step, and she wrote it all down.

The next to last day of the year, a Saturday, was Joe, Mike, and Frank's last day on the premises. When the diner reopened under new management on January 2, a reporter from the *Berkshire Record*, a weekly, came around and wrote a friendly changing-of-the-guard story. Ramona was quoted as saying ("with a chuckle"), "It's been a harder day than any I ever had at Berkshire Medical Center, and I worked in intensive care." By the time the story was published three days later, she was no longer in the diner business. In the wake of her startlingly abrupt departure, there was speculation that Ramona had been defeated by the exigencies of preparing the Thursday special, corned beef and cabbage, which was widely regarded as Joe's pièce de résistance. It seems more likely that she realized what she'd gotten into, in general, and had a vision of herself imminently back in intensive care, as a patient. The staff received calls telling them that they were no longer employed, and Joe's lawyer got a call telling him that the purchase agreement, which hadn't yet been consummated, wasn't going to be. Ramona exited in such haste that she left behind the spiral-bound computer-printed notes of all the instructions Joe had given her. When he found it, he said, more or less with a chuckle, "Yeah, I should hold on to that. Someday I might want to open up a diner."

By the time I went to Lee to get a status report, the inhabitants had spent almost two weeks coping with the town's new identity as the erstwhile home of Joe's Diner. Joe, a fleshy, pleasantly handsome fellow in his late sixties, with swept-back black hair that was gray at the temples, thick eyebrows, and dark brown eyes, agreed to meet me at the diner. The mood inside was crepuscular, and the air felt chilly. I sat at the counter, Joe stationed himself in his accustomed position, on the other side, and we spoke for several hours, during which he made it plain that he failed to detect much humor in the situation. On the topic of Ramona Hamilton, he was circumspect; he felt bad, she felt bad, and he didn't want to say anything that would hurt anyone's feelings. He happened to be negotiating with a new potential buyer, and if the lawyers could agree on certain details the place might be up and running again any day. But he still couldn't get over the tormenting fact that he'd been a party to circumstances that had deprived innocent victims of their weekly rations of home-fried potatoes, scrod Sorrentino, and sparerib patties on hard rolls.

"It hurts," he said. "This place has never been closed since 1939. Now it's closed. Say you're used to coming here every night. Now you've got to find another place. You do that, and you're going there two or three weeks. You hear that Joe's sold his place, but you don't know who the new owners are, and you're happy with your new place, so you wind up staying there."

The import of his remarks — the notion that forty-five years' worth of accumulated goodwill could disappear in a matter of days — struck me as highly unlikely. Too many people in Lee depended on the diner as much for fellowship as for sustenance. The reality was that the townsfolk wanted a diner called Joe's Diner just as it was, and stood ready to give the benefit of the doubt to anyone with a clear-eyed grasp of how hard the Sorrentinos had worked to make the enterprise seem effortless.

In the midst of Joe's lamentations, Theresa dropped in — a small woman with intelligent eyes, a halo of gray curls, and the bemused contentment of someone who hadn't needed to travel far to see it all. Any competent new operator who had enough common sense to rehire Joe's old staff would do fine, she said. "As soon as the customers find out that your help is back, they're going to come back."

Joe looked at her with a mixture of hope and skepticism, and after she'd left he said, "You know, I never sat down here and ate a meal. I'd go home for that. Theresa prepared dinner every night."

Mike Sorrentino, who had been around for most of the conversation, said, "I'd leave here at two or three in the morning and go home and eat."

"If people came in and saw us sitting down, then we weren't putting out their dinner," Joe continued. "I wouldn't let those guys" — Mike or Frank — "cut the meat to put on the dish. I'd push them out of the way. I had to make it look good, make sure they got the right cut. If I know you're a big eater, I'll give you a bigger cut. If you come in here and don't eat everything, next time you get less. Until I know your capacity. Because I don't like to see food wasted. You see some guy six-six, you've got to put a half pound of meat on there, for six bucks. Every time the girls took an order, I had to know who it was for."

Mike: "You knew how each customer liked their food."

Joe: "Don't other places do that?"

THE NEXT TIME I saw Joe, six days later, a large cardboard "Open" sign had been taped to the front window and his spirits had greatly improved. We met back at the diner in the late morning, as the early-lunch crowd was arriving; it was a Tuesday, tortellini soup day. In the meantime, he'd closed a deal to sell the place to people whom, in retrospect, he realized he should have approached in the first place — two brothers, Chuck and Gordon Hebler, and their partner, Terry Shapiro. They had successful restaurants in Lenox and Pittsfield, and many years of experience catering backstage at big rock concerts and stadium shows. When the diner reopened the previous day, Joe and Mike and Frank were all present and in uniform — short-sleeved white shirt, white apron, black and white checked trousers — because they'd agreed to work for a week, explaining the ins and outs. All the old help was back except for Margaret MacDowell, who'd taken a job at the paper mill next door. As regular customers repatriated, Joe introduced them to the new guys, who said all the right things: they might cut back the nighttime hours a bit, but otherwise everything would remain the same.

Everything that was supposed to happen on a Tuesday did. Aldo Pascucci, one of the town selectmen, came in for the tortellini soup, and he and Joe agreed that his recent bout with the flu could probably have been avoided if he hadn't gone soupless for two weeks. Joseph Scapin Sr. from Lee Hardware Store sat at the counter with his grandson, ordered a meat-loaf sandwich, and went through a familiar routine with a waitress named Pat Read: he asked how her dog was, she said the dog was fine, and he urged her to deliver it to the kitchen because he had an appetite for what he called "polenta bowwow." Charlie Flint, an antiques dealer, sat at a table and ordered a dish named after himself, the Charlie Chef Salad.

"Hey, Charlie, how ya doin'?" Joe greeted him.

"You smell like mothballs," Charlie replied. "But, you know, Joe, you look rested."

I stuck around until dinner because I wanted to meet the Higgins brothers, Bill and John, eighty-one-year-old twins who for almost twenty years had been making the trip from Pittsfield five nights a week. They always sat at the end of the counter, where there was a photograph on the wall that showed them in that exact spot. As they were settling on their stools, Jackie Nicholas approached and wordlessly put out paper napkins, silverware, glasses of water, and buttered bread. Bill had just tucked the napkin into his crewneck sweater when she delivered two plates of salad, followed by turkey, mashed potatoes, broccoli, and cranberry sauce, and a small pitcher of yellow gravy. When I asked how she knew to bring the turkey and not the meat-loaf special, Bill said, "Last night they asked us. We told them."

Joe dropped by. "You gotta eat what's on the table," he said. "Just like home."

"Right, Joe," Bill said.

The light had dimmed outside, and, without anyone's having touched a switch, it seemed brighter inside. The diner was almost full now. Doris Day had come on the jukebox, singing "Whatever Will Be Will Be." "Once I know these guys have been fed, I can go home," Joe told me. He disappeared into the kitchen, and when he came out he was wearing a blue windbreaker and a Yankees cap.

"You be in tomorrow?" he asked the Higgins brothers — a rhetorical question.

"Yeah," Bill said. "Roast pork."

"Okay," Joe said. "I'll see you tomorrow."

TIME TO KILL

Terre Haute, Indiana

MAY 2001

I T WASN'T AS IF I'd especially been looking forward to the day of Timothy McVeigh's execution. I understand that when you decide to kill someone in a manner that's likely to attract a large crowd, you want things to proceed smoothly and so you plan ahead. (McVeigh himself had certainly done that when he murdered 168 people in Oklahoma City on April 19, 1995.) Still, many of the ground rules devised for the ceremonies in Terre Haute, Indiana, struck me as gratuitously onerous. Leaving nothing to chance — except, of course, the is-this-a-great-country-or-what possibility that the prospective executee's arch-nemesis, the Federal Bureau of Investigation, would disgrace itself in the eleventh hour with a revelation of incompetence worthy of the Department of Motor Vehicles — the Federal Bureau of Prisons had scripted McVeigh's farewell with an inflexible specificity that even the most exacting anal compulsives could marvel at. The micromanaging extended well beyond the fifty-one-page "Execution Protocol," which delineated the killing ritual in language intended to reassure taxpayers that they were getting their money's worth: "The Warden will then advise the Designated United States Marshal that, 'We are ready.' A prearranged signal will then be given by the Designated United States Marshal to the Warden, who will direct the executioner(s) to administer the lethal injection." Fine. But what about those of us for whom the logistical dictates were a source of personal inconvenience? Whose idea was it, anyway, to inject McVeigh with potassium chloride at seven o'clock in the morning?

Eight days before the execution date (and three days before it was postponed), the Bureau of Prisons set up a media-registration center on the first floor of the Terre Haute Holiday Inn and began distributing press credentials — a laminated plastic "Media Center Official Press Pass," to be worn on a nickel-chain necklace along with a photo ID. Even if what McVeigh called the "suicide-by-cop deluxe package" had been delivered to him as originally scheduled, these were patently worthless party favors. The press pass would allow access not to the confines of the U.S. penitentiary but to a precisely demarcated ghetto almost a half mile outside its razor-wire-topped fences. From that vantage point, a very limited range of options would be available. A camera equipped with a telephoto lens could capture static images of the brown brick exterior of the federal lockup, but nothing about those images would particularize that an execution was taking place inside. With or without a camera, one could interview pro– and anti–death penalty advocates who would gather on-site. The opposing groups would be separated from each other and cordoned within plastic-fenced zones a few hundred yards from the main media-briefing tent. No one could predict how many demonstrators would show up in Terre Haute, but it seemed likely that they would be far outnumbered by members of the Fourth Estate. Under the circumstances, representatives of the press would be reduced, as is inevitably the case in such situations, to interviewing each other. Many of the requisite components of an American macabre extravaganza would be assembled, but what the audience lusted after would be hidden from view, rather like a Roman Colosseum frolic in which the arena remains empty until a herald arrives with the news that the lion, offstage, has enjoyed his meal.

When I claimed my press credentials at the Holiday Inn — by then, I'd already been domiciled on the fourth floor for several days, testing the hypothesis that a life sentence in tight quarters in Terre Haute was sufficient punishment for any crime — I volunteered to be a media-pool representative in the execution witness room. Ten of the twenty-five witness slots were allocated to the press, two to the "print media." Gore Vidal, it turned out, had come by his reserved seat not because he would be reporting on the event for *Vanity Fair* but because the soon-to-be-deceased was allowed to invite five guests. I was curious when I first heard that Vidal and the most homicidal man in America were acquaintances; a byproduct, perhaps, of a shared enthusiasm for the novels of Dawn Powell? Not quite. Actually, they'd become pen pals after Vidal published, in 1998, an intermittently coherent essay alleging a general assault by the federal government on the Bill of Rights, an argument McVeigh found philosophically compatible with his own beliefs — the same beliefs that to this day undergird his nauseating certitude that bombing the Alfred P. Murrah Federal Building was the right thing to do.

As for the rest of us scribblers, the Bureau of Prisons had mandated, "The method for choosing or selecting press pool witnesses is a matter that is completely determined by those media representatives involved in the selection process." So we would settle this among ourselves, no doubt in a spirit reminiscent of *Lord of the Flies*. I probably stood a better chance of winning the Powerball lottery, but I would never have forgiven myself if I failed to make the effort to be an eyewitness to a historic event for which — assuming that one believed the assurances of Attorney General John Ashcroft — no visual record would be preserved. The dreadful part was that the selection process would take place at four A.M. To be present, one would have to arrive an hour or so earlier at an off-site location and then be transported to the prison outskirts by shuttle bus. The net result would be little or no bed rest on the eve of the execution. In that regard, I shared McVeigh's resentment of the federal government's heavy hand. When, deus ex machina, the FBI disrupted millions of people's ardent expectations, I appraised the upside: at least we could all sleep in.

AMID ALL THIS, one still felt, constantly and acutely, for the victims' families, the survivors, and the citizens of Oklahoma City, who were so desperate to blot McVeigh out of their consciousness and who would now have this chapter of their nightmare prolonged for weeks, or possibly months or years. The mood in Terre Haute, however, ran more toward exasperation than aggrieved outrage. What these two communities, 650 miles apart, had in common — besides their flat landscapes and their deep familiarity with the trappings of the homogenized Middle American quotidian — was the arbitrariness with which they had become settings in the twisted chronicle of McVeigh's twisted existence. Before electing to ruin thousands of lives in Oklahoma, McVeigh had pondered potential targets in Arizona, Arkansas, Missouri, Texas, and Washington, D.C. Oklahoma City was an erstwhile oil boomtown and cowtown, the capital of a state distinguished by the fact that, during its relatively brief history — Oklahoma joined the Union less than a century ago — events of national consequence tended not to occur there. McVeigh fixed that. Passively, Oklahoma City had become defined as The Place That Got Bombed.

Terre Haute, meanwhile, had enjoyed several decades of civic satisfaction as the home of a federal penitentiary with a population that now numbers almost two thousand convicts. During the Depression, the town fathers lobbied vigorously for the prison to be built there because of the hundreds of permanent jobs it would create. The first occupants arrived in 1940. In 1994, the United States criminal code was expanded to include several new categories of misdeeds punishable by death. The last federal execution, in 1963, was accomplished by hanging, an untidy method no longer in vogue. The official explanation from the Bureau of Prisons was that Terre Haute's central location made it an ideal home for the country's only state-of-the-art federal execution apparatus; after all, the town called itself "The Crossroads of America." People in Terre Haute claim not to be pleased to have achieved celebrity in this fashion, not even the majority that supports capital punishment in general and the extermination of McVeigh in particular. On the other hand, there's no question that the prospect of his unnatural demise has been good for business.

During a press briefing a week before the proceedings got put on hold, the mayor, Judy Anderson, was asked how she felt about her city's moment in the international spotlight. "It's not something we chose, but because it's going to happen we're trying to put a positive spin on the activities that will take place here," said the mayor, a gracious lady in her late fifties. "We want people who come here, most of whom will be leaving and not returning, to know that this is a beautiful, friendly city. We're on the Wabash River, we have lovely parks. We want visitors to go away feeling that the people they've met here are polite, friendly, and helpful. We want you to go away knowing that we personally feel that the penitentiary is a very good partner of our community. The death chamber just happens to be part of that facility."

Previously, Mayor Anderson had told the *Times*, when asked about the prospect that souvenir venders would be hawking T-shirts and buttons, "We have no control over what they sell. We're just asking that it be in very good taste." After the press briefing, I visited a tattoo and body-piercing parlor in central Terre Haute, where commemorative T-shirts were priced at twenty bucks. The most popular item showed the front page of a mock newspaper, the *Hangin' Times*, with a photograph of McVeigh under the headline "DIE MOTHERFUCKER DIE!"

*   *   *

THE MAYOR WAS NOT ALONE in confronting a daunting spin-control challenge. One afternoon, I drove to the town of Bloom-field, southeast of Terre Haute, for an appointment with Roger Stalcup, the brigadier general of the Southern Indiana Regional Militia, which consists of twenty county militias with a combined membership, according to Stalcup, of more than a thousand peo-ple. The government's investigation of McVeigh placed him and his co-conspirator, Terry Nichols, at militia meetings in the vicin-ity of the Nichols family farm, in Michigan. It was one thing to agree with McVeigh that the odious forces of gun control posed a grave threat to the sacrosanct Second Amendment. However, McVeigh's shrill rhetoric — inspired by William L. Pierce's *The Turner Diaries*, an anti-Semitic novel whose protagonist bombs the FBI headquarters in Washington — proved a bit much for the folks in Michigan, and he never officially joined a militia. Never-theless, in the aftermath of Oklahoma City, militia groups every-where, never popular to begin with, became the object of greatly increased hostility.

For someone like Stalcup, a forty-nine-year-old family man and professional bail-enforcement agent ("It's a fancy term for bounty hunter"), everything connected to McVeigh was anath-ema. We met at a Dairy Queen. Stalcup had brought along his wife, Janice, and their daughter, Sarah, a twelve-year-old who looked like her mother — round-faced, with a brunet pageboy haircut — but was dressed like her father, in jeans and a camou-flage jacket. Sarah, who told me that she wants to be an army drill sergeant when she grows up, is the commander of her county youth militia.

I'd heard about Stalcup from a German public television crew that had gone to see him a couple of days earlier — a visit that, all agreed, had not been worthwhile. "The Germans tried to talk us into bringing out some automatic rifles and handguns and dem-onstrating them on camera," Stalcup complained. "That's some-thing we wouldn't do ordinarily and certainly wouldn't consider when we're right on the verge of the McVeigh execution and people are in a panic as it is. Even though all our weapons are perfectly legal and we have nothing to hide. Some people just associate guns with evil, and they don't understand the whole story."

Our conversation made detours into topics like the Antichrist and the specter of one world government, but there were moments when, if I closed my eyes, I might have fancied I was chatting with an Upper West Side liberal. Stalcup was opposed to capital punishment — "I've never been for the death penalty, because there's a lot of flaws in the justice system. Look at all the DNA evidence that has set people free" — and he assumed that McVeigh's execution would backfire. "There are several more radical fringe groups out there, and we're giving them one more date on the calendar to do something," he said, echoing the compelling logic that locking McVeigh away for life would deprive him of the capacity for martyrdom.

"The way I see capital punishment, two wrongs don't make a right," said Sarah, demonstrating the thoroughness of her political indoctrination.

"We're one of the few nations in the world that has capital punishment," her father added. "What's that say about us?"

US. IN PRINCIPLE, all of us have a stake in the decision to take or spare McVeigh's life, a binary choice with uncountable caveats. Those among us who want McVeigh to be executed — a group that includes many who profess a belief in forgiveness — insist that the motivation isn't revenge but justice. It's really quite simple: he did it to us and so we're entitled to do it to him.

And he did do it. From the get-go, he had admitted his guilt to his lawyers. He told them the story again and again, until the tale didn't so much leak as hemorrhage to the newspapers before his trial. Convicted, condemned to death, done with his appeals, he guided his biographers step by step through the epic of his transfiguration, explicating without remorse how and when and why.

A week before the execution date, a combination of reportorial and homing instincts drew me from Terre Haute to Oklahoma City. I grew up in Oklahoma in the 1950s and sixties, left after high school, and returned to live there for a couple of years in the early eighties, renting a house in Oklahoma City a mile from ground zero. Two or three times a week, I used to run on an indoor track at the YMCA, diagonally across the street from the Murrah Building. For my literary purposes, Oklahoma had usually served as a comic foil, an endearing, amusing, anthropologically rich subculture that I understood as well as any. The bombing catastrophe didn't fit into any narrative around which I could wrap my imagination or my treasured sense of where I came from.

Which is why, until my most recent visit, I had avoided going near the bomb site. When I finally forced myself to take a look, the sobering reward was a stunningly well-conceived memorial museum and park that filled two square blocks downtown. A pair of two-story polished bronze walls, separated by a reflecting pool, stand at each end of the park: on one is engraved "9:01" and on the other "9:03" — the moments before and after the explosion. Arranged on a gently sloping lawn alongside the reflecting pool are the now famous 168 empty chairs. I spent two hours there, during which, it later occurred to me, I thought about the lives of the dead and not at all about McVeigh. Then I got into my car and drove a hundred miles north, to Enid, to the office of Stephen Jones, the lead defense lawyer during McVeigh's trial.

JONES OCCUPIES A POSITION very high on the list of McVeigh's least favorite people. Lou Michel and Dan Herbeck, the authors of the best-selling *American Terrorist*, who spent seventy-five hours interviewing McVeigh, have written that one of the reasons he agreed to talk with them was that he had become "enraged" by

Jones. The dispute between Attorney Jones and his former client boiled down to this: McVeigh insisted that he was the brains, brawn, and guts behind the planning, building, and detonation of the bomb; Jones asserted that McVeigh was a dedicated soldier in a terrorist scheme arranged and financed by . . . um, well, exactly who remains a mystery. In 1998, Jones published his own book, *Others Unknown*, and it was decidedly not a bestseller. The title was drawn from the government's original indictment of McVeigh and the weak-willed Nichols, which referred to "others unknown" who might have aided and abetted their crimes. The most sought-after phantom co-conspirator was "John Doe No. 2," whom some witnesses — most notably the three employees of the Ryder truck-rental agency in Kansas where McVeigh picked up the vehicle used to transport the bomb — reported having seen in the company of "John Doe No. 1," a.k.a. McVeigh. In his book, Jones described an early meeting with his client during which he asked, point-blank, "Mr. McVeigh, who is John Doe No. 2?" and McVeigh replied, "John Doe No. 2 doesn't exist." This was not the answer Jones wanted to hear.

While not absolutely opposed to capital punishment, Jones didn't favor it in McVeigh's case — or any other case, presumably, in which he was the attorney of record. Confident that the line of defense McVeigh had urged him to pursue — that it was necessary to bomb the Murrah Building to prevent the federal government from perpetrating future Ruby Ridges or Wacos — was a guaranteed loser, he settled for an equally doomed red-herring strategy. As a court-appointed counsel, Jones succeeded in globe-trotting, on the government's dime, to the Philippines, Israel, England, Syria, and Hong Kong, an odyssey predicated on the existence of an international intrigue involving John Doe No. 2 and others unknown. Nothing emerged, however, to illuminate anyone's understanding of the bombing beyond what the prosecutors, the twelve jurors, and McVeigh himself have agreed on.

Jones is an intelligent if rather pompous fellow whose conduct in the McVeigh case has tarnished his previously respectable reputation, and I doubt that he genuinely doubts that McVeigh essentially acted alone. We had been having a cordial conversation for an hour and a half — not so much about the case per se as about McVeigh's imminent extinction — when he received a phone call alerting him that CBS News had just reported that the FBI, five years too late, had delivered to McVeigh's appellate attorneys more than three thousand pages of field reports from their investigation of the bombing. Then a receptionist entered the wood-paneled office — the only room in Enid, Oklahoma, decorated with autographed pictures of Richard Nixon, Nelson Rockefeller, Dan Rather, and Yasir Arafat, as well as a portrait of the Virgin Mary that once hung in Timothy McVeigh's grandfather's home — and handed Jones a dozen urgent phone messages. Whereupon he got to work doing what he most enjoys, uttering quotable quotes.

Between calls, I asked what he made of this development. "I must honestly say that I'm not surprised," he replied. "We argued before and during the trial that we hadn't received the discovery material we were entitled to. What's not clear is what's in this new material. We don't know that it exculpates McVeigh. All we know is that they were supposed to give it to us and they didn't."

The collateral damage, to use McVeigh's pet phrase, from the FBI's blunder was certainly not that the moldering field reports would prove exculpatory — his confession obviated the possibility of a new trial — but that it would serve the agendas of other obstreperous enemies of the so-called federal juggernaut. Staggering ineptitude, inevitably, would be exploited as proof of sinister behavior. Twenty minutes later, as I drove back toward Oklahoma City, I turned on the radio and there was Jones, bloviating. He popped up again and again over the next few days, enjoying himself at the expense of both McVeigh and the numbskull feds. During an appearance on *Larry King Live*, he heard another guest, Gore Vidal, pronounce *Others Unknown* a "marvelous book." It is, in fact, just the opposite — tendentious, self-serving, bloated with irrelevant details that bespeak its lack of substance. Worst of all, it is a dangerous book, because it encourages all the right-wing lunatic conspiracists out there who insist that the bombing was a plot hatched by the Bureau of Alcohol, Tobacco, and Firearms (the diabolical coauthors of the Waco disaster) and that McVeigh was a patsy. The most entertaining of these future supermarket-tabloid fantasies is the notion that whoever gets the lethal injection in Terre Haute, whenever that should come to pass, won't actually be McVeigh but an even more unfortunate patsy. McVeigh, it seems, will be granted a new identity, which means we have McVeigh-at-large sightings to look forward to. No doubt he'll be traveling with Elvis.

THE LAST PERSON I spoke with in Oklahoma City had had as good an opportunity as anyone to crawl inside McVeigh's mind. Dr. John R. Smith is a psychiatrist who, at Jones's request, rendered an opinion of McVeigh's fitness to stand trial. In the spring and early summer of 1995, he conducted twenty-one hours of psychotherapy with McVeigh and found him, he told me, "competent, depressed but not psychotic" and "fully aware" of what he was doing when he planned and carried out the bombing. (Our conversation was permissible because McVeigh had previously waived the doctor-patient privilege, allowing Dr. Smith to be interviewed by Michel and Herbeck, the authors of *American Terrorist*.) We met at his house — three blocks from my old house — in a comfortably furnished living room with louvered windows, one of which had shattered when the bomb exploded.

Who, I asked Dr. Smith, is Timothy McVeigh?

"A young man who is both child and man," he said, "and who has, as Gore Vidal says, a sense of justice. But it's misguided. He probably should have lived in the eighteenth century. He's so identified with some of the Founding Fathers and the Constitution, the warriors of old, that he believes he's going to save this country. Mostly he's just a human being who made some decisions that caused a lot of pain and suffering to people for reasons that seemed right to him at the time. He stood up for his ideals, but in a way that no one who is decent could agree with."

What were the causal links between the events of McVeigh's white-bread suburban upbringing and the moment he lit the fuses of his 7,000-pound bomb? It was a less than ideal boyhood — his parents quarreled, separated, reconciled, and eventually divorced, and during his adolescence his mother disappeared from his life. At school, he was picked on by bullies, but he also made some friends. (A slightly dubious authority, Ted Kaczynski, the Unabomber, with whom McVeigh was incarcerated for a year in Colorado, wrote a letter to Michel and Herbeck that included a testimonial to McVeigh's "excellent social skills.") In any event, Dr. Smith agreed with McVeigh's own assessment that "he didn't blow up the building because of the effects of the divorce."

Indeed, it's safe to say that we all knew children who were bullied at school or whose parents divorced, and who yet managed to avoid becoming mass murderers. What made McVeigh different? Wasn't the quality of our horrified fascination with McVeigh rooted in our recognition that he was both the personification of evil and one of us? The German television producer who had led me to the militia family made a similar observation: "As a German, I know that they're still talking about the monstrosity of the crime committed in my country. And the size of McVeigh's crime — the number killed — is why people are talking about it. But in my opinion there's more to it. The American sense of security was compromised. Had it been an Arab, a Chinese, a German, it would have been a matter of 'Oh, *they* do that, those kind of people.' But how could an American do that?"

What happened to McVeigh, Dr. Smith believed, was this: When he was a small child, his parents' squabbles, audible on the other side of his bedroom wall, transformed into frightening monsters, which he combated with superhero fantasies derived from his imagination and, later, from comic books. The school-yard bullies were also monsters. When he was very young, his paternal grandfather introduced him to guns, and having weapons enabled him to cope with his fears. Later, gun control activists enraged him by threatening to take away his constitutional rights as well as his psychological armor. As a young adult, he graduated from comic books to texts like *The Turner Diaries*, in which the federal government assumed the role of bullying monster. Ruby Ridge and Waco brought this fantasy to life. Other people who conjured revenge fantasies after those events kept them in check, but McVeigh did not.

Dr. Smith repeated something he had told Michel and Herbeck — that McVeigh, in describing his role in the bombing, "reminded me of a high school student whose science project has been very successful."

Oh, really? Why couldn't he have just grown some fuzzy stuff in petri dishes, scrutinized the rings of Saturn, vivisected frogs?

"He'd been depressed for a long time," he added, "and this project gave him a focus and enabled him to relieve the depression. Most people are not capable intellectually of putting the project together. You have to have someone who's motivated, who's fearless, who has the experience of being a warrior, and who views himself as a warrior."

And if the death penalty is carried out?

"I think it demeans the United States as a government to have a federal death penalty law. For the most powerful democracy in the world to rely on the death penalty to control its citizens is an indication of its weakness, not its strength. There's no one on death row who would have been deterred because of the death penalty. We don't need it here."

I HAD BEEN BACK in Terre Haute less than half an hour, once again under house arrest at the Holiday Inn, when Attorney General Ashcroft announced the one-month reprieve that McVeigh might or might not have desired. When he finished, I left the TV on with the sound muted and settled in. I had work to do and suspected that this would be a quiet place to get it done. A family crowd materialized for the Mother's Day buffet downstairs, but by that evening, when all of Terre Haute was supposed to be eyebrow-deep in the pregame festivities of the closest thing to a Super Bowl the town was ever likely to witness, I pretty much had the run of the joint. Some traumatized hotel operators, flooded with cancellations, announced that anyone reserving a room for the next round of the deathwatch would have to put up a non-refundable deposit. Antifederalist sentiment ran quite high at the chamber of commerce when the realization dawned that the new execution date conflicted with the state beauty pageant. The Miss Indiana Celebrity Miniature Golf Tournament and Pizza Party was scheduled for the night before McVeigh's medical appointment. Someone, by God, was going to pay for this.

When I first arrived in town, I had driven out to look at the prison and immediately discovered the best candidate for the title Local Merchant Destined to Be Interviewed Most Often. This was Raoul David, the friendly eponymous proprietor of David's Food Center, a small grocery store that specialized in the major weekend food groups — meats, sliced cheeses, pickles, chips, salsa, beer — and the most conspicuous business establishment on State Road 63, right across the street from the pokey. The morning after the postponement, David's photograph turned up on the front page of the *Indianapolis Star*, along with a tough-luck account of how the perishable provisions he had stocked up on were going to result in a $3,000 loss. Later that day, I went back to see him and was relieved to find him in a sanguine frame of mind.

"It's not really that bad," he said. He'd bought a lot of pint containers of whole milk and chocolate milk, and he'd take a hit on those. Also, he'd invested heavily in sandwich rolls and some refrigerator products called Lunch Maker Bologna Fun Kit and Lunch Maker Turkey Fun Kit — fifteen cases' worth that he might have trouble moving. But the shish kebab meat he'd been planning to grill for the hungry journalists and death penalty debaters was still in the freezer, and the eighty cases of bottled water would last indefinitely. Memorial Day weekend was coming and his Budweiser distributor had promised to send out a couple of girls in bikinis who would serve beer in the parking lot, and that would boost his cash flow. One area of uncertainty was snack foods. He had a major oversupply of potato chips, nachos, pretzels, cheese curls, and the like, some with expiration dates in September and some in late June. If McVeigh's attorneys decided to seek another delay — well, who knew? Another death row inmate, a drug dealer and murderer named Juan Raul Garza, is now scheduled for lethal injection eight days after McVeigh. Should Garza somehow get the juice first, that will attract a certain amount of interest, but nothing of shish kebab proportions. It's McVeigh's expiration date, God bless America, that matters, for all the right reasons and all the wrong ones.

Timothy McVeigh's unwanted reprieve lasted one month, and on June 11, 2001 — precisely three months before the attacks on the World Trade Center and the Pentagon, events that would eclipse McVeigh's place in the annals of terrorism in America — he was executed according to the prescribed protocol.

For the occasion, Raoul David defrosted and grilled his inventory of shish kebab meat. The price was right — three dollars a skewer — but David had overanticipated the demand; he lost about $250 on the kebabs. The last time I spoke with him, he still held out hope for a bonanza, if only the federal death chamber could attract higher-caliber tenants. "What we need is somebody like Osama bin Laden or Saddam Hussein locked up over there," he said. "That would be a hell of a thing. With bin Laden, my business would jump ten times."

HOME IS HERE

Iɴ ᴛʜᴇ sᴜᴍᴍᴇʀ of 1988, a young Arab-Israeli woman named Maha Mahajneh visited the United States at the invitation of an organization of Palestinian-American women who were holding a convention in New Jersey. It was Mahajneh's first trip to America. At the convention, she gave a talk, the topic of which was, indirectly, the story of her life: the challenges confronted by Arab citizens of Israel. Mahajneh happened to be an anomalous specimen of upward mobility. Growing up in Umm al-Fahm, a small city in the Galilee, she had longed for three things, at least two of which were out of the question: "I wished I was Jewish, I wished I was a man, and I wished I was rich." Clearly, however, she possessed ample self-confidence and self-awareness. Her family was Sunni Muslim, but far from devout. At eighteen, she left home. By twenty-four, she had a university degree, had settled into a cosmopolitan life in Tel Aviv, and had become the first Palestinian woman certified public accountant in Israel.

Mahajneh went on to deliver the same lecture in Chicago and Detroit, where one member of the audience was Roy Freij, a businessman whose Arabic given name is Raed. At the time of the Six-Day War in 1967, he was three years old and living in Jerusalem. In its aftermath, his parents decided to follow a well-traveled path to southeastern Michigan, where 250,000 Arabs now reside — other than Paris, the largest concentration outside the Middle East. Months of letter writing followed Maha and Roy's first encounter, and in the spring of 1989 he flew to Israel and asked her to marry him. Within three weeks they had wed and Maha had obtained a visa. "I wasn't thinking to come to America at all," she told me. "I came for a man I loved." In 1992, she became a United States citizen.

Maha is the chief financial officer of ACCESS, an Arab social service and advocacy organization that operates out of eight locations in Dearborn, Michigan, offering, among other things, medical care, psychological counseling, job training and placement, adult education, and after-school programs. Dearborn has a population of 100,000, more than a quarter of which is Arab; in the public schools, the figure is about fifty-eight percent. For its clients — Lebanese, Syrians, Iraqis, Palestinians, Yemenis, Jordanians, Egyptians, and North Africans — ACCESS, with a comparatively modest annual budget of $10 million, is a more vital presence in the community than the Ford Motor Company. Maha's office is in ACCESS's main facility, a converted school building in Dearborn's south end, a dingy district along the perimeter of Ford's gargantuan River Rouge plant.

On the morning of September 11, she awoke at six o'clock and took a two-mile walk in Livonia, the affluent suburb west of Detroit where she lives with her husband and their two young sons. She had dropped the boys at school and was driving to the office while listening to National Public Radio when she heard the first news bulletin about the World Trade Center. Soon after she reached her desk, Maha knew that, while no work would get done that day, she and her colleagues, for symbolic and practical reasons, had to keep the doors open at all of ACCESS's facilities.

Except for a three-hour bomb-scare evacuation of one building and a four-day suspension of the after-school program, they succeeded.

The names of Maha and other ACCESS executives are listed on the organization's Web site, and two days after the attack she received an e-mail from a man who attached an inflammatory newspaper column, written by Nolan Finley, an editor at the *Detroit News*, which had appeared in that morning's paper. The "least [Arab and Muslim Americans] can do for their neighbors," Finley insisted, would be to "help in every way possible to smash the network within their own communities that provides money and shelter to terrorists." In other words, what the United States government's intelligence gathering and law-enforcement apparatus had failed to accomplish before September 11 (or since), the law-abiding Arab citizens of Detroit, in a vigilante spirit that would validate their patriotism, should undertake themselves. The e-mail sender appended his own opinion: "Talk is cheap! If you really love America, turn over the terrorist sympathizers in your midst."

Intemperately, Maha responded in kind: "Your thinking is cheap. It seems to me that you have an IQ of 10???"

In his next message, her pen pal took off the gloves: "Your remark makes it clear you support the vermin that murdered thousands of innocent Americans in New York. . . . I will forward your response to the *Detroit News* and the local FBI. Terrorist scum like you have no right to be in our country."

"I'm the one who's going to forward your stupid remarks to the FBI," Maha replied. "As far as the *News*, I will not be surprised if they have more space for racist remarks from people like you. The way they did from racists like Nolan Finley."

When I paid her a visit a week later, she seemed burdened by deepening preoccupations.

"The main thing I'm thinking now," she said, "is, after September 11, how is it going to be for my kids? They were born in this country, and they are totally like other kids. I want my kids to be the President of the United States. Or one will be President. The other will be the adviser. I really want to believe that. At home, the day of the attack, my husband and I sat down with our sons and told them that a bad thing happened and that there might be Arabic people who caused this. We said, 'If someone at school bothers you, you answer back that these people are not representative of the Arab community. You say, "We are Americans, so don't be small-minded and include us in this." ' And I keep thinking about the possible retaliation our government might take and the consequences. All our work and accomplishments — are they shattered by what happened in New York? Because we look a certain way? We are not even allowed to grieve like everyone else. People look at us like we are the enemy. I want to say, 'No, I didn't do it. I was on my way to work.' It's like Palestinians living in Israel. They're always under suspicion. And I feel that our situation here might become the same way. And if that happens where do we go? There is no place."

As narratives of immigrant journeys go, Maha's, because it is a love story, seems paradigmatic, even though it is driven neither by economic nor by political urgency. The willingness to uproot oneself and come to America and partake of what it has to offer expresses — more than any appetite for material comfort — a passion for possibility. There has always been a dark side to this evergreen tale, a shadow of dread, a xenophobia rooted not so much in fear of assault from outside aggressors as in a dull-witted suspicion of those among us who look or sound or somehow seem as if they "don't come from around here." Now that the United States actually has been assaulted from the outside, the license to feel suspicious of certain of one's neighbors has been sanctioned as an unfortunate price that the country, at war with an indiscernible foreign enemy, is willing to pay.

*   *   *

THE MIGRATION of Arabs to Detroit in measurable numbers began in the early twentieth century. The first wave of immigrants were mostly Christians from Syria and what is now Lebanon. Muslims, attracted by job opportunities in the automobile industry, started appearing not long thereafter, and since the 1960s they have predominated, arriving in ripples that emanate from cataclysms in the Middle East — an influx of Palestinians after 1967, followed by Lebanese refugees during the late seventies and early eighties, and Iraqi Shiites in the early nineties. Nothing about the local scenery reminded the earliest arrivals of home, but today certain run-down pockets of southeast Dearborn look as if they might have been grafted on from the West Bank, and in the middle-class neighborhoods there are long commercial stretches with store signs in both Arabic and English. An average of five thousand new Arab immigrants make Detroit their port of entry each year.

In Dearborn, as in New York City, September 11 was a mayoral primary election day. Unlike New York, Dearborn kept its polls open. The incumbent, Michael Guido, was seeking a fifth term, and although he received sixty percent of the vote, the rules mandate a November runoff against the second-place finisher, Abed Hammoud, a thirty-five-year-old assistant prosecutor, who got eighteen percent. Hammoud, who is Lebanese, immigrated to the United States in 1990 and likes to say that he landed in America "three days after Saddam moved into Kuwait." This dash of rhetorical color won't hurt with the Iraqi refugee vote, but he would pick that up anyway. Not that it will be enough. No one, with the possible exception of Hammoud himself, expects him to win.

For a small-city mayor, Guido, a stocky fellow in his mid-forties who favors pinstriped suits, suspenders, and monogrammed shirts with French cuffs, has been quite adept at cultivating an old-school big-city mayoral persona. During his first campaign in 1985, he circulated a blunt-talking pamphlet that referred to

Dearborn's "Arab Problem," in which he disparaged bilingual classes for Arab children in the public schools, "new neighbors [who] neglect their property," and the " 'gimme, gimme, gimme' attitude" of "the so-called leadership" of the Arab community. Some Dearborn Arabs with long memories place Guido on a continuum that extends back to the heyday of Orville Hubbard, an unapologetic segregationist who was mayor from 1942 to 1977. (Hubbard is most often remembered for promoting the unsubtle motto "Keep Dearborn Clean" and for his role during the 1967 race riots in Detroit, when he took to the street to prohibit blacks from crossing into his city.) Guido has sufficient finesse to have befriended many members of the older Lebanese business establishment. But no one would accuse him of being overly solicitous toward the larger Arab population, and they are grossly underrepresented in the municipal workforce — about 2.5 percent.

Dearborn is arguably the most likely city in America where a mayoral candidate, after outlining his position on streetlight maintenance, might be tossed questions about national security and would be expected to answer. Guido knows that most voters aren't all that concerned with local politics at the moment and that the less he says the better. The terrorist attack, he said, "clouds what you can do to separate yourself from your opponent." He continued, "You don't point out that your opponent is Arab-American. You talk about what you can do. What I've done for my city — I blow this guy out of the water. That should be the contest. But, you know, I have people saying, 'I'm voting for you because I don't want to vote for an Arab.' Three people have told me that in the last week. Three people telling you that out loud is like getting ten letters. And the politician's rule of thumb is that ten letters means a thousand people are thinking about it."

Or, as Hammoud said to me the week after the attack, "You think I can go knock on doors now? It's not a good time to campaign."

*   *   *

IN THE SPRING of 1991, after participating in uprisings against the government of Saddam Hussein, Abu Muslim al-Hayder, a Shiite college professor of computer control engineering who was then in his mid-thirties, fled Iraq with his wife and four children. They had not been long inside a Saudi Arabian refugee camp when it became evident that it was hardly a refuge. The camp population was infested with spies for the Saddam regime and "the Saudis don't look at us as full human beings — they look at us as prisoners." After the family spent a year and a half in detention, a relief agency called the Church World Service resettled them in Washington State. There al-Hayder went back to school and subsequently tried and failed to find a job in the computer industry. Confident that his bilingual abilities made him employable, in 1995 he moved the family to Detroit.

On September 11, al-Hayder, who has been a citizen for five years, happened to be one of the federal observers dispatched to monitor the municipal election in the town of Hamtramck, ten miles northeast of Dearborn, where there had been discrimination against Arab voters in the past. He was supposed to spend that night in a hotel and file a report the next morning, but he was allowed to leave at nine P.M. and return to his wife and (now six) children in Detroit.

"I found all my family scared, afraid that somebody would attack the house," he told me. Most of his neighbors had American flags displayed on their porches, and when he went to a flag store the next day it was sold out. As a short-term approach to making his allegiance plain, he tied an American-flag balloon to his balcony.

Before September 11, al-Hayder said, he felt happy and secure. He was delighted with his children's progress in school and, in his work as ACCESS's professional liaison to the Iraqi community, he was gratified by the chance to help his newly arrived countrymen. He counts himself far more fortunate than many other erstwhile Iraqi professionals — the college teacher who now delivers pizzas;

the widely published literary critic who, having failed at carpentry, is now on welfare. But he is also greatly disturbed by the American media's depiction of Muslims, most of all because of how it might affect his children's perception of themselves.

Al-Hayder has a long familiarity with, and an exceptional equanimity in the face of, the consequences of dissent. In 1978, he was imprisoned by Saddam's predecessor, Ahmad Hassan al-Bakr, and sentenced to death for his political associations, then released a year and a half later when Saddam came to power and issued an amnesty for most political prisoners. Al-Hayder remembers regarding the gesture with skepticism. "I didn't trust Saddam," he said, "because I knew that even if he gives you something he will take a lot of things more valuable."

If he saved your life, I asked, how could he take from you something more valuable?

"There are many things more valuable than your life. There is your dignity, your respect. If you live a life with no respect, it's better to die. And this is why I agreed to come to America as a refugee — better than to stay in Saudi Arabia or go to another country. But this crisis we are in is making many people, especially the media, turn away from the values that I know. If someone comes and tries to insult me for no reason, I cannot tell him thank you. A lot of people now who are colored and are American citizens, and who have a right to have weapons, may go and get a license to have weapons to defend themselves. I may even lose faith in law enforcement agencies because they target people who are Arab and Muslims. And this is very disturbing. None of this is why I came here. I came here to be a respected human being."

ON A RAINY AFTERNOON eight days after the attack, I went to the New Yasmeen Bakery, a popular establishment in north Dearborn, where John Dingell, the Democratic congressman who has represented Detroit's Downriver suburbs for forty-six years, was meeting with more than twenty Arab community leaders, mostly

Lebanese businessmen and professionals. The group gathered around a square of tables in a brightly lit room and listened as Dingell praised Dearborn's Arab and non-Arab populations, noting with relief that the city had avoided the bloody spasms of anti-Arab violence (or mistaken-identity violence, as in the case of a murdered turban-wearing Sikh) that had erupted elsewhere. A couple of law enforcement people attended, Mayor Guido sent a representative, and a tone of mutual goodwill prevailed. "I can't think of a single criticism of what you've done and I can't think of a single thing you haven't done that you should have," Dingell said. "This community has made me proud. You have shown yourselves to be exemplary Americans, and I apologize to you for any of the hurts that have been inflicted upon you."

That was the good news. The ominous downside was implicit in several questions posed to Dingell: What about government proposals to expand wiretapping authority? What about the ratcheting up of racial profiling and the broadened application of "secret evidence" (the tactic authorities use to detain immigrants without explanation)? Abed Hammoud cited a fresh Gallup poll, which showed that fifty-eight percent of Americans favored requiring Arabs, United States citizens included, to go through "special, more intensive" security screenings at airports.

Dingell didn't gloss over any of these concerns. "I can tell you," he said, "that the events of last Tuesday are not going to be useful to us in terms of protecting basic liberties."

Inauspicious in a different way were snatches of conversation I overheard before the meeting got under way — a sifting through rumors that reflected the awfulness of feeling marginalized, a grasping at anything remotely self-exculpatory. Hadn't there been news reports that some of the alleged terrorist pilots had turned up alive in Saudi Arabia? (And if they hadn't been flying the planes, who had? Europeans, perhaps?) For days an e-mail had circulated concerning the newsreel footage, first shown on CNN, of Palestinians celebrating in East Jerusalem in the hours after the attack;

it was ten-year-old videotape, several people assured me, recycled from the Gulf War, when Iraqi missiles landed in Israel. (After I returned to New York, I checked CNN's Web site, where conclusive evidence was posted that the claim of hoax was a hoax.)

The next day, I dropped by the office of the *Arab American News* and met with the editor, the inconveniently named Osama Siblani, who'd been collecting factoids as well as incendiary phone messages, some of which he played for me. Many were bizarrely disgusting (e.g., the rant from a fellow whose favorite television programs were being preempted by the prime-time news blanket: he wanted Arab corpses fed to the sharks in Florida), but most were just plain chilling. Siblani also expressed dismay at the half dozen e-mails he'd received urging him to publish the "fact" that four thousand Jews had mysteriously not shown up for work at the World Trade Center on September 11. Was Dearborn a place where, unavoidably, two startlingly divergent realities had taken root? Or was the nuttiness symptomatic of a profound urge to insulate oneself from reality altogether? More than once I heard Arabs express the fear that a "Dearborn connection" to terrorism might materialize.

Alas — the law of percentages dictated as much — that had already occurred. The day of the gathering at the New Yasmeen Bakery, a screamer headline in the *Detroit Free Press* said, "TERRORIST TASK FORCE ARRESTS 3 IN DETROIT." Federal agents looking for Nabil al-Marabh, a presumed associate of Osama bin Laden, had raided an apartment on the southwest side, just outside Dearborn. Al-Marabh wasn't present (he was captured later in the week, near Chicago), but the three men who were arrested reportedly had false identification papers as well as a notebook that made reference in Arabic to an American base in Turkey. As the story unfolded over the next few days, it emerged that last year, in Dearborn, al-Marabh obtained licenses to drive large trucks with hazardous cargoes. Two of the other suspects, Ahmed Hannan and Karim Koubriti, attended a commercial truck-driving school this past summer. Their tuition of $3,300 apiece had been paid by ACCESS, a revelation that obviously pained Ismael Ahmed, the executive director. "We send people to all kinds of training programs and we don't check their political credentials," he told the *Free Press*. "All they have to do is come here looking for a job." In fact, Ahmed told me, he is working with the authorities. "There's a legitimate investigation of terrorism, and we think people should be cooperating," he said. "But we're not telling our community to march into the ovens. I just read a survey that shows sixty-one percent of Arab Americans agree that profiling is justified. That's a symptom of plain fear. That's not what they truly believe, but when they're asked about this in the context of national security, that's what they're going to say."

AHMED MOHAMED ESA is a short, slightly built, soft-voiced forty-eight-year-old man with a cropped white beard, black hair, a gap between his front teeth, and thick dark rings beneath his eyes. Since 1976, he has divided his life between Yemen and Dearborn, where he shares with two other Yemenis a $500-a-month three-room flat. In Yemen, Esa has a wife and six sons. They live three hours from the city of Taiz in Makbana, a village with no telephone and no electricity. None of them has ever seen America. Until the day after the attack on the World Trade Center, Esa had worked at a small welding company for fifteen years — longer than everyone except the company's owner, Paul Rakoczy. He earned $12.36 an hour and usually put in an eight-and-a-half-hour day. Whatever money he saved he sent to his wife, unless he was bringing it in person; each year, he spends at least three or four months with his family.

On September 12, Esa told me, he arrived at the welding shop at 5:40 A.M. — around the time the muezzin at his neighborhood mosque was uttering the morning prayer call — and punched the clock. Then: "I go take my work uniform. When I hear the whistle for the work, I take my coffee and go to take my gloves and go to see Mr. Paul what I work on today. He say complete the job from yesterday. I start to work. I'm working twenty minutes, a half hour, and he say to me, 'Don't work. Go home.' I tell him, 'Why I go home?' He say, 'You are Arabic, you are Muslim. You don't see what happened in New York, in Washington? You don't see how many people your people killed?' I tell him I not do nothing. I work here. I have been here fifteen years. How I can go home? He say, 'I can see your face. Go pray in your mosque. Go pray with your leader. I don't want you to work here.' For a half minute or a minute, I thinking what I can do. He say, 'If you don't go, I get the police for you.' I hear that, I say maybe there is trouble, so I go. I have my check coming the next day, but I don't go get it. I'm too scared. I think maybe if I go there he do something, I don't know."

After finding his way to an ACCESS counseling center, Esa told his story to me and to a reporter for the *Free Press*, who in turn tracked down Rakoczy. Though Rakoczy disputed elements of Esa's account — he had not fired him outright but had told him to take the rest of the week off — he made no attempt to conceal his feelings about Islam. "As far as I'm concerned, their religion is done," he said. "When these guys ran their plane in there like that and hurt all those people, that was the end of it right there. That made their religion — you might as well write it as I say it — the scum of the earth." (Last week, a lawyer for Esa filed a discrimination suit against Rakoczy.)

I asked Esa whether his wife knew that the family no longer had an income.

"I speak to her sometimes once a week, sometimes once a month," he said. "If she come to the city, she will call. She doesn't know what happened with my job. She maybe doesn't know what happened in New York. I maybe will talk to her today. Maybe tomorrow."

When I asked whether he had plans to look for another job, he smiled, shrugged, and said, "How can I face an American guy and ask him to work? How can I knock the door and say I'm an Arabic guy? He might kill me."

So what was he planning to do next?

He smiled and shrugged again.

"America has changed like the weather. You not see America how is it? I sleep on Monday. I get up in the morning on Tuesday. Now I don't know what tomorrow will happen. Tomorrow. I don't know. Tomorrow is too far."

I PLEDGE ALLEGIANCE

Madison, Wisconsin
NOVEMBER 2001

Even Scott Jensen's detractors concede that the Speaker of the Wisconsin State Assembly has done a skillful job of consolidating his reputation as a patriotic fellow. In 1995, Jensen, a Republican who represents the Milwaukee suburb of Waukesha, proposed to amend an existing law in a way that would have placed an American flag in every classroom and required students in all public and private schools to recite the Pledge of Allegiance or sing the national anthem every day. The vote in the Assembly, where Republicans held a slight majority, was 95–2. The bill then made its way to the Senate, where a committee chairman, in effect, stuck it in a drawer. Jensen was back at it in 1999, with an identical result — nearly unanimous approval in the Assembly, followed by a quiet death in the Senate. Earlier this year, the same thing happened. By then, the Speaker no doubt had a clear picture of what was really going on. "We all vote for Jensen's flag bills," a Democratic assemblyman told me, "because we know they'll get killed somewhere else, and why put yourself through a tough vote?"

After the most recent setback, Jensen resorted to a tactic so effective that many of his colleagues wondered why he hadn't tried it before: he attached his proposal as a rider to the state budget bill. Routinely, hundreds of statutes that have virtually nothing to do with the budget per se, and that often possess dubious public policy value, get appended to the budget bill. As co-chair of a joint Assembly-Senate committee that determined its precise content, Jensen was ideally situated to protect provisions he cared about. Not coincidentally, the budget bill is also the one piece of legislation that is certain, eventually, to get signed into law.

Another distinguishing feature of Wisconsin politics is that its capital city, Madison, is also the home of its largest public educational institution. The same thing is true of Texas, Ohio, and a few other states, but the cultural climate engendered by the University of Wisconsin sets Madison apart. When the rest of the country began drifting to the right during the seventies, Madison held its ground, and it has remained an island of liberalism — or, if you prefer, of gray-bearded soft-in-the-middle leftie-pinko Commie-symp delusional behavior. The dominant Madison worldview is a lineal descendant of the Wisconsin Idea, the philosophy championed by Robert La Follette, the congressman, governor, senator, and, in 1924, Progressive Party presidential candidate. It survives and thrives, often in amusingly exaggerated ways, no matter how many red-meat conservative politicians seek to advance themselves by "running against Madison." Twenty-three years ago, a moderate Republican governor named Lee Dreyfus referred to Madison as "fifty-two square miles surrounded by reality." It's a tribute to Madisonians' appetite for lively, usually friendly debate that nowadays this characterization tends to be cited at least as often by the left as by the right. Certain conspiracy-minded folk in Madison believe that Jensen opportunistically engineered the passage of his pet amendment with the confidence that Madison would find a way to fail his patriotic litmus test. Jensen himself says, "People think I'm this extremely clever strategist who set them up. But, actually, I just wanted every school day to begin with the Pledge of Allegiance."

The new law mandating the pledge or the national anthem every day was supposed to have gone into effect September 1, at the beginning of the current academic year. Because of some benign bureaucratic confusion, however, a few weeks went by before state officials got the word out to local school districts. By then, September 11 had happened and Americans had begun to think in unprecedented ways about what it meant to salute the flag or publicly express one's love of country. This proved no less true of Madison than anyplace else. Nevertheless, the city was soon caught up in a not at all friendly debate of the only-in-Madison variety, a controversy that in its most heated moments succeeded in overshadowing the national crisis that had provoked it.

DURING THE FINAL WEEK of September, parents of Madison public school students read newspaper reports and received formal notification that, come Monday, October 1, the Pledge of Allegiance or the national anthem would become part of the daily ritual. That weekend, some members of Madison's seven-seat school board received phone calls from apprehensive parents and teachers. The new law stipulated that "no pupil may be compelled, against the pupil's objections or those of the pupil's parents or guardian, to recite the pledge or sing the anthem." Apparently, however, that language wasn't good enough. When a retired Madison high school English teacher and school board member named Bill Keys fielded such calls, he gave his standard response: "Come to the next school board meeting." As it happened, one was scheduled for the evening of October 1. Ten parents showed up to spell out their opposition to the law, which amounted to this:

Requiring the Pledge of Allegiance, with its reference to "one nation under God," violated the doctrine of church-state separation. Furthermore, members of certain religious groups never say the pledge because they're forbidden to utter oaths other than to

God. Then there was the tricky business of what "God" connoted. A University of Wisconsin psychology lecturer with children in elementary and middle school told the board, "While it may seem that the words 'under God' do not endorse a particular religion, they in fact do. Those words imply a certain type of God, a male god, a singular god. There are families in Madison that do not believe in a supreme being, there are families that believe in a Goddess rather than a God, and there are families that believe in a spirit world populated with multiple deities." On balance, "The Star-Spangled Banner" was deemed less offensive than the Pledge of Allegiance, but its militaristic imagery did pose a problem; "the rockets' red glare, the bombs bursting in air" wasn't the sort of poetry Quakers and other committed pacifists wanted their children declaiming each morning. Above all, leaving aside questions of minority rights (why should non-Americans be placed in a position that marginalized them even more than they already were?), what the law really amounted to was an unsubtle form of coercion, one that smacked of McCarthy-era loyalty oaths and defined patriotic self-expression in narrow and unimaginative terms.

Those, anyway, were the arguments, and they raised questions that couldn't be resolved in a single evening. The board president, Calvin Williams, decided to call a special meeting to address the topic. When it took place, a week later, a different group of ten parents attended. On neither occasion did any Speaker defend the new law. After an hourlong discussion, the board approved, by a 3–2 vote (two members were absent), a resolution put forward by Keys: every school would offer, every day, a wordless, instrumental version of the national anthem. Period. The two dissenters, a University of Wisconsin Law School dean named Ruth Robarts and a Hmong immigrant social worker named Shwaw Vang, were not defenders of the pledge. Rather, they felt that Keys's compromise still didn't adequately protect nonparticipants. "I'm just very uncomfortable with anything that does not remove the coerciveness of the classroom," Robarts said. Why not comply with the law, she asked, by offering the pledge or the national anthem at a specified time each day in a gymnasium or auditorium? Because, the majority agreed, such an approach would be too time-con-suming and cumbersome.

As it turned out, time-consuming and cumbersome barely de-scribed the unwelcome consequences of the board's vote. A head-line in the next day's *Capital Times*, the more liberal of Madison's two daily newspapers, said "PLEDGE BANNED IN CITY SCHOOLS." In the days that followed, as hostile reactions to the decision rained down on the school board, Keys and his defenders would maintain that the reference to a "ban" was inaccurate and had triggered the backlash. The resolution, they pointed out, made no mention of the pledge. Semantic sophistry, the critics countered; whether or not the pledge was actually mentioned, the result was, de facto, a ban. The air war in Afghanistan was two days old when the mes-sage went out over the right-wing talk radio airwaves: "In the Madison, Wisconsin, public schools they have — get this — *banned the Pledge of Allegiance. Banned it! Unbelievable. Un-American."*

The day after the vote, Art Rainwater, the superintendent of the Madison Metropolitan School District, and Calvin Williams, the board president, were publicly stating that the board would reconsider its decision. Though Williams had voted with Keys, he called a press conference and said, ruefully, "We did not consider all the ways it could have been interpreted or misinterpreted." Then he announced yet another special meeting, to be held the following Monday — during which, it seemed foreordained, the board would reverse itself. Commentary by Matt Drudge, Rush Limbaugh, and the like prompted acolytes to flood Rainwater's office with complaints. Temporary employees had to be hired to answer the phones. Angry e-mails arrived at the rate of a thousand per hour, until the e-mail system began returning them unread.

ON OCTOBER 15, 1,200 people jammed the auditorium and an overflow cafeteria in one of Madison's four public high schools for an event that lasted from five o'clock in the afternoon until two-thirty the following morning. Depending on who was offering the postgame analysis, what transpired was a nasty spectacle of bullying jingoism or a stirring display of pure participatory democracy — or both. Just as the meeting got under way, a large contingent of the audience rose and, as if taunting the school board members gathered on the auditorium stage, shouted the Pledge of Allegiance and followed that with fist-waving chants of "U.S.A.! U.S.A.! U.S.A.!" Then came the speakers, each allotted three minutes — 166 opinionated citizens, by turns pro, con, eloquent, inarticulate, sentimental, arrogant, humble, coolly analytical, belligerently nationalistic, self-righteous, philosophical, and, of course, unassailably patriotic. Another 683 people submitted written statements. When it was all over, the board voted 6–1 to undo its previous decision. Individual principals would decide whether to offer the pledge or the national anthem in their schools, and the ceremony each day would include this preamble: "We live in a nation of freedom. Participation in the pledge or anthem is voluntary. Those who wish to participate may stand; others may remain seated."

The lone holdout was Keys, who, ironically — but, because this was Madison, perhaps not so surprisingly — happened to be the only white male member of the board, which also included two women, two African-American males, a Hispanic male, and Shwaw Vang, the Hmong immigrant. A great deal of vituperation was directed at Keys, and, in an especially creepy way, at Vang. During the in-your-face recitation of the pledge, Keys and Vang had remained seated. Before the members of the public gave their three-minute statements, Vang, a soft-spoken father of three in his mid-thirties, took the microphone and said, "As Americans, each of us has a right to do what he feels is right, and I have as much right as anyone else. I won't be forced to do something against my will. That's a right I have as a citizen. I also believe in the Pledge of Allegiance. I say it because I believe in it and when I want to say it — not because a group of people forces me to say it. Now I'm going to say the pledge. I invite everyone to stand and say it with me. Those who don't want to do so, I respect your right not to, and I hope you have the courage to remain seated." Whereupon he faced an American flag, stage right, and, along with virtually the entire audience and all the other school board members except Keys, recited the pledge.

The next time Vang spoke was hours later, after a local talk radio shock jock named Chris Krok took the floor and attacked him, saying, "You've been called Seesaw Shwaw. You've said 'yea' and 'nay.' You say the pledge promotes war, but this is not Vietnam — this is America." Vang was not unprepared for this sort of idiocy. On his home telephone answering machine, he had recorded greetings in both English and Hmong, for which his reward had been messages from callers saying things like "I can't even understand what you're saying. You don't belong on the school board." Vang's only direct response to Krok was a terse "I just want to correct one fact: I wasn't born in Vietnam." Then, toward the end of the meeting, before the board voted, he elaborated. He had been born, he explained, in Laos, the son of an officer in a special guerrilla unit funded by the CIA. "I was never a soldier," he said. "But I was a child living in the midst of war. As a parent, and as somebody who had gone through that experience, I prayed that my children would never be placed in that situation, that no children would be placed in that situation. I've seen a lot of what war can do. I question whether patriotism only means serving in the military or whether it isn't possible to serve the country in a different manner. I can tell you that in Thailand or Laos, if the pledge or the national anthem is being said, no matter where you are you'd better stand up straight and salute. There's a feeling of fear that goes with that, the fear of a government that wants to control every single move a person makes. In Laos you have to have total respect for the government or you will be persecuted.

Almost every Laotian teacher and student says the pledge, but does that teach them to be more patriotic? I don't think so."

And what was Vang's emotional reaction to what he'd just witnessed? "I've never been so scared for myself and my kids in all the years I've been here."

EVEN BEFORE the vote was taken, the next round in the battle had begun. That same evening, in the same building, an organization that had incorporated itself as the Madison School Board Recall Committee held a press conference and announced plans to try to remove from office Bill Keys, Calvin Williams, and Carol Carstensen, the third board member who had first voted to "ban" the pledge. A statement by the group's chairman, a former Republican congressman named Scott Klug, made plain that, while he normally had little interest in education policy, this situation was extraordinary. A recall campaign posed a logistical challenge: almost 32,000 petition signatures would have to be collected before a special election could take place. Regardless of the outcome, for conservatives here was an irresistible opportunity to score points at the expense of Madison's liberal hegemony. "This is Madison," Klug told reporters. "Before this is all over, there'll be somebody somewhere holding a bake sale for Osama bin Laden, saying he's been misunderstood and is the way he is because he didn't have mittens as a child in Saudi Arabia."

Within a few days, the recall activists had refined their strategy: they would go after Keys, and they would time their petition drive so that a vote could take place next February, when Williams and Carstensen, should they choose to run again, will likely face a re-election primary. The people I spoke with in Madison tended to agree with John Nichols, an editorial writer for the *Capital Times*, who said of Keys's antagonists, "I know these people. Most of them are sincere. They honestly believe the school board went off the deep end. Most of Madison believes that the school board made a mistake. But it's not a recallable offense." Keys himself struck me as neither contrite nor distressed. "I still have a good relationship with all the members of the board," he said. "I'm not carrying this on my back. My election committee has already met. I've received lots of mail from people saying 'When can I contribute? What can I do?'"

Even by Madison standards, Keys lacks the aura and demeanor of a politician. He's sixty years old, pink-faced and freckled, with red hair that's completing the transition to white. His drooping mustache, wire-rimmed glasses, plaid shirts, and blue jeans give him the overall look of a lean Wilford Brimley. The conventional wisdom is that Keys stands a far better chance of defeating a recall than Williams or Carstensen do of winning reelection, because, when confronted with an angry mob à la *High Noon*, he didn't blink or budge. "It's most important that you affirm your principles and live your principles in a time of crisis," he told me. "Otherwise, you don't really believe in them." Consistency, it seems, is Keys's most consistent trait. His first teaching job, in the mid-sixties, at a high school in suburban Maryland, ended after the principal wandered into his classroom during a discussion of *The Canterbury Tales*. In the principal's estimation, Keys's pedagogy threatened to undermine the morality and religious beliefs of the students. "Change or leave," the principal advised, so he left. He found a more congenial atmosphere in Madison, where, for thirty-one years, he taught English literature, film criticism, and writing at West High School, in a leafy, tidy neighborhood near the University of Wisconsin campus. During a graduation address at West several years ago, Keys, who for three years was president of the local teachers' union, referred to teaching as a "sacred ritual."

Keys retired in the spring of 1999, was elected to the school board the following spring, and for the past year has spent every Wednesday as a volunteer at a mental health facility, where he teaches classes in English and citizenship to members of the local Hmong community. He happened to be teaching on the day that the *Wisconsin State Journal,* Madison's other daily newspaper, published an editorial fulminating against him. "Someone in class that day asked about the word 'reputation.' And I used the newspaper editorial as an example. I said, 'A reputation is what people say about you. But it isn't necessarily an indication of who you are. Who you are is what you do.' "

Would the school board have acted as it did, I asked, and would Keys be in the position he finds himself in, if September 11 hadn't happened?

"That's the road not taken," he said. "I don't think what we did blew up in Madison's face. I think the nation blew up in Madison's face. I was asked on TV, 'Why did you tackle this issue now?' I said, 'We didn't tackle it, it tackled us.' The law was passed before September 11 and implemented after September 11, and what could we do?"

From my meeting with Keys, I went to an appointment with Bill Geist, a freelance tourism consultant who has become Scott Klug's co-chair in the recall campaign. As we sat in his dining room, Geist, a broad-shouldered fellow in his mid-forties, said, "I like the fact that when my friends and I gather around this table I have raging progressives on one side and raging conservatives on the other. That's what makes this a wonderful town. But the minute somebody slams the door and says, 'Nope, you can't salute the flag or sing the national anthem in school,' then Madison isn't such a wonderful place.

"This whole thing isn't about religion, it isn't about patriotism. It's about 'Do these people on the school board represent this community's best interests?' There are those who try to paint us as trying to shove our nationalistic views down people's throats. That just isn't the case. There's no coercion here. If anything, we think the board overstepped its bounds in telling principals and teachers that they could not lead their class in the pledge. That's a form of coercion.

"Maybe I've got too much faith in today's kids, because I think they do honor tolerance and diversity. I realize there's the chance that somebody might feel ostracized in one way or another, but so do the kids with zits, so do the dweebs, so do the stoners and the jocks. Everybody has a little of that. I think kids today respect each other better than we did. I understand the issue, but to take away rights from ninety-seven percent of the kids to protect what might happen to three percent, I've got to question that one."

The next morning, I went to West High School, Keys's former place of work, to test Geist's hypothesis. Because I was physically incapable of being in more than one classroom during the national anthem, what I observed was hardly definitive. Nevertheless, if Geist had been a fly on the wall in the media studies class I visited, I imagine he would have been surprised. At 9:20 A.M., the student council president, speaking over the public-address system, read the preamble ("We live in a nation of freedom," etc.), and then, of the twenty-five students in the room, only one, a husky blond boy, stood at attention during a tinny rendition of "The Star-Spangled Banner." Four boys made a point of leaving the room before the music began. Two others walked in a bit tardily, self-consciously surveyed the scene for a few seconds, and then slid into their chairs. Some kids rested their heads on their desks. Others had that vacant why-am-I-here-oh-yeah-this-is-high-school look. After the music stopped, and after the announcements about wrestling tryouts, the state soccer tournament, the Asian Club, the bake sale, the gospel choir, and the swing-dancing club, we talked about what it was all about.

"I believe in the Pledge of Allegiance and the national anthem, but if we have to do it day in, day out, it loses its value."

"It's promoting militarism and nationalism in the classroom, and I'm strongly against that."

"What's the difference between standing and sitting? Does standing mean that you appreciate it more?"

"If we were required to recite the pledge each day instead of listening to the national anthem, I would have found a stronger form of expression than leaving the room."

"Sitting isn't going against the government. When I sit during the national anthem, I'm probably thinking more about my country than those who stand. I'm thinking that I'm grateful to live in a nation where I have the ability to sit or stand. But I still disagree with many of the things our government is doing right now, and by sitting I'm making a statement to that effect."

"I know of another school in Wisconsin where they've tried hard to come up with a more musically interesting version of the anthem. There's a Whitney Houston version, I think, and a Marvin Gaye version, and a Jimi Hendrix version."

"I'd stand up for Jimi Hendrix."

LAST WEEK, the Madison School Board Recall Committee formally launched a petition campaign, starting a clock that gives them thirty days to collect the nearly 32,000 signatures necessary to force Keys into a February election. February is soon enough that whoever runs against him will have no trouble remembering the closing paragraph of a profile of Keys that was published in the *Wisconsin State Journal* in late October: "Does he love his country? Well, he's glad he has the rights he does. Then he paused. 'I can't love anything that is so much in the abstract.'" Even Keys's allies winced at that, though the idea he was trying to convey could be found a couple of paragraphs earlier. Being patriotic, he said, is "not about what you say. It's what you do to help make life better for the people around you."

That Keys's primary skills aren't political is a boon to the vast number of Madisonians, left and right, for whom politics remains a diverting spectator sport. What other American community, after all, can boast a city council that debated and then passed, by an 11–8 vote, a resolution of support for the September 11 attack victims in which the phrase "thoughts and prayers" lost out to "thoughts and sympathies"? How connected, these days, is Madison to the reality beyond the city limits? I wonder if the bloody-minded urge for a fight is not a local phenomenon but a symptom of the anger that arises from our impatient uncertainty about how to prevail in the war against terrorism. In Madison, more than in most places, the unbloody culture war — political correctness and all that — has served as a curious catalyst. Underlying the noble rhetoric about what a valuable civics lesson Madison has witnessed, there's a less noble quality, a failure to acknowledge the self-indulgence implicit in all the carping. The semiotics of the Pledge of Allegiance and the national anthem and the schoolhouse are abstractions that one has the luxury to dwell on when the World Trade Center and the Pentagon and dense concentrations of grieving survivors happen to be several hundred miles away. In the abstract, "democracy" is the way this dialectic gets defined. So be it. The most salutary byproduct of "democracy," it turns out, is the messy reality of democracy.

★

This story generated more mail than any of my other "U.S. Journal" dispatches, mostly from readers who took issue with its ending, especially the last two sentences, which originally read: "'Democracy' is one way to define the dialectic. Other terms apply as well." My critics found this sentiment not only peevish but self-contradictory. With sufficient distance from 9/11, I came to agree with them, and so I amended it to read as it does here. In "Song of Myself," Whitman wrote, "Do I contradict myself? Very well, then, I contradict myself." There are worse self-indulgences, I think.

The effort to recall Bill Keys failed before ever coming to a vote, as petition gatherers collected only about one third of the signatures required to put the recall question on the ballot. After the regular school board election the following spring, Keys's fellow board members chose him to be president. In 2003, he was reelected to the board without opposition.

Scott Jensen no longer holds a leadership position in the Wisconsin

State Assembly, a consequence of having been indicted, in the fall of 2002, on four counts of corruption and election law violations, including allegations that he required staff members to engage in political activities on taxpayer time. While awaiting trial, he remained a member of the Assembly but was forced to resign as Speaker.

WHO KILLED CAROL JENKINS?

Martinsville, Indiana

JANUARY 2002

Carol Jenkins arrived in Martinsville, Indiana, on the foggy and damp afternoon of what proved to be nobody in that town's lucky day. This was September 16, 1968. Although no one in Martinsville was able to get to know her well, thirty-three years later most of its adult population remains familiar with certain vital facts about Carol Jenkins's brief and abrupt experiences there. She was twenty-one years old, a shy, polite, slender, and pretty woman. As the newspapers in Martinsville and Indianapolis reported at the time, "She was a Negro," or "a Negro girl." Growing up in the rural community of Rushville, Indiana, she had nurtured an adolescent fantasy of moving to Chicago and pursuing a career as a fashion model. That dream, however, metamorphosed into the reality of an assembly-line position in a factory that made large appliances. If the factory hadn't been idled by a strike, she wouldn't have taken the job that brought her to Martinsville — selling encyclopedias door to door. Or, perhaps, had she and her coworkers not got a late start, they might have been able to reach their intended destination of Vincennes, ninety miles farther down the road, and therefore wouldn't have bothered canvassing in Martinsville — then a working-class town of 10,000 situated about forty minutes southwest of Indianapolis. Or, had she consulted and heeded her stepfather, Carol Jenkins never would have set foot in Martinsville, in which case she might very well still be alive.

I recall, more than a decade ago, while reporting a story in Indiana, hearing Martinsville mentioned tangentially and being told that it had an all-white population and that black people made a point of not stopping there. That was my first encounter with the legend of Martinsville — the notion that it's a racist town where no African American, much less a solitary and attractive African-American woman, would want to be caught after dark. In the years since, Martinsville's civic burden has, in many respects, worsened. Discussing Martinsville with reporters from other Indiana cities, I've found that the conversation never gets very far before references to the Ku Klux Klan creep in. Last August, an *Indianapolis Star* columnist named Ruth Holladay wrote a couple of stories about Carol Jenkins and described Martinsville as having been in 1968 "a Ku Klux Klan stronghold." Seeing the name of their town and those three K's in the same context invariably evokes a complex reaction from the town's loyalists — a mixture of anger, frustration, denial, and weariness, nourished by a suspicion that the rest of the world is inexplicably determined to punish Martinsville for transgressions it had nothing to do with.

Considerable scholarship has been devoted to the history of the Ku Klux Klan in Indiana, especially to the 1920s, when the Klan was more active there than in any other state. In some towns, between forty and fifty percent of the native-born white men paid the Klan's ten-dollar membership fee; statewide, the figure averaged almost thirty percent. In 1923, the city of Kokomo, population 30,000, hospitably welcomed a national convention of 100,000 Klansmen and their families. The Indiana Klan had a distinct political agenda to go along with its anti-immigrant, antiblack, anti-Catholic dogmatism, and at its peak, after the elections of 1924, it controlled the state Republican Party. Klan-endorsed candidates were elected to the governorship, the majority of both houses of the legislature, and almost all the congressional seats. The steep decline that followed was caused by political corruption and infighting and by the 1925 conviction of Grand Dragon D. C. Stephenson on charges of rape and second-degree murder. The last reported racial lynching in Indiana took place in 1930, in the city of Marion.

But in Morgan County, where Martinsville is the county seat, something lingers. On a visit there not long ago, I met with Jo-anne Raetz Stuttgen, a local resident and a doctoral candidate in folklore at Indiana University. When I asked about the present-day relevance of the Klan, she said, "When I travel and people say to me, 'Oh, Martinsville. That's the headquarters of the KKK,' I tell them, 'Listen. Martinsville's so disorganized it couldn't be the headquarters of anything.'" In 1995, a local bank underwrote the publication of a boosterish pictorial history of Martinsville and enlisted Stuttgen to provide the text. She knew better than to duck the issue of race, but she put it off until the very end — a two-page coda titled "The Legend We Live With," in which she maintained that, whatever Morgan County's Klan infatuation might have been seventy years earlier, it amounted to "no more than [that of] other Indiana counties." Martinsville, Stuttgen suggested, was itself a "minority victim: a small, all-white central Indiana town maligned for its supposed racism just as minorities themselves are maligned." Rather than attempting to pin down how that had come to be, she posed a double-edged rhetorical question: "That Martinsville — or any town — should become the scapegoat for America's painful sensitivity about its racist and supremacist past is not so unusual. But why Martinsville?"

WHEN PAUL DAVIS married Elizabeth Gooden in 1949, her daughter, Carol Jenkins, was a toddler. Referring to Carol's natural father, Davis told me, "She went to see him when she was fifteen or sixteen, but she called me Daddy." Together, the Davises had five more children, two boys and three girls, and he regarded Carol, no less than the others, as his own. The family resided in Rushville, a classic corn-and-soybeans farming community an hour east of Indianapolis, where Davis has spent his entire life. For forty-eight years, he worked as a machine repairman at a Ford Motor Company plant. Now in his mid-seventies, he lives alone — the Davises divorced in 1967 — in an impeccably kept three-bedroom house that he built himself.

As a child in Rushville, where blacks made up about three percent of the population, Davis attended integrated schools, with no ill consequences. "I never really had any problems," he said. "Myself, I've always been real respected here." During the forties, when he was in high school, a black friend went to Martinsville to play in a basketball game and reported afterward that he'd been verbally harassed. Martinsville was more than seventy miles away, and Davis had never had reason to visit. But he filed away that information and remembered it two decades later, in the fall of 1967, when a group of Rushville football fans decided to make the trip to watch a game. Davis was reluctant, but his older son, Larry — Carol's half brother — was Rushville's star running back, so he went. What he witnessed in Martinsville appalled him. "They called Larry all kinds of names," he told me. "It wasn't just the players — it was the fans, too. When he had the ball, there was a lot of 'Get that nigger!' Or stuff about 'that darky.' And it wasn't just the kids. Some of those adults was just as bad." Davis vowed never to return.

Evidently, Carol never got the message. Or it's possible that she did but felt uncomfortable with the thought of telling her supervisor, on what happened to be her first day of work, that she was afraid to knock on doors in a benign-looking little city. There was, after all, nothing particularly striking about Martinsville, a nineteenth-century settlement that gave the impression of having moseyed indifferently into the twentieth. In the decades since the Depression, a number of enterprises, including the many "health spas," or sanatoriums, that materialized after the discovery there of artesian wells in the 1880s, had been dwindling toward extinction. The most conspicuous landmarks were the old sanatoriums, several churches, and a grand red-brick Italianate courthouse that occupied the central square.

It was four-thirty P.M. when Carol and the other members of her sales crew — another young black woman from Rushville and two white men from Indianapolis, one of whom was the supervisor — reached Martinsville. They selected a residential area east of downtown — mostly tidy neighborhoods of brick bungalows and two-story wooden frame houses — and split up, agreeing to rendezvous at ten o'clock at a gas station not far from the square. Around seven-thirty, when it had been dark for about a half hour, Carol knocked at the door of a couple named Don and Norma Neal and apologetically explained that she was frightened. Some men in a dark sedan were following her and had yelled at her, she said, though she couldn't make out what they were saying. When Don Neal went outside, he didn't see the car she had described, but an unfamiliar light-colored sedan was parked near his house. The car's parking lights were on, but he couldn't see the occupants. He approached and got close enough to make a mental note of the license number. As he returned to the house, the car drove away.

The Neals telephoned the Martinsville Police Department, which dispatched a patrolman, who stuck around for about ten minutes, long enough for Carol to repeat her story. After he departed, Norma Neal drove Carol around the neighborhood for several minutes in an unsuccessful effort to spot one of the other salespeople. Back at the Neals', Carol turned down their offer to remain with them until it was time to rejoin her colleagues. "We tried to get her to stay. But she said she had been a bother long enough," Norma Neal told a reporter. "That sounds like her,"

Paul Davis reflected, thirty-three years later. "I always felt like she was a very sweet, sort of naive girl. She had a smile for everybody. She never was in no kind of trouble, never gave me no trouble. Carol didn't like imposing on anybody."

At eight, she thanked the Neals and departed. Not quite an hour later, ten blocks away — near the corner of Morgan and Lincoln Streets, a block shy of her destination — she collapsed on the sidewalk. A teenage boy who lived across the street discovered her and ran into a nearby restaurant to call the police. She was alive when they arrived but dead shortly after an ambulance delivered her to the Morgan County Hospital. Only then was her brown wool jacket removed, and her barely bloodstained white turtleneck sweater, revealing a single stab wound on the left side of her chest. The next day, Paul Davis broke his vow and returned to Martinsville, where he paid a visit to the office of the Morgan County coroner, who had already conducted an autopsy. The killer had punctured her heart.

IN THE YEARS SINCE, the mystery of how Carol Jenkins died, the whodunit, has competed with the mystery of why the whodunit has never been solved. The official investigation had, at best, an inauspicious beginning. The Martinsville Police Department employed no detective-grade personnel, so the county sheriff and the Indiana State Police were summoned immediately, which turned out to be too late. Not the least complication was that the crime scene had not been secured, mainly because it wasn't clear that a crime had occurred until Carol was examined at the hospital. Don Kuster, the first state police detective to work on the case, told me that, when he arrived, "there were about fifty people hanging around the crime scene. One of them came up and handed me a pair of glasses and said, 'I think these are her glasses.' Somebody else handed me her notebook." (The notebook had been lying near the entrance to an auto-repair shop, more than half a block from where she fell.) That it was raining steadily didn't help matters. The dark-colored automobile that had been trailing her before she sought refuge with the Neals was tracked down. Its teenage driver and a friend admitted having followed Carol but denied having yelled at her; before long, the police decided they weren't suspects. Because Don Neal hadn't accurately remembered the license number of the light-colored sedan, that lead never went anywhere. No murder weapon was ever found.

Out-of-town journalists who came to Martinsville discovered that information was remarkably hard to come by. "The town became a clam," an Indianapolis newspaper reporter told me. "I got the impression real quickly that there was something funny. I began knocking on doors to see if anyone had seen this gal, and I got nothing from the townspeople. After a while, we learned that nothing was going to happen. And, even if somebody knew something, they were afraid to talk. They really didn't want outsiders coming around. It cooled and cooled, until it was futile. So we ended up just making routine calls, and when you called you got the standard 'The investigation is continuing.' You knew if anything was going to happen it would have to be an anonymous tip. After a while, the thing just petered out."

Well, not exactly. Six weeks after the murder — by which time there had been an accumulation of news stories bearing headlines like "NO PROMISING LEADS IN MURDER PROBE" and "CLUES, MOTIVES SCARCE IN MARTINSVILLE SLAYING" and "POLICE PUT 'LID' ON FATAL STABBING CASE" — the Indianapolis chapter of the National Association for the Advancement of Colored People sent a telegram to the attorney general, Ramsey Clark, requesting an investigation by the Department of Justice. The telegram stated, "Morgan County has historically been associated with Ku Klux Klan–like activities." This was, of course, technically true. And, indeed, the previous year — in the summer of 1967 — a Klan motorcade had made a newsworthy tour of several central Indiana towns, which culminated in Martinsville. There, on the courthouse square, thirty or so robed Klansmen carried placards and distributed literature. The *Indianapolis Star* reported that the group's spokesman "said Martinsville was chosen for a demonstration because there is a strong local chapter in Morgan County." (Which is not to say that any of the Klansmen actually lived in Martinsville or that anyone from Martinsville had joined the motorcade.) Whether this episode had any connection to the murder was as much a matter of conjecture as most of the other elements of the case. The federal government never undertook a formal investigation, but the NAACP request helped plant in the minds of people — especially black people — in Indiana and beyond the belief that the Jenkins murder was racially motivated and that no one should be surprised that it had taken place where it did.

THE FIRST ANNIVERSARY of the crime was the occasion for feature stories of the "Anybody Know Carol's Killer?" variety. After that, more than three decades went by with virtually no substantial media coverage. Still, the crime had lodged in the collective memory of people who could never quite stop speculating about it. The prime suspect, a construction worker whose whereabouts on the night of the murder were unknown, left the state not long afterward and, it was said, later died in a shootout in Illinois. Another suspect had been the owner of the auto-repair shop near where Carol's notebook was found, a circumstance that gave rise to a widely held screwdriver-as-murder-weapon theory. Both men were among several to whom the police administered polygraphs, and all "passed" (which, given the fallibility of polygraphs, proved and disproved nothing). Talking among themselves, Martinsville residents named names; often, these conversations took place after a few drinks. Beyond Martinsville, the scuttlebutt was that the police were unwilling or too inept to make the case — a point of view that, in time, the victim's family subscribed to.

What stray facts and factoids have surfaced across the years have tended to deepen rather than illuminate the mystery. After Paul and Elizabeth Davis divorced, she married a man named

Gene Scott, and they adopted an infant named Phillip. In 1998, Phillip Scott, by then thirty years old, went to see his half sister Laura Davis Watkins — Paul's youngest child — and told her that, through friends, he had met people who knew who had killed Carol and how. "They took him to somebody's house in Martinsville," Laura told me. "They said everybody in Martinsville knows who killed her. He said he was amazed at how much these people knew. But, for whatever reason, Phillip wouldn't tell us any more than that." Actually, Phillip did convey one other piece of information: the murder weapon could be found in an underground gasoline tank at the site of the long-defunct auto-repair shop. Laura's brother Robert contacted the Federal Bureau of Investigation, and soon Paul Davis heard from a Martinsville police detective. When, a few months later, the gas tank was unearthed, a chisel was found inside, but it didn't match the dimensions of the fatal wound.

Two years later, the family received another provocative tip, from a woman who refused to give her name. She was six years old at the time of the murder, she said, but she knew what had happened because she had heard about it from her father. The scenario she described involved more than one guilty party, as well as a screwdriver. When Paul asked for her name and phone number, she said, "I'm sorry. I have a family. I fear for my life." She never called back. Again, one of Paul's sons got in touch with the FBI, and again a Martinsville detective followed up. By then — the summer of 2000 — Paul had long since become disaffected with both the Martinsville police and the state police, who, he felt, had for years arbitrarily withheld information from him. He hired his own private detective, a former state trooper named William McAllister. It took McAllister "about five minutes," he told me recently, to ascertain that the prime suspect, the construction worker, had not died in Illinois but was alive and living in Florida.

Coincidentally, as McAllister was getting to work, the Indiana State Police were mobilizing a new investigative unit devoted to old homicides, and two detectives were assigned full-time to the Jenkins case. That fall, Paul Davis, accompanied by an attorney and some other family members, made one more trip to Martinsville, for a meeting with the new team. Eventually, Paul became convinced of the detectives' sincerity, and he authorized McAllister to share his files with them. This past summer, when they had been working on the case for more than a year, the Morgan County prosecutor decided to publicize the reopening of the investigation. When I asked the prosecutor, Steve Sonnega, for a prognosis, he said, "I think we're making progress. I'm not willing to say how much, because I really don't know. I think people think that if this case is going to be solved, now is the best time." In fact, the best time would have been in the fall of 1968, when the physical evidence was fresh, potential witnesses were available, and memories were less impeachable. The suspect in Florida, after initially refusing to cooperate, has reportedly become more talkative, but only in the interest of exculpating himself. Shy of an outright confession, any defendant convicted at this point would have to be approximately as unlucky as Carol Jenkins.

PAUL DAVIS seems far less interested in the formality of a trial than he does in finding some peace. "Once they figure out who committed the crime, I don't know what they'd do about it," he said. "But, once I find out, then that will bring the family and me closure. We just want to know who done it and why.

"I pray every night that something comes, maybe some new DNA test. Because, if they don't get some new concrete evidence, the guy is still going to be walking around free, in Martinsville or wherever he is. But even solving the murder can't solve Martinsville's problem. It'll just help to take a little of the pressure off them that's been on them for so many years. To solve their problem, they're gonna have to diversify. They're gonna have to make it where black people can come in there living, working, and not having fear."

Four years ago, Martinsville attracted a lot of national publicity — once again, none of it desirable — in the wake of a high school basketball game. A team with several black players came to town from Bloomington, and afterward its fans complained that they had been subjected to racial taunting and to dirty play on the court. (One black Bloomington player wound up on the floor, retching, after being violently elbowed.) The subsequent punishment levied by the Indiana High School Athletic Association — a one-year probation, which, among other things, forbade all Martinsville interscholastic teams to host conference home games — still provokes lamentations in Martinsville about unfairness and humiliation. (Not to mention that the out-of-town coverage inevitably dragged in references to the Klan and the Carol Jenkins murder — QED.)

A FLAP with an identical resonance occurred in late October, after the assistant police chief of Martinsville, Dennis Nail, who was unhappy with television news coverage of errant American bombs falling on civilians in Afghanistan, wrote a letter to the *Martinsville Reporter-Times* in which he railed against the networks for being sympathetic to the Taliban, Osama bin Laden, and liberal pieties. The letter wasn't racist per se, but it didn't brim with goodwill toward one's fellow man. Among other complaints, Nail bemoaned the outlawing of organized school prayer "because it might upset Hadji Hindu or Buddy Buddha," and he followed that up with a homophobic rant: "Our country was founded on Christian principles. Talk about majority. When I look around I see no Mosque, or fat, bald guys with bowls in their laps. I see churches. I'm offended when I turn on a television show and without fail a queer is in the plot just like it's a natural thing. America put God in the closet and let the queers out. When the planes struck the twin towers I never heard anyone utter, 'Oh, Ellen.' I heard a lot of, 'Oh, my God.' . . . It's time the dog started wagging the tail. Let's not be led around by a minority of weirdos and feel gooders. I, for one, am tired of it." The mayor of Martinsville and the police chief said that, while Nail's remarks might be offensive to some, he had made them as a private citizen, not as a public official, and therefore wouldn't be disciplined. During a meeting of the city council nine days after the letter was published, only one of the citizens present criticized Nail, who was in attendance and received a standing ovation.

One of Nail's most outspoken critics was Joanne Raetz Stuttgen, the folklorist. I asked her whether she could imagine a scenario in which Martinsville might rehabilitate its image. "Legends die hard, if they ever die at all," she said. "Facts don't matter much. If people believe a legend, that's enough. If Martinsville could be magically proved to be the most gracious, charitable, humanitarian, loving Christian community on earth, there would still be people that would continue to believe that it's not. Belief will always be stronger than the truth."

The party line in Martinsville, among civic leaders and people in law enforcement, is that the Jenkins murder was motivated not by race but by sex. According to this rationale, Carol Jenkins died because she spurned her killer's advances. This is, of course, a wishful hypothesis. (How could anyone but the killer know?) Nevertheless, the impulse is understandable. In the aftermath of the Dennis Nail outburst, more than 700 Martinsville residents signed a full-page newspaper ad that said, "We respect and affirm the dignity of all people," but it's unlikely that any of them imagined this gesture encouraging African Americans to move there. By now, the people of Martinsville are possessed of few illusions about the rest of the world's opinions. It might be that places like Martinsville end up performing a perverse public service for those of us who live in racially diverse communities: they make us more than a little smug and spare us the trouble of examining our own bigotries. In a town burdened with Martinsville's history, an ugly basketball game, a public official having a very bad day — incidents that anywhere else might seem like peccadilloes — easily become caricatures of evil. Martinsville is a familiar landscape, but one less sunny than the one that most of us inhabit. And Carol Jenkins, who was only passing through, has taken up permanent residence there — a moment, a memory, a stigma, as fixed as the rhythm of her telltale heart.

★

In January 2002, approximately two weeks after this story was published in The New Yorker, *a woman named Shirley Richmond McQueen confronted her father, Kenneth Claude Richmond, who then resided in an Indianapolis nursing home, about his role in the death of Carol Jenkins. McQueen, it was later reported, had a long-dormant memory of the murder, which occurred when she was seven years old. That night, she said, she had been a back-seat passenger in a car driven by her father; another passenger, in the front seat, was a man whose identity she couldn't recall. In Martinsville, she told investigators, she had witnessed the stalking of Jenkins and then, as the other man held the victim's arms, had watched her father stab her in the chest with a screwdriver. Back in the car, McQueen said, her father gave her seven dollars and told her not to tell her mother what she'd seen.*

In May 2002, when Richmond was formally charged with first-degree murder, he was seventy years old and suffering from bladder cancer as well as, apparently, dementia. At a hearing three months later, a judge in Martinsville, after reviewing conflicting medical and psychiatric testimony, along with a documented history of Richmond's alcoholism and proneness to violence, ruled that he was not medically or psychologically able to assist in his own defense. Eight days after this ruling, Richmond died. The identity of his alleged accomplice has never been determined.

Richmond had indeed been a racist and a Klan sympathizer, but no evidence emerged of any broad conspiracy in the Jenkins murder. The predominant reaction in Martinsville to Richmond's unmasking was grateful relief — that the crime seemed to have been solved and that the perpetrator was not from Martinsville. The response of Carol Jenkins's loved ones was altogether different. Speaking for the family, Laura Davis Watkins, told me, "We believe Shirley McQueen was telling the truth. We're very sorry her father never stood trial. It's important to remember that there's still another man out there who was responsible for my sister's death. As far as we're concerned, nothing is resolved."

THE HAVES AND THE HAVES

Norfolk, Connecticut
AUGUST 2003

I FEEL SLIGHTLY guilty mentioning that, earlier this year, *Connecticut Magazine*'s annual survey of towns with populations under 5,000 rated Norfolk, a Berkshires village in northern Litchfield County, the most livable in the state. This is an accolade that would, of course, delight any chamber of commerce, except that Norfolk happens not to have one — a function of a lack of commerce rather than a lack of civic spirit, which Norfolk possesses in abundance. Unlike the boosters in other ostensibly charming New England communities within weekend-commuting reach of New York City, however, many Norfolk citizens give the impression that it would suit them fine if their town, twenty miles east of the New York state line and five miles south of Massachusetts, disappeared from road maps. The timing of the publication of the *Connecticut* survey — February, with several weeks of a particularly brutal winter still ahead — did offer some consolation: come spring, it was hoped, readers might not remember. A Norfolk retiree who logs weather data has urged me to point out that on June 2 the temperature was thirty-eight degrees.

Usually, at this point in midsummer, casual conversations in Norfolk incline toward a predictable and reassuring range of topics: mosquito woes, black bear sightings, preparations for the annual fair at the Congregational Church and the book sale at the Norfolk Library, critiques of the chamber music concerts at the old Battell Stoeckel estate (now occupied by a Yale University summer arts program). The white eighteenth-century church, the red stone library, and the crenellated brick wall that borders the Yale property all adjoin Norfolk's triangular village green. At one end of the green is a faux-vintage mileage marker that notes the distances to Winsted, Hartford, Torrington, and Goshen and offers an implicit invitation to keep moving.

But the temptation is to stick around, whether for reasons of affinity or anthropological curiosity. Much of the money in Norfolk (and there's much money in Norfolk) is old, lineally descended from nineteenth-century industrial fortunes. By the turn of the century, Norfolk had established itself as a white-shoe summer retreat. It attracted the gentry from New York, Hartford, and Boston, plus the occasional Philadelphia banker or Pittsburgh steel magnate, as well as tuberculosis sufferers whose doctors had prescribed the air at the highest-altitude town in Connecticut. The winter population (1,700) still doubles during July and August, but the summer hotels have long since burned down or been demolished. While a fair number of Gilded Age trophy homes survive, ostentation is nowadays deemed a cardinal violation of the social code.

Generously spaced along the shady lanes that radiate from the village green, or else partially obscured along unpaved roads that wind through dense woods, are handsome, roomy but unassuming Colonial, Georgian, Victorian, and Adirondack-style houses. What defines Norfolk as much as its graceful architecture is its natural milieu. Eighty percent of the town's 30,000 acres has been designated as forest, agricultural, or tax-exempt land (including four state parks). In an era of naked and shameless real estate lust,

Norfolk is an anomalous throwback, a place where the phrase "conservation easement" gets uttered with what seems like lubricious enthusiasm. Overall, the ambience and physical details render a rare distillation of haute Yankee style — the unmistakable trappings of a real-deal WASP preserve (not to be confused with, say, the Ralph Lauren variety). The poet James Laughlin, who was also the publisher of the New Directions imprint, lived and worked in Norfolk for almost sixty years; his friend, biographer, and fellow poet Hayden Carruth composed a collection titled "The Norfolk Poems." In "A Short-Run View," Carruth wrote:

> There are a number
> Of millionaires in Norfolk, which adds a good deal
> To the scenery, but also a number of people who are
> Content not to be millionaires, which adds even more.

Norfolk is home to many varieties of artistes and aesthetes, among them sundry born-lucky folks who don't have to work a forty-hour week to get by and whose gratitude for their inheritance manifests itself as a potent desire to maintain the town, and the rhythm of their lives, just as is. Whenever change occurs in Norfolk, it tends to get scrutinized down to its molecular particulars.

Recently, a couple of macroscopic alterations to the landscape have occurred. Last month, a pizza place relocated, shifting two hundred yards, from next door to a liquor store — one of Norfolk's half dozen or so retail businesses — to a spot on Route 44, the main thoroughfare. And the granite Battell Memorial Fountain, which in warm weather burbles at the southern end of the green, has been out of commission ever since it got whacked by a truck. Otherwise, Norfolk looks exactly as it did a year ago (and the year before that and the year before that). Take away the Volvos, Saabs, and Subarus, and the clock might have stopped circa 1955 or, plausibly, 1925.

Which belies the fact that, for several months, among a large segment of the populace, reassuringly predictable casual conversations have been superseded by anxious speculation that the whole place is at risk of going to hell. A high-dollar land development scheme has been proposed for Norfolk and, in classic Not In My Back Yard fashion, has provoked an alarmed response from the community's self-anointed conservators. Unlike most NIMBY conflicts, however, the source of the distress isn't a proposed rehab clinic or industrial polluter. Oddly, for a place with a long history of devotion to genteel leisure, the perceived lethal weapon aimed at Norfolk's soul is a luxury golf course.

THE OFFSTAGE VILLAIN in this story — or, perhaps, more catalyst than villain; in any event, *way* offstage — is Gamil al-Batouti, the EgyptAir pilot who, on Halloween 1999, deliberately crashed a jet bound from New York to Cairo into the Atlantic Ocean. Of the 217 who died, three were from Norfolk, including Henrietta Mead, one of the town's most beloved citizens. Henny Mead had settled in Norfolk in 1958, the year she married Robin Mead, who was a grandson of Helen Hartley Jenkins, a summer resident from 1898 until her death in 1934. "One of the wealthiest women in the country" was how one history of Norfolk described Jenkins, whose father, Marcellus Hartley, founded the Union Metallic Cartridge Company, which later became the Remington Arms Company. Though she had formidable competition, Jenkins was one of Norfolk's grandest dames. "The townspeople of her day often misinterpreted her actions" — no doubt because she appeared to work at cross-purposes. When she wasn't acquiring old farmsteads in her capacity as an "avid conservationist," she was buying antiquated factory buildings and tearing them down "to rid the town of its traces of industry." Eventually, her holdings exceeded 1,500 acres, including a 300-acre parcel that in 1732 had been deeded by the Connecticut General Assembly to the then fledgling Yale College.

Well before Robin Mead received his inheritance — following the death of his mother, Jenkins's daughter — this real estate and several contiguous properties were collectively known as Yale Farm. For most of his adult life, Robin taught at a private school in nearby Salisbury. Summers he spent at the farm, clearing fields with his brush hog and tending a herd of Polled Hereford cattle. In his early fifties, he retired from teaching, became a gentleman farmer, and, in a community that placed a premium on volunteerism, chaired the planning and zoning commission. In 1992, the Meads sold more than 800 acres to a single buyer. When, six years later, Robin died of cancer at sixty-five, Yale Farm — 780 acres, about one fifth in pasture and cornfields and the rest in hemlock, pine, and hardwood forest — and its buildings had an appraised value of almost eight million dollars. The EgyptAir crash occurred a year and a half later. That Henny was only sixty-three years old and in good health explains why her immediate survivors — three sons, Robert, Slade, and Winter — weren't prepared to deal with the tax implications and ancillary complications of settling her estate. In twenty years, maybe, but not so soon after the death of their father. Slade recalls that at his mother's funeral he was approached by, and appalled by, a real estate developer.

NOT THAT NO ONE ELSE in Norfolk had considered the possibility that Yale Farm, or some portion of it, might come on the market. The Mead boys had inherited enough cash and securities to pay estate taxes, but they were left with a valuable, expensive-to-maintain asset that yielded very little income. Robert and Winter were both teachers, and Slade was a professional sports agent; all three had left Connecticut. Before long, Robert announced that he wanted to be bought out, but he agreed to give Slade a year to devise a strategy for the disposition of the property.

About two thirds of Yale Farm fell within the boundaries of Norfolk, and the balance was in North Canaan. As Slade was trying to come up with a development plan that wouldn't offend the neighbors (something other than a cookie-cutter housing subdivision), he happened upon a copy of the 1999 North Canaan town report: a light-bulb-over-head moment. North Canaan has a distinct blue-collar identity, but for some reason the report was illustrated with photos of golfers. That Slade himself had little interest in golf didn't stop him from suddenly envisioning fairways where the cattle had grazed. And, as long as the bulldozers were revved up, how about a hundred four-acre home sites on the course perimeter?

Slade conferred with golf course developers around the country, including one in Phoenix, where he lived. The consensus was that Yale Farm, with its diverse topography, broad meadows, mature trees, and plentiful water sources — not to mention its proximity to New York, Albany, and Hartford — had excellent potential. Opinions varied about what to construct along with the golf course. The Phoenix developer, evidently inspired by the notion of networking in a woodland setting, talked about a conference center instead of private homes. Someone else proposed a multisport resort. Most developers discussed buying Yale Farm outright, but Slade wanted to establish an ongoing partnership; he figured he could make more money that way and also influence the design. He was especially concerned about the homestead, which his paternal grandparents had built in 1938. Slade imagined it as a clubhouse or, better yet, a guesthouse, where Mead family members might stay during summer visits.

One afternoon in the spring of 2001, a friend phoned from the Denver airport. The friend had just got off a flight where, fortuitously, he had been seated next to Roland Betts, the creator and developer of Chelsea Piers, the immense sports and entertainment complex on the Hudson River in lower Manhattan. It turned out that Betts owned a weekend house in North Canaan, played about forty rounds of golf a year — all over the world, with a four handicap — and was eager to hear Slade's pitch. When they met in New York a few weeks later, the result was mutual enthusiasm. The resort or conference center concept didn't grab Betts, but he could foresee a large number of ten-acre house lots and he was willing to preserve the homestead. For Betts, much of the appeal, clearly, lay in the challenge of building something he'd never previously attempted. Chelsea Piers had been his first venture as a developer and it had succeeded grandly, both as urban amenity and business proposition. What he had in mind for Yale Farm wasn't a mere golf course but a world-class golf course, a links that could someday be mentioned in the same breath as Augusta National and Pebble Beach, with a cachet that would entice members who would be delighted to pay an initiation fee of $100,000 or more.

It wasn't only what Betts had to say that excited Slade's optimism but who he was and who he knew. Before Chelsea Piers, he had organized a series of investment partnerships that financed scores of Hollywood movies, among them *Outrageous Fortune*, *The Color of Money*, and *Escape from New York*. (Before that, he practiced entertainment law.) He had a reputation for enriching not only himself but his partners, most famously when he assumed a lead role in the 1989 purchase of the Texas Rangers baseball franchise. That deal had an incalculable domino effect: Betts netted more than $20 million when the Rangers were sold nine years later, and his old Yale fraternity chum and best friend, George W. Bush, parlayed an up-front stake of $600,000 into $15 million. Along the way, Bush had established himself in Texas as a seemingly successful businessman and viable political candidate.

One can easily picture Slade's gears turning: He was a sports agent who represented baseball players, and Betts knew lots of people in the world of baseball. A Republican, Slade was contemplating a run for the Arizona state senate; having a business partner whose best friend was the tenant of the White House couldn't hurt, could it? As soon as a partnership agreement was signed — Slade and Betts would become co–general partners, but

Betts would handle most of the details — the Meads would no longer bear the burden of Yale Farm's taxes or of its maintenance costs. Betts would line up the other investors, who would eventually kick in $20 million; the Meads would contribute the land but no cash. Once the technical plans were drafted, formal approvals from state and federal regulators and from the planning-and-zoning and inland wetlands commissions in both Norfolk and North Canaan would be necessary before a shovelful of dirt could be moved. This process could take years, but it would be worth the wait. In the end, Slade figured, he and his brothers stood to make far more than they'd inherited. And, instead of being land poor, they'd be cash rich.

SLADE NOW SAYS he assumed that the plans for Yale Farm Golf Club would trigger modest resistance, "because there's always a group against any sort of change." Possibly, his anticipation of a bonanza clouded his judgment, or maybe living in Arizona allowed him to lose sight of how a large-scale luxury anything aimed at wealthy outsiders would viscerally offend people in Norfolk and the Canaan Valley. Betts has said of the antagonism, "The whole thing has me astounded." One senses that members of the opposition camp have surprised even themselves with their vehemence. The fight against the golf course, it seems, has given a lot of people in Norfolk a renewed raison d'être, a chance to affirm their shared values and, in the bargain, to infuse their lives with some otherwise missing drama. In the process, a narrative has evolved in which Slade and his brothers have been reduced to minor roles — regarded as casualties, certainly, of their own cupidity but mainly as dupes of Betts, who has been cast as a manipulative opportunist. "The Mead boys are going to lose both ways," one Norfolk resident assured me. "This guy's a master of Hollywood accounting, and their share comes off the back end. My guess is the town gets fucked and they do, too."

The first objections arose in the autumn of 2001, after Slade met with three neighbors and outlined the basic plan. One of the three, Scott Asen, later tried to persuade Slade to give him time to come up with an alternative bidder. A studious-looking private investor who lives in New York and spends weekends in a house he grew up in and inherited from his parents, Asen hoped to induce a land trust or conservation organization to buy the farm. The price that Asen had in mind, however — $4 million — Slade briskly dismissed. Eventually, Asen and the other neighbors constituted themselves as the Canaan Conservation Coalition and hired lawyers and technical experts to appear at public hearings and rebut the lawyers and experts hired by Betts and his partners. The group also retained a public relations firm and posted yard signs around North Canaan (but not in Norfolk, where, by ordinance, that sort of thing is a no-no) with slogans like "Cows Not Caddies," "Berkshire Hills Not Beverly Hills," and "Gophers Not Golfers."

In Norfolk, a somewhat less combative entity, the Coalition for Sound Growth, materialized, qualifying as an intervener with Norfolk's inland wetlands and planning-and-zoning commissions. For the past year, a Web site created by a coalition supporter has tracked the minutiae of the Yale Farm Golf Course battle. In addition to posting extended commentaries about land-use practices, the site has provided a forum for just barely polite jousting between Betts and his critics as well as less polite fulminations about his insidious designs. ("Do these super-rich nomads with their multiple residences remember what it's like to have only one home, or to be a member of a community?") Yet another protest group, which includes neighbors and former friends of Betts who believe that, after spending twenty-two years as an amicable enough weekend resident of North Canaan, he's now going to ruin the neighborhood, has occupied itself by writing letters to the editor impugning his judgment and character.

The opposition's overarching theme, after the ad hominem gibes and the scientific verbiage have been pruned, is that the golf course represents the beginning of the end, the harbinger of a permanent violation of the environment for the benefit of nou-veau-riche boors who long ago spoiled places like the Hamptons, Martha's Vineyard, and Nantucket — vulgarians who assume that anything, even a landscape, can be had for a price, and who con-gratulate themselves when, indeed, the price of everything in the vicinity, especially real estate, subsequently escalates. Thus, early on, after Betts promoted the golf course as a boon to property val-ues during a presentation before the North Canaan board of se-lectmen, Wheaton Byers, one of the abutting landowners, told him, "But I don't *want* my property values to rise."

According to Byers, a retired diplomat whose family settled in North Canaan in 1938, "Betts told me, 'Your children will appre-ciate it.' I said, 'No they won't.' And he said, 'Then you'll just have to learn to live with it.'" (Betts denies that this conversation took place.)

Learning to live with it, the opponents maintain, would mean not only enduring an aesthetic insult (they anticipate scores of "McMansions" surrounding the golf course) but having to cope with extra traffic (from resident and nonresident golfers) and in-creased demands for municipal services (schools, fire and ambu-lance, roads). I also once overheard a couple of Coalition for Sound Growth members toying with the idea of having helicop-ters buzz over Norfolk to simulate President Bush and his Secret Service detail descending for a round of golf. Betts, who dis-putes the McMansion scenario, replies that Yale Farm Golf Club's homeowners would be predominately weekenders (or, even if they moved in year-round, would send their children to private schools), and that the golf course and the new housing would yield multiple dividends: tax revenues would rise (giving existing prop-erty taxpayers relief); local businesses would benefit; jobs would be created.

An incontrovertible fact that neither Betts nor the Coalition for Sound Growth wants to dwell upon is that Norfolk already suffers from a dearth of so-called affordable housing. Whatever gets built at Yale Farm Golf Club would skew that statistic even further. The fear in Norfolk is that, at some point, the state will take note of this inequity, and (gasp!) a developer of low-cost multifamily housing or a downscale subdivision will get his foot in the door.

ONE IRONY of the contretemps — beyond Betts's characterization of it as "a titanic struggle between the haves and the haves" — is that a public relations strategy that he plotted has become a public relations bungle. Before Slade Mead encountered Betts, he discussed his plans with Arthur S. Rosenblatt, a close friend of his parents as well as, for six years, Norfolk's first selectman — de facto, the mayor. A jocular, sardonic man of Falstaffian girth, Rosenblatt grew up near Boston and settled in Norfolk in the early eighties (having first visited more than twenty years earlier with a friend whose family had been there for three generations). He quickly became an energetic volunteer, serving on various local boards before running for office in 1993. Among his accomplishments as first selectman was securing a large federal grant to help fund the felicitous renovation of the center of town. But he was consistently frustrated in his efforts to increase the commercial tax base — why was it that Norfolk couldn't even support a hardware store? — and that experience, he says, spurred his enthusiasm for the Mead-Betts vision for Yale Farm.

In the spring of 2002, at which point Rosenblatt was no longer first selectman but was still a member of the select board, he signed a contract as a public relations consultant to the partnership — Betts having grasped that Rosenblatt, an avid gossip, could help him keep tabs on who in Norfolk opposed the project. Before proceeding, Rosenblatt had solicited an opinion from the town attorney, who concluded that he didn't have a conflict of interest, because the board played no substantive role in reviewing the golf course proposal. However, as first selectman, Rosenblatt did have the authority to make appointments to the inland wetlands commission; I spoke with a number of Norfolk citizens who said that they didn't oppose the golf course and yet felt that Rosenblatt had burdened himself — and, by association, Betts — with an appearance of impropriety. Nor did Rosenblatt help matters with his occasional barbed public comments. In one interview with the *Litchfield County Times*, he referred to the opposition campaign as "pathetic" and "lacking in wit," which prompted an editorial rebuke from the paper.

During a June meeting of the inland wetlands commission, a lawyer for the Coalition for Sound Growth, in a sporting attempt to embarrass Rosenblatt, submitted a letter intending to disqualify him from speaking (though it was safe to assume he wouldn't be doing so anyway). I happened to be seated in front of Rosenblatt. Earlier, as the room filled — about eighty people attended — I had asked him whether he knew everyone present. "Not only do I know them," he replied. "I can tell you who's for and who's against."

Rosenblatt is the source of Betts's attempt to spin the opposition to Yale Farm Golf Club as, fundamentally, elitist sour grapes. When the coalition was forming, Rosenblatt discerned a significant overlap between its membership and that of the Norfolk Country Club, a deliberately unprepossessing establishment with six tennis courts, no swimming pool, and a spottily maintained nine-hole golf course. ("It's not well irrigated and the grasses are, shall we say, highly varied," a member told me.) In my first phone conversation with Betts, he said, "What I find interesting is that Norfolk already has a golf course attached to a very exclusive private club, and almost everyone opposed to us is associated with it." According to this logic, the hostility to Yale Farm Golf Club has nothing to do with its potential impact on wetlands, water quality, myriad varieties of flora and fauna (including human), or the texture of life in a community rooted in a deeply conservative ethos of land stewardship. Nor does anyone in Norfolk sincerely object that the new folks in town wouldn't be likely candidates to volunteer for the school board, fire department, emergency medical squad, library, or historical society. Rather, it seems, it's all about vanity and wounded pride.

THERE ARE, to be sure, many unalarmed people in Norfolk — those who accept Betts's fiscal prognosis, or who believe that private property rights are sacrosanct, or who view the conflict as an intraclass squabble that doesn't concern them. Within this last category, the opinion also prevails that, never mind what the regulations mandate, the project will be approved simply because its principal investor is a close friend of the President of the United States. Last month, both North Canaan commissions conditionally approved Betts's application, and the Canaan Conservation Coalition initiated an appeal. This fall, the Norfolk commissions are expected to deliver their verdicts, which either the proponents or the interveners are virtually certain to challenge. Meanwhile, Slade Mead is on record to the effect that if the golf course is ultimately turned down his Plan B is to build a high-density housing development.

When I went to see Betts in New York a few days after the meeting of the Norfolk inland wetlands commission, he surprised me by downplaying the importance of the housing component. "I've given serious thought to what if I eliminated the houses," he said. "If I did that, would it calm folks down? Or what if I take the fifty to sixty homes down to twenty? We'd just increase the size and the price of the lots. It's a wash."

We met in Betts's office at Chelsea Piers, two miles north of the World Trade Center site. In November 2001, around the time Betts and the Meads were negotiating their partnership agreement, Betts was appointed to the Lower Manhattan Development Corporation, and he subsequently supervised the architectural competition to redevelop Ground Zero. Among his other not-for-profit endeavors, he is a trustee of Columbia Law School and of Yale, and a member of the United States Olympic Committee.

Both in his work and in his domestic life, he has peripatetic habits, and if he becomes persona non grata in the Berkshires he can always retreat to one of his other homes — in Manhattan, New Mexico, Wyoming, or Tortola.

At one point, Betts began discussing traffic patterns. "There's this tremendous hubbub about how this golf course is going to completely change Norfolk," he said. "But I think Norfolk will be completely unaware of it. The whole orientation of the people using the golf course will be toward the west. That's how you get there from New York, or even from Boston — and Norfolk is to the south. Like in a stream, it's a back eddy. Physically and psychologically, Norfolk's the back door. It's isolated, it's not on the way to anywhere."

In the nineteenth century, the area west of the Canaan Valley was an iron producing center, and Norfolk's forests supplied charcoal that fueled the smelters. By the time the iron industry moved elsewhere, the timber harvest had denuded the landscape, at which point a small group of remarkably farsighted conservationists got busy, buying land for a song and committing themselves to its regeneration. Their descendants, Norfolk's fiercely protective inhabitants, don't consider it an accident that their town has the look and feel of not being on the way to anywhere in particular. They consider this an unalloyed virtue. The accident, in their minds, was the EgyptAir calamity, and the consequence is that they must now confront the likes of Roland Betts.

Betts has a disarming style of gamesmanship. It's often noted, in references to his bond with George Bush, that he's a Democrat, but more important from Norfolk's perspective is his comportment as a plutocrat. He's a large, affable man — he played hockey at Yale and kept it up until a shoulder injury slowed him down a while back — who presents himself as the soul of reasoned compromise. But he also exudes the air of someone whose experience has taught him that by being persistent and thorough he'll usually get his way. Even among his adversaries in Norfolk, the consensus goes, "Why does Roland Betts want to build this thing? Because he can." As for the deeper question of why, at one point while we were talking his assistant interrupted him: "I'm sorry — Mr. Betts, it's Condoleezza Rice calling." Betts slipped away for a few minutes. Upon returning, he said, "She wants a membership. What can I tell you?"

Bismarck, North Dakota
FEBRUARY 2002

NORTH DAKOTANS who favor changing the state's name tend to be realists. They readily concede that many evocative and desirable alternatives (Florida, Tahiti, Martinique) are unavailable, while certain other options (Southern Manitoba, Lower Saskatchewan) are not advisable. The name-change advocates make no attempt to be boldly original; they want to call their home Dakota, period — minus the directional modifier that was appended in 1889, when Dakota Territory (adapted from the name of the Dakota tribe, which means "alliance of friends") was divided and North Dakota and South Dakota simultaneously joined the Union. During the deliberations that preceded statehood, sentiment ran high on both sides of the forty-sixth parallel, the anticipated border-to-be, to lay claim to the name Dakota. When neither the southern nor the northern pioneers proved willing to yield, the result was a compromise that seemed mutually unsatisfactory — but not, evidently, mutual enough. The frequency with which some North Dakotans have revisited the question across the years plainly reflects an aggrieved belief that their state came up short in the deal.

Further confirmation that members of the Dakota lobby — a loose confederacy of businesspeople, politicians, and journalists — are grounded in reality: they don't expect to prevail. Or, as some among them, hedging their skepticism, will say, "not in our lifetime." The presumed futility of the enterprise, however, is a goad rather than a deterrent. Hunkering down and trying to devise new and improved reasons that Dakota would be superior to North Dakota is a diverting pastime, an indigenous sport no less absorbing than ice fishing or curling, and it offers the deep satisfaction that comes with committing oneself to a perpetual struggle. Bucking the very long odds — trudging toward the infinite horizon with a head-bowed-into-the-stiff-wind doggedness — is, after all, the quintessential North Dakota experience.

At least four times since the end of the Second World War — in 1947, 1983, 1989, and 2001 — the name-change debate has made headlines. As Mike Jacobs, the pro-Dakota editor of the *Grand Forks Herald*, noted not long ago, "For a state with very little that brings it national attention on a regular basis, this is the one thing we can do that gets people to acknowledge we're out here." Because North Dakotans are congenitally earnest, hardworking, and sincere, one naturally hesitates to impute cynical motives.

The 1947 undertaking was the imaginative handiwork of John Fleck, an automobile dealer and a member of the North Dakota House of Representatives, who one January day introduced a resolution postulating that "countless numbers of tourists who have not visited or even passed through North Dakota" would do so if only the place sounded less Arctic. Fleck's effort dovetailed with an editorial crusade that the *Bismarck Tribune* was then waging to do something about the local weather, an endeavor that consisted mainly of complaining about it.

It's unclear whether the peevish tone of Fleck's resolution

("Whereas, the State of North Dakota through adverse publicity has been ridiculed because of its climatic conditions; and whereas, such publicity has been unwarranted; and whereas, much of such unwarranted publicity has been caused by the use of the term 'North' in the name 'North Dakota' . . .") was responsible for its failure. In any event, it had been long forgotten by 1983, when a Bismarck advertising man named Mylo Candee spontaneously reinvented the wheel. According to Candee, who is now an aide to Kent Conrad, North Dakota's senior United States senator, he and "some poker-playing buddies" were discussing how North Dakota might improve its image and attract more industry when Candee "impetuously said that if the state of North Dakota wanted to change its image a good place to start was to change its name."

Soon Candee had coined a catchphrase ("Let's Drop the North and Call It Dakota") and an outdoor-advertising company had donated billboard space in Fargo and Bismarck. Candee's logic was straightforward: "North Dakotans yearn to be known for something other than the North. It is a wintry, cold, snowy climate up here, but we wish to be recognized for some of our other attributes. In my travels, when someone asks me where I'm from, I'm in the habit of saying, 'I'm from Dakota,' and their eyes light up and they say, 'Oh, a cowboy.' But if I say the full name they talk about the cold. I liken it to Bill Cosby's character Fat Albert. Sure, he was overweight, but why rub his face in it by calling him fat?"

A Bismarck radio reporter saw the billboards and called some people in South Dakota, who rewarded him with unhappy sound bites, and from there the story made its way to the Associated Press national wire. Within hours, Candee, upon returning to his office from a funeral, discovered thirty telephone messages. He also discovered that his brain trust had scattered. ("We're still friends, but they all said, 'Don't drag my name into this!'") The same day, he accepted an invitation to fly to New York to appear on *The CBS Morning News* — a dubious decision.

"My image of North Dakota is the Badlands, the beautiful area in the southwestern part of the state, where I grew up," Candee told me recently. "While I was on the air talking about the beauty I was accustomed to, those stinkers at CBS were running a video of a blizzard."

"Was it a blizzard in Georgia or Alabama?" I asked.

"No, it was a North Dakota blizzard, I guess. But, still, that juxtaposition bothered me."

I'D BEEN HOPING for a blizzard myself, heavy weather I could write home about, when I flew to Bismarck last month. Instead, I arrived during a thaw so startling (daytime highs *in the forties!*) that it provided fodder for every conversation I had until I got on a plane again. I timed my visit to coincide with a gathering in Grand Forks of participants in the New Economy Initiative, an ambitious industrial development strategy-in-the-making, orchestrated by a statewide coalition of chambers of commerce, whose goals include increasing and diversifying the population, enabling businesses to become more technologically sophisticated, and creating more high-paying jobs. My first morning in Bismarck, I had breakfast with Katherine Satrom, a travel agency owner who is active in the New Economy Initiative's "tourism cluster." Tourism entrepreneurs, unlike, say, wheat farmers, find themselves in the hypothetically enviable position of having nowhere to go but up; North Dakota ranks forty-ninth in tourism revenues (ahead of Delaware).

"They encouraged us to think outside the box," Satrom told me, by way of explaining what prompted her, a year ago, to proffer a "Let's Call Our State Dakota!" initiative. "I prefer to think of this as shortening the state's name rather than changing it. Not everyone's comfortable with change." Satrom, a solicitous and friendly woman in her middle years and a lifelong North Dakota resident, was aware of the John Fleck and Mylo Candee precedents. "Just because an idea fails once or twice doesn't mean it isn't worthy of perseverance," she said. Nor was she discouraged by the cautionary experience of Tim Mathern, a state senator from Fargo who in 1989 drafted two name-change resolutions, held hearings before the legislature's constitutional revisions committee, and had the majority of the committee members in his corner, only to see the full Senate trounce the idea. Mathern felt that embracing Dakota would have been a way of honoring Native Americans, and Satrom agreed. "What could be more true to our heritage?" she said.

But there was a tentativeness in her tone, a media-shyness that I attributed to the repercussions last spring when her proposal received a premature public airing. The immediate consequences were the usual get-a-load-of-this stories in the national press, late-night-television monologue jokes, and a flood of you'd-*better*-not-change-the-name-of-my-home-state letters to the editor, many from expatriates in California, Arizona, Colorado, and other un–North Dakota latitudes. Dave Barry wrote a column ("Changing names is a sound idea, an idea based on the scientific principle that underlies the field of marketing, which is: People are stupid"), the mayor of Grand Forks retaliated by inviting him to come for a visit and promising to name a sewage lift station in his honor, and Barry wrote a second column ("North Dakota is calling me. 'Come on up!' it says. And then it adds: 'Bring thermal underwear!'").

Satrom had thoughtfully arranged for me a two-day itinerary that seemed designed to curb any inclination I might have had to caricature the state as a flatter-than-flat treeless prairie. (Typical flatness knee-slapper: "North Dakota is so flat you can watch your dog run away for three days.") My guide the first day was Jim Fuglie, a lapsed journalist and former director of the state tourism department who now works for an advertising firm. Fuglie's pro-Dakota credentials include testimony before Senator Mathern's committee. He also made a name for himself during the 1980s as the author of what could best be described as a campaign of government-sanctioned ironic boosterism, when he posted billboards at the borders with messages like "Welcome to North Dakota — Mountain Removal Project Completed" and "Stay in North Dakota — Custer Was Healthy When He Left."

We hit the road right after breakfast, crossed the Missouri River, and drove west a couple of hundred miles. Along the way, the elevation subtly rose and the terrain shifted from plowed wheat fields to short-grass rangeland. The air temperature also rose — a local phenomenon. Typically, Bismarck, in the center of the state, is five degrees warmer than Fargo, on the Minnesota border, and Dickinson, sixty miles from Montana, is five degrees warmer yet. "That's why this part of North Dakota's called the Banana Belt," Fuglie said. By the end of the day, I'd had a good look at the Badlands, an expanse of buttes and ravines carved more than half a million years ago by the Little Missouri River and covering thousands of square miles — a vista more majestic, it occurred to me, than several lifetimes' worth of truck commercials. I'd also met some rancher friends of Fuglie's, mingled with a herd of bison who hospitably refrained from charging us, and visited Medora, a restored Western town situated at the entrance to Theodore Roosevelt National Park, which draws 450,000 visitors a year.

Fuglie told me that, by coincidence, shortly before Katherine Satrom decided to champion the Dakota idea, he'd been having discussions with executives at a software company called Great Plains, whose president, Doug Burgum, was willing to underwrite market testing of the name change. For several years, Great Plains has been North Dakota's most conspicuously successful entrepreneurial venture; last spring, in a $1.1 billion stock deal, it was acquired by Microsoft and renamed Microsoft Great Plains. Burgum, a homeboy and happy philanthropist, sees the Dakota opportunity as, in effect, a product placement scheme on a grand scale, a way of rebranding the entire state.

"What people like Doug Burgum and I are interested in is the message that we're willing to change the name of our state just to survive in this century," Fuglie said. "If this actually happened, it would be a signal to the world that something powerful has taken place. That's how I think we could sell this. You know, there's a lot of identity confusion between North Dakota and South Dakota. People who aren't from here don't know which is which. They say, 'The Badlands. Oh, those are in South Dakota.' So we just haven't marketed our Badlands as well as they have. If we could change our name, a generation from now we'll be identified as the genuine Dakota, and South Dakota will seem like the pretender. Our research shows that it would be the same thing as Virginia versus West Virginia. Where would you rather say you're from?"

THE NEXT DAY, I rode from Bismarck to Grand Forks, completing a traverse of the state, in the genial company of Katherine Satrom's husband, Joe, who works for Ducks Unlimited, a conservation organization that protects ducks (in part) so that folks wearing camouflage gear and carrying shotguns can wait for them to fly by. We stuck to back roads, and I got to contemplate the prairie pothole region, a forty- to sixty-mile-wide band of elevated glacial remnant, pocked with thousands of small ponds that make North Dakota the state with the finest waterfowl-nesting habitat on the continent. The day after that, I sat down for a conversation with Doug Burgum in his office at the Microsoft Great Plains headquarters, a cedar, glass, and brick low-rise campus on an interstate frontage road in Fargo. Burgum, who is forty-five, grew up thirty miles from Fargo, in the tiny town of Arthur, where the grain elevator has been owned by his family for four generations. After college at North Dakota State University, he did what most of his contemporaries did — left the state. (North Dakota high school students are, by a wide statistical margin, more likely to attend college than high school students in any other state. But this salutary fact is offset by a grievous migration of the state's youngest and brightest. Fifteen of its fifty-three counties have fewer than twenty new births annually. The population in the 2000 census was 642,000 — 40,000 less than in 1930.)

In 1983, Burgum was living in Chicago and working as a management consultant at McKinsey & Company. He joined Great Plains, a developer of software for small and medium-size businesses, when it was a startup, because he was "specifically interested in doing something in North Dakota." After mortgaging farmland that he inherited from his father, Burgum literally "bet the farm" by providing the seed capital for the fledgling company. A year later, together with other members of his extended family, he bought the rest of the company.

North Dakota, Burgum said, has coal reserves, plenty of water, and roughly the same latitude as the Ruhr Valley in Germany. "But there's no industrial base here," he said. "That's not the result of a lack of resources; it's a function of the distance to markets." The state leads the world in the production of durum wheat, for pasta, but when Burgum was in high school a bushel of durum sold for seven dollars, and now it's less than half that price. "When your economy is so tied to agriculture, you're dependent not just on the weather but, increasingly nowadays, on global market forces. There's so much you can't control."

That sense of being marginalized, of struggling to master one's destiny, has a long history. It's a syndrome traceable to the settlement of Dakota Territory, which was an economic development scheme hatched by the railroad interests. The railroads built an infrastructure for millions of people — a town every twenty miles — only a small fraction of whom showed up. For decades, of course, the towns have been dying or barely hanging on. "On top of that," Burgum continued, "we have this deep-seated Scandinavian, Teutonic outlook — a combination of dark Lutheranism and German Catholicism, which adds up to a primal sense that somehow we're not worthy. This is also a place where people get the message that if they do well they're not supposed to say anything about it, because it's not nice. You never want to do well at the expense of anyone else. The grocer in a small town wants to look like he's broke so nobody thinks he's charging too much.

"When we convened focus groups in Fargo and Bismarck last summer, we found that most people don't care for the idea of changing the name. They don't want to be made fun of, they don't want to have to explain it to their out-of-state relatives, so they talk about what it's going to cost. But math doesn't speak to the heart of the issue.

"Words are powerful, names are powerful. The word *north*, for instance — unless you're a polar explorer, there's nothing that excites the mind about the word. Some people think it's intellectually dishonest of us to drop the 'North.' But we're north only in relative terms. We're north of South Dakota, but we're not north of Winnipeg or several major European countries. The geographical center of North America is in Rugby, North Dakota. But people look at weather maps that don't show Canada, and in the American mindset we're thought of as the end of the road.

"No state has ever changed its name. It appeals to me for that reason alone — that it's never been done before. One definition of an adventure is an uncertain outcome. Why not just do it for ourselves?"

FOLLOWING MY CHAT with Burgum, I hurried up the interstate to Grand Forks, where, as it happened, back-to-back events were taking place that clearly fell into the doing-it-for-ourselves category. At the Alerus Center, a city-owned convention facility, the New Economy Initiative was holding its winter meeting. This was to be followed by the Marketplace of Ideas, an annual business opportunity and employment networking bazaar, organized by Senator Conrad and the state agriculture commissioner. I arrived at the Alerus Center in time for a PowerPoint presentation on "nature-based tourism" led by a woman who made the perhaps not scientifically provable observation that businesses that cater to bird watchers have a lot of growth potential because "many birders live in warm places, and they look forward to coming to North Dakota for a few days and being cold." I liked that — and the cheerful, benign self-delusion that it implied — because I had also come to realize that North Dakotans generally know better than to fool themselves or anyone else. More than once, my hosts mentioned what a lucky break it was for North Dakota that the National Weather Service had recently recalibrated the wind-chill index. What used to feel like thirty-five below now feels, officially, like a mere fifteen below. No telling what a boon that might be to the economy.

The next afternoon, back at the Alerus Center, I made a point of touring the arena where the Marketplace of Ideas exhibitors had set out brochures and samples of their wares. There were a couple hundred booths, occupied by promoters of products and enterprises large and small: monster windmills ("North Dakota: the Saudi Arabia of wind energy"); flax producers ("Flaxseed: almost too good to be true"); the revolutionary bidirectional Dakota Sno-Blade. Elsewhere in the building, throughout the day, citizens treated themselves to dozens of seminars with titles like "Profit by Welcoming Vacation Guests to Your Farm," "Emus — Status of the Industry Today," and "Grant Writing: Where Is the Money? How Do We Get It?"

Tantalizing possibilities, but I hadn't quite made up my mind to relocate permanently. If I did, I knew that finding work wouldn't be a problem. "Jobs are so plentiful in North Dakota," I'd been told, "most people have two." And yet, for all their self-deprecating affability, North Dakotans have a canny suspicion of certain types of outsiders. Yes, the state could really use more people, more investment capital, brighter entrepreneurial ideas. At the same time, its citizens prefer, in many ways, to be left alone. A grave distrust of corporations — a lesson learned from the experience with the railroad builders — is explicitly encoded in state law. (It is still illegal, for example, for big corporations to own farmland.) The progressive Nonpartisan League, which thrived during the years of the First World War, was created in response to dissatisfaction with the major national political parties, and it established an enduring tone for political debate. Two of its vestiges are the Bank of North Dakota, in Bismarck, which was founded in 1919, the only state-owned bank in the country, and a state-owned mill, which was built in Grand Forks, in the early twenties, in response to the predatory ways of the Minneapolis grain-processing oligopolists. A great deal of native pride is invested in these curiosities, each, in its way, a declaration of independence from the mainstream way of doing business. Increasingly, that pride mingles with recognition of the discomfort of marginality. Which is not to say that the prospect of change seems either desirable or inevitable. At the Alerus Center, I had a conversation with Lloyd Omdahl, a retired political science professor and former lieutenant governor, who was bragging, tongue in cheek, about his hometown of Conway. According to the 2000 census, Conway had suffered a net loss of only one person since 1990. "We went from twenty-four to twenty-three," Omdahl said. "We feel it's a victory compared to other communities. My theory is that the young people aren't leaving — the old people are dying."

The wind blows, winter overstays its welcome, most experiences are horizontal, and that's the beauty of the place. A new idea comes along, and nobody's really sure what to do with it. Same with old ideas. North Dakotans possess a sublime talent for talking to the brink of death just about any subject that pertains to North Dakota — because the rest of the world isn't much interested, and there aren't that many North Dakotans to debate the topic. Eventually, it feels so old that they reach a consensus to forget about it. After a few long winters of hibernation, the time arrives for it to resurface. When it does, it's a brand-new idea all over again.

SO LONG, READ ABOUT
YOU TOMORROW

Las Vegas, New Mexico
JULY 2002

CAROLYN GILBERT has no trouble remembering where she was when she came up with what, in all modesty, she still regards as an excellent idea — the First Great Obituary Writers' Conference. She was in North Dallas, in a bar "a lot like Cheers," with a bunch of like-minded friends, among them a federal judge, a couple of attorneys, and some other professionals, who made a point of getting together once or twice a month. "Sort of like a salon for news junkies" is Gilbert's description of the gatherings of her coterie, which seems somewhat misleading, given that the group spent far less time chewing over the front-page fodder served up by the *Dallas Morning News* than they did indulging their collective fascination with who had died recently and what had been written about them.

Gilbert isn't an obituary writer herself (unless you count the one she wrote and sent to five Texas newspapers last winter, after her father, R. C. Milford Jr., died). She could be most accurately described as an obituary gadfly, a self-selected advocate for obituary writers and readers. Every day, after digesting the obits in the *Morning News* — clipping and filing the ones she might want to refer to later on — she proceeds to read the obituary pages of the *Times*, the *Washington Post*, the *Fort Worth Star-Telegram*, the *Houston Chronicle*, the *Archer County* (Texas) *News*, and the *Electra* (Texas) *Star-News*. Most American newspapers treat obituaries more as a revenue source than as a literary opportunity. The obits in the *Morning News*, for instance, usually take up two pages, but a page and a half of that is occupied by paid obituaries, a gray expanse of pallid prose that, for the most part, sounds as if it had been written by a platoon of undertakers, which it generally is. Gilbert finds this shameful, but she is, by nature, an optimist, and her optimism extends to the future of the obituary, which she believes should be elevated to its proper place as an art form. That belief inspired her spontaneously expressed intention to convene the First Great Obituary Writers' Conference.

"I just said it as a lark," she told me not long ago, when I called to inquire about the upcoming Fourth Great Obituary Writers' Conference. "I'm not even sure what I meant — whether I meant great obituaries, great writers, or great conference." The first one, which took place on a May weekend in 1999 in Archer City (the north-central Texas destination made famous by the film version of Larry McMurtry's novel *The Last Picture Show*), was a strictly Texas event, to which only obituary writers and editors from the state's major dailies were invited. The Honorable Jerry Buchmeyer, Gilbert's federal judge friend, gave a speech, sharing selections from his vast collection of obituaries. He also recited excerpts from a compendium of euphemisms for *died*: "was ushered to the angels," "passed from this plane to a higher plane," "made his transition," "passed into life's next adventure," "received his final marching orders," "departed this life on his Harley-Davidson," "graduated to phase two of God's eternal plan," "became a handmaiden of God," "was royally escorted into her heavenly home," "teed up for Golf in the Kingdom," and — my favorite — "went fishing with Christ!! on Friday."

Gilbert's Second Great Obituary Writers' Conference, held in the town of Jefferson, was the occasion for a disquisition on a collection she had begun of paid obituaries of people who had been photographed wearing hats. "I'd noticed that, for some reason, there'd been a rash of all these folks wearing caps from Jim's Truck Stop and the like," she told me. That year's conference generated enough publicity that she began thinking of expanding beyond Texas. She gave her cottage organization a big-sounding name (International Association of Obituarists) and began collecting dues to help support a Web site (www.obitpage.com), a source of memorable obits, reviews of books with obituary-related themes, and practical advice on how to spice up one's death stories. She also founded the Obituarium, which is a word that she and a colleague coined without quite deciding how to define it. "It's conceptual at this point," she said. "It's the name of the concept of everything that gets associated with obituaries — historical, literary, genealogical." (For the moment, the Obituarium doesn't exist, except as a letterhead and a T-shirt.) Meanwhile, friends of Gilbert's had bought and restored a historic hotel in Las Vegas, New Mexico, north of Santa Fe, and she calculated that if the next conference were held there more out-of-staters would show up. That proved true in 2001, so she decided to return for this year's event.

"We're a small but elite group," Gilbert explained when I told her I was thinking of attending. "We really study the art and science of the obituary. The purpose is serious, but we have great fun. This year we have the added attraction of Nigel Starck, who, even as we speak, is on a round-the-world trip to gather more information about the global obituary." Barring unforeseen circumstances, I promised, I'd be there.

ANYONE WHO PAID the $135 conference registration fee, Gilbert decided, would automatically become a member of the International Association of Obituarists. Though I wouldn't be laying out any cash myself, I imagined how I might qualify for membership under some vague grandfather clause. Not only do I turn first to the obituaries in the *Times* each morning; my sense is that I've been reading obits for approximately as long as I've been reading. I vividly recall being seven or eight years old and encountering in my hometown dailies, the *Tulsa World* and the *Tulsa Tribune*, terse accounts of men in their early forties who had "succumbed" to heart attacks.

In the middle of midlife, I read the *Times* obits for pleasure, a pleasure that arises from the contemplation of a completed cycle of accomplishment or notoriety, concisely wrought. An almost conspiratorial escapism animates this daily exercise — my own guilty escape from having to think about, say, trade policy toward China or more bad news on the global-warming front, coupled with an envy of the freshly deceased, who have become immune to tomorrow's probably even worse news. I also make a point of reading the agate-type paid memorial tributes in the *Times*. My preference is for souls I've never heard of. Good for you, I think, whoever you were, whose loved ones loved you so well . . . and special congratulations for dying in the autumn (especially the autumn), amid the drifting leaves (drifting lives?) that will soon mingle with the drifting snow, in deepening, soothing silence.

It long ago occurred to me that my obituary habit derived from the same instinctive curiosity, the same blithe inquisitiveness — okay, nosiness — that made me a reporter. When I read the obits as a young boy, however, it was with a palpable dread. The death I feared most was my father's, and when he turned forty (I was nine at the time) my worrying intensified. But then, obligingly, he didn't die. Year after year, as I got older he got younger. I kept reading the obits, absorbing subliminal clues about how to live life, while my father and mother both kept offering their own examples. They kept not dying, and at some point I realized that my anxiety about losing them had transmuted into gratitude that they had stuck around for so long.

A week before the Fourth Great Obituary Writers' Conference was scheduled to get under way, I flew to Oklahoma for a family gathering. My father had, at last, made his transition, slipped the surly bonds of earth, joined the legions of Oklahoma Sooners football fans in the ultimate luxury skyboxes. Died. Always a charitable person, he had with characteristic munificence outlived by more than forty years my primal childhood fear. We gave him a sendoff with far more laughs than tears, spent several days plundering his admirable wine collection, and pronounced ourselves lucky.

Which is why I was in a reflective but not especially somber state of mind when I arrived at the Plaza Hotel in Las Vegas, where checking in ahead of me was Carolyn Gilbert. Though she's now a freelance public policy and communications specialist, Gilbert spent many years as a high school English teacher, and I wasn't surprised to find that she resembled a composite of my high school English teachers — a neatly groomed sixty-one-year-old woman with big eyeglasses, wavy auburn hair, a pearly North Texas drawl, and a howdy-do affability.

The conference wasn't officially set to begin until the next afternoon, but I got more than a preview during dinner with Gilbert that evening and a postbreakfast conversation with her the next morning. On both occasions we were joined by Carolyn's daughter and aide-de-camp, Ashlee Gilbert, an aspiring actress and fellow obituary devotee, and by the globetrotting Nigel Starck, an Australian journalist turned university professor, who was immersed in research for a doctoral dissertation on Australian, British, and American obituaries since the late eighteenth century. Starck's enthusiasm for his subject was such that he couldn't resist scooping his keynote address, which he'd titled "Revival of a Dying Art."

He was particularly eager to share some recently acquired artifacts — photocopies of two October 1892 articles from the *At-*

lanta Constitution, one a deathbed scene starring Caroline Harrison, the wife of the twenty-third president, Benjamin Harrison, and the other a postmortem dispatch that, strictly speaking, wasn't an obituary. " 'Mrs. Harrison's body was laid out in the room in which she died, and this afternoon it was placed in a casket, in which it will finally repose,' " Starck read. "Now, here's the part I like: 'She shows in her emaciation the effects of the long wasting illness of eight months that has reduced her large, matronly figure to a thin, frail form.' "

"That's what I want in my obituary," Carolyn Gilbert said.

"There was a flowering of ornate bereavement in the 1880s — a Victorian phenomenon," Starck explained. "In the latter part of the nineteenth century, they were extremely graphic and intrusive in their death journalism. They would describe suicides, brains being splattered on the ceiling." But in the 1920s the obit died — according to the most popular theory, because, after the First World War, people were sick of death. A renaissance didn't occur until the 1980s, when several British newspapers, notably the *Independent* and the *Daily Telegraph*, decided to treat obituaries as feature stories and hired talented editors to oversee them. Suddenly the obituary pages offered leisurely narratives, lots of photographs, and a refreshing aversion to hagiography — what Starck calls "the posthumous parallax, a bending of life histories toward all that is light and wholesome, away from anything that might reflect unfavorably on the dead." Hugh Massingberd, a former editor of the obituaries page of the *Daily Telegraph*, recalled the unwieldy challenges posed by a refusal to capitulate to the seductions of the posthumous parallax. "One day, an injunction arrived from on high that we were to make a point of including the cause of death," he reminisced in the *Spectator* last year. "As it happened, a candidate for the morgue of the morrow, a priapic jazzer, had handed in his dinner pail after a penile implant had unfortunately exploded. We duly complied with the editorial diktat."

So popular are the *Daily Telegraph*'s obituaries that in 1995 the paper began publishing obituary anthologies, and many have been bestsellers.

AT TOO MANY American newspapers, writing obituaries is considered a second-class calling, the pasture where reporters whose legs have given out are sent to graze before being consigned to even more distant pastures. As it happened, the journalists who attended the conference — from the *Denver Post*, the *Arizona Republic*, the *Cleveland Plain Dealer*, the *Atlanta Journal-Constitution*, the *Point Reyes (California) Light*, and the *Valencia County (New Mexico) News Bulletin* — were all natural storytellers who, for various reasons, had volunteered for the obits desk. (The nonjournalists included a married couple who worked for competing Dallas funeral homes, along with several serious amateurs who, à la Gilbert, devote major chunks of their lives to scrutinizing the obits.) With the exception of a presentation by Michael Putzel, a former journalist who is the vice president of Web operations for the National Obituary Archive, a service that provides what amounts to an Everyperson's cyber obits database (the dearly departed rendered accessible, in perpetuity, for $29.95), the conference business sessions didn't dwell upon the technical aspects of respectfully memorializing the dead. The main attraction, it seemed, was camaraderie — a chance to swap war stories with other scribblers who have confronted the challenge of summoning the mots justes to convey that the deceased was a megalomaniac or a colorful deadbeat or an unindicted felon.

After the opening session (an effusive, gesticulating performance by Nigel Starck), as the crowd headed toward the bar, I intercepted Susan Little, a college administrator and obituary collector from Georgia, who had brought along a scrapbook filled with some of her favorites. Little traced her fascination with obituaries to having grown up next to a cemetery in Atlanta. Opening the scrapbook, she said, "I've always been very comfortable around death issues. I've taken courses on death, grief, and dying. I started collecting these stories about seven years ago, and this was the first one I saved: William M. Yancy. He was a founding member of Justice for Janitors. It says here, 'He was a pioneer in the recycling business and very enterprising, even before it became fashionable or politically correct. He could not stay still.' There's a novel in there. It's a life that had meaning. And look at this. John Scandalakis. He joined the Greek Resistance during the Second World War, at the age of seventeen. He fought against both the Nazis and the Greek Communists. He was captured by Communists and witnessed the beheading of his father. He was going to be executed the next morning, but he escaped and joined the Resistance movement. I've never had a bad day compared to this man's life. Notice that it says he was surrounded by his family at the time of his death. What a wonderful full circle to have come."

The headline above an obit of an Atlanta numbers racketeer identified him as "WESLEY MERRITT, JR., 69, BUSINESSMAN," and a headline on an adjacent page in the scrapbook said, "HARRY WATTS, 76, RECEIVED HIS WISH TO DIE WHILE IN CHURCH." Several of Little's keepsakes had been written by Kay Powell, the obituary editor of the *Journal-Constitution*, who was attending the conference for the second consecutive year. Powell's May 2000 obituary of David Robeson Morgan, Little said, was "the one I've given to more people around the country than any other." It read:

> David Robeson Morgan was a brilliant man whose future looked good, until he had a frontal lobotomy in 1947. . . . "He was such a delightful person. He was bright and articulate. He had a nimble mind both for his age and lobotomy. He was forever inquisitive." . . . His life was spent, his sister said, "struggling with his curtailed brain." . . . One constant in his life was his joy in singing, and he sang tenor in the choirs at the First Baptist churches in Hogansville and in Stockbridge. . . .

He also returned to writing. On his word processor, he produced a thirty-thousand-word manuscript on the philosophy
of religion.

Stored in Little's computer are obituaries that she's prepared
for all her family members — husband, children, parents, siblings.
"I've got these things ready," she said, "because when someone
dies at two o'clock in the morning and the funeral home's calling
to say that the newspaper has to have the obituary, you can't necessarily think coherently. And, yes, I have written my own obit. I
left plans with our minister for my memorial service. Willie Nelson will be singing 'Precious Memories,' though probably not in
person, because he's about to keel over."

STEVE MILLER, the editor and publisher (indeed, the entire staff)
of *Goodbye! The Journal of Contemporary Obituaries*, also grew up
next to a "particularly nice" cemetery in Montclair, New Jersey,
and often hung out there as a teenager. But his interest in the literary aesthetics of the dead probably originates in an obit routine at
the *Paterson News*, one of several uninspiring newspaper jobs he
held in his twenties (he's now forty). "The *Paterson News* had a
form we filled out for obituaries," he told me. "And on slow news
nights I'd occasionally put fake obituaries in the paper. I followed
the form exactly, made them seem innocuous. But I was putting
my friends' names on them and giving them unlikely hobbies —
like making them Scoutmasters."

A few years later, after a couple more career missteps, Miller
wound up on Wall Street (specifically, in the World Trade Center), working for a Japanese bank, and once he reestablished fiscal
solvency he realized that he missed "a creative outlet." He was a
regular reader of biographies and, he knew, a skillful writer. The
result was *Goodbye!*, an eight- to sixteen-page all-obituaries illustrated newsletter. "What I've done from the start is cull the best
dead people I could find," he said. "Then I do my own research

and make the obits more interesting than the standard fare. My ideal obit is somebody you've barely heard of. In the last issue, I did Grover Krantz, the authority on Bigfoot. Everybody knows about Bigfoot, but how many people know about Grover Krantz? So I read his books, researched his career, and developed a point of view about his life that doesn't necessarily adhere to the traditional life trajectory." The result is a droll essay about an obsessed anthropologist laboring at the margins of respectability. "Krantz had a paranoid streak," Miller writes, and "was convinced that many of the giant footprints he documented were faked by people whose motivations he could never understand." Every failure was blamed on the careerism and timidity of his colleagues — "the closed-minded bastards want to run me out of the profession." And the essay ends with an allusion to Krantz's final, crushing rejection: "A physically imposing specimen himself, Krantz nevertheless failed in his last wish to have his body accepted for display at the Smithsonian Museum."

When Miller spoke at the Third Great Obituary Writers' Conference, his theme was the philosophy of the obituary. This year, he talked about September 11, and how his view of writing obituaries was altered by having been in his office on the eightieth floor of the World Trade Center's south tower, when the attacks began. Miller was halfway down the fire escape when the second plane hit.

"I've told the story of my escape so many times, in so much depth, it's made me reflect about storytelling and what you can know and what kinds of effects you can try for," he said. "It's fascinating to me how our stories are shaped by our lack of knowledge." Miller's own story of escaping with his life was fashioned in his unawareness that his life was in danger. "Not knowing that it was a major attack, and that hundreds of people were already dead, gave us a confidence and a sense of purpose, sort of like a willful agnosticism.

"Someone told me that the first couple of issues after the attack

weren't as humorous as the ones before. I don't know that I'm
conscious of that." Actually, the most recent issue is humorous,
but its humor is of a very dark kind. And it's also unusually frag-
mentary. "It's just one anecdote after another, where I'm not even
trying to create a narrative." The anecdotes are organized themat-
ically. There are deaths associated with animals ("Newark, NJ —
A man who collected monitor lizards, as well as a menagerie of
other exotic animals, was discovered half-eaten by the monitor
lizards. . . . Spared in the carnage were a bunch of two-inch-long
Madagascar hissing cockroaches, meant to be the monitor lizards'
food"). There are deaths by mayhem ("A man who sawed down a
tree in his garden accidentally killed his wife when the tree fell on
her. The woman was standing in the street to warn passing cars
when the tree crushed her" — the headline is "TIMBER!"). And
there are deaths by "Darwinian Events," including this account,
published under the title "What a Knockout," of a young girl's
death: "A car knocked down and killed a teenage girl while the
driver was distracted by a billboard advertising women's lingerie.
The man's car careened onto the pavement when he took his eyes
off the road to stare at a giant poster of a woman clad in a revealing bra and panties." Miller is also intrigued by people who live to
be more than 110 years old. "I found out that not much is known
about them," he said. "What's most typical is that most of them
didn't party and they never went far from home. Clearly, the best
way to grow old is never to leave your house."

TWO DAYS before the conference, the *Dallas Morning News* had
run two different paid obituaries of the same person, along with
two different photographs and the announcement of two different funerals. During a morning session on the final day, Carolyn
Gilbert deconstructed the two obituaries. The deceased was
Melodi Dawn Knapp, a twenty-seven-year-old emergency room
nurse. Each obit had a different list of survivors, and the two funerals were planned, on consecutive days, at different churches —

one at a Baptist church, the other at a predominantly gay nondenominational church. An exegesis of the text revealed a lot of piquant information: Knapp's parents were divorced; both had remarried; her father, who evidently had difficulty accepting that his daughter was a lesbian, was affiliated with the Baptist church; her partner was a woman named Tina Merritt. It wasn't clear which funeral would feature an empty casket.

Careful readers had some familiarity with Knapp from a news story in the *Star-Telegram*, which identified her as the driver of a car that on a Saturday night had been traveling the wrong way on a Dallas freeway before hitting five other vehicles and killing three other people, including a seven-year-old boy. What neither obit mentioned, of course — and technically couldn't have, because a toxicology report wasn't yet available — was that Knapp had a blood alcohol reading four times as high as the legal limit.

In light of these complicated facts, it's hard to say where in the Melodi Dawn Knapp story one would situate what Carolyn Gilbert calls the "defining line, an insight into the heart and soul of the life." When the defining line is missing — this is a common pitfall, she says, of paid obituaries — the result is mediocrity, a long list of survivors but not much in the way of color. She addressed this topic during the conference's concluding session, which was held in a classroom on the campus of United World College, a ten-minute drive from Las Vegas, in the town of Montezuma. (One of the school's main benefactors was Armand Hammer, the former chairman of Occidental Petroleum, whose 1990 obituary in the *Times* avoided the posthumous parallax by noting an improper payment to a Soviet Minister of Culture and the suit brought by his own wife after he managed to abscond with part of her art collection.)

By chance, I had with me in the pouch of my laptop computer case a laminated copy of my father's obituary, with the Twenty-third Psalm printed on the other side, a bit of lagniappe from the funeral home in Tulsa. I pulled it out to see whether my brother

George, who had written it, had met Gilbert's standard. This was the first time I had focused properly on the obituary — I hadn't adjusted to the thought of Alex Singer's well-lived life being reduced to eleven column inches and encased in plastic — but now I saw that George had captured our father well. There were two defining lines: "His numerous friends knew him best for his great generosity and his terrific sense of humor," and "His nearly 60-year marriage to Marjorie was the center of his life." In what might have been an oversight, or perhaps a well-intentioned fastidiousness, my brother had omitted the untidy cause of death, emphysema. (Nor was there any reference to our father's having been a cigarette smoker for more than forty years.) The nicest touch, probably, was the photograph — Dad had a particular talent for smiling when photographed — though I regretted slightly, along with one or two other regrets, that he didn't happen to be wearing a Jim's Truck Stop cap.

DAY STRIPPERS

Wilmington, Vermont
OCTOBER 2002

I<small>T's NOT</small> Phil Markham's or Joanne Ruppel's fault, nor is it mine, that I've never seen them naked. On a global scale, I'm still in the majority, but a *lot* of people out there have been present on occasions when Phil and Joanne weren't wearing clothes. (Most of these people, not by chance, were themselves naked.) Phil and Joanne live in Albany, New York, and they spend a good part of each summer in southern Vermont, a latitude where the opportunities to lounge around comfortably outdoors in the nude are delimited by the air temperature and the biting insect population. During the eight years that they've been a couple — they met in bundled-up circumstances, while skiing, also in Vermont — they've managed to make the most of those opportunities (especially Phil).

In 1980, Phil Markham began making regular pilgrimages to the Ledges, a scenic and popular destination for clothing-optional recreational swimming — what used to be known, in the pre-postmodern era, as skinny-dipping — in the town of Wilmington. He'd been skinny-dipping in western Massachusetts when he first heard about the Ledges, which was by then a not very well-kept Vermont secret. To get to the Ledges from the center of Wilmington, you drive a mile and a quarter east of town on a paved, numbered highway, then head south for a mile or so on a dirt road that terminates in a parking lot next to a sinuous eight-mile-long lake called Harriman Reservoir. From there, it's a hike of several minutes along a root-veined forest trail that leads to a small sandy beach and a quarter-mile stretch of easy-to-negotiate granite shelves, some of them excellent diving platforms, which give the Ledges its name. The view is a 180-degree panorama of lake, sky, unspoiled shoreline, and timbered mountains.

On a midweek morning in May or September, when the place is barely occupied, or on a crowded midsummer Sunday, when the panorama would typically include two or three hundred naked bodies — male and female (usually more of the former), in various states of fitness and decrepitude — it's a genuinely idyllic spot with a remarkable capacity for evoking proprietary feelings. Markham wouldn't be so bold as to suggest that he owns the Ledges, but he clearly thinks of himself as the site's protector and caretaker. Which is why he was deeply disappointed late last spring when the Wilmington governing council, the Selectboard, passed the Wilmington Public Indecency Ordinance by a 4–1 vote. In explicit language, it stated that what Markham and other well-behaved but naked visitors to the Ledges were engaged in was unlawful. Anyone who knew Markham — and regulars at the Ledges already knew him well — understood that this was not the sort of reproach he would be likely to take, literally or figuratively, lying down.

According to Markham, removing one's clothing in public on a regular basis, even in a secluded spot, does not make a person a nudist. "I don't call myself a nudist, and most people who participate in nude recreation don't call themselves nudists," he said recently. "Although one in four Americans, based on a Roper poll, go skinny-dipping, it's something people like to keep private about themselves. A 'nudist,' by way of Webster's, belongs to a cult. And I'd hardly call one in four Americans doing something cult behavior. The proper term is 'naturist,' which I don't mind, but, basically, I despise labeling of any type. I'm simply not clothing-obsessed."

This nomenclature distinction matters to Markham because he feels that misinformation has been at the heart of the battle over the Ledges. Ostensibly to remedy that problem, during the summer of 2001, in his capacity as a regional representative of the Naturist Action Committee — an offshoot of the Naturist Society, an organization whose membership consists of individuals whom clothing-obsessed types have a careless tendency to refer to as nudists — he founded the Friends of the Ledges. Markham, who has defined the FOTL's mission as "solving problems," "communication," and "facilitation," is now in his late forties. Lean, with graying hair, an angular face, and skin that tans easily and deeply, he has a habit of chain-smoking when he contemplates what he regards as the unscrupulous schemes of his adversaries, the proponents of the indecency ordinance. In the past, Markham has had careers in real estate, home remodeling, landscaping, and Christmas tree farming, but for the last several months he has devoted his energies full-time to Ledges-related activism, which he's able to do because his partner, Joanne Ruppel, a trim, healthy-looking dark-haired woman in her early forties, is employed full-time as a government research analyst.

Markham strives for a please-we're-here-to-help-you demeanor, a tone that might persuade the citizens of Wilmington to rededicate themselves to the classic Vermont live-and-let-live spirit, the ethos that for decades tolerated the social rituals of the Ledges. But more and more frequently — especially when Markham dwells on his opponents' determination to interfere with his pursuit of happiness — he has had difficulty containing himself. The fundamental fact that often seems to elude Markham and many of his fellow Friends of the Ledges (for the most part, summer visitors who legally reside in other states) is that Wilmington is no different from any other Vermont community. And if there's one Vermont creed that trumps live-and-let-live it's the belief that the locals can get along just fine without flatlanders from Albany or Boston or New York City, naked or not, offering them unsolicited advice on how to manage their affairs.

MARGARET FROST, the person most clearly responsible for the passage of the Public Indecency Ordinance, no longer speaks to reporters, so it's hard to say precisely what goaded her into action. For more than forty years, the Frost family has owned a small summer cottage on Harriman Reservoir, a rustic abode with an outdoor privy. The cottage sits on less than a quarter acre, in a cluster of similarly modest dwellings, set back a few hundred feet from the water's edge. The Frosts don't have title to actual lakefront property, because the reservoir and its perimeter belong to USGen New England, a utility company, which uses it to generate hydroelectric power. Nevertheless, Frost, not unlike Markham, came to think of the sliver of shoreline down the path from her cottage as "her" beach, and she was routinely offended by the scenery about two hundred yards away. What she could see — although, without binoculars, discerning much of anything must have been a challenge — was the result of an informal Balkanization, whereby Ledges users had sorted themselves into peacefully coexisting populations. Heterosexual males and females dominated the section nearest the parking lot trailhead and gay men gravitated farther along the trail to a shoreline area that happened to be within view of the Frost family. Some of the gay men were also retreating into the woods for purposes other than mushroom hunting. Evidently, the presence of naked men so close to her property disturbed Margaret Frost. Or was it the particular fact that these naked men slept with other men?

Frost's family had for years lodged complaints with the police department, but Margaret took their concerns public in the summer of 2001, when she began dispatching letters to the editor, making calls to public officials, and distributing shrill handbills. "We own a cabin just north of the infamous Ledges at Harriman Reservoir," one of her broadsides began.

> What we see every time we go down to the shore is disgusting, embarrassing and very upsetting. . . . In the cove in front of our cabin there is a large group comprised only of males. . . . We also see nude water skiers, boaters, wind surfers, jet skiers, and shoreline hikers. If you use the lake you can't help but see it. There is no escaping it. There is NO LAW AGAINST NUDITY ANYPLACE in Vermont, EXCEPT RUTLAND. . . . ANYONE can walk down the Main Street in YOUR town STARK NAKED. Unless they touch themselves in an inappropriate manner (who is to say what that might be?) it is perfectly legal. They can stand outside your schools, undress on the sidewalk in front of you (just as males undress in front of us in our cove) and there is NOTHING anyone can do. If you do not believe me, call your local police department and ask them. You and I have as much right to use the Ledges WITHOUT EMBARRASSMENT AS THE NUDIST. We must not allow these people to jam nudity down our throats. I for one am choking on it!!!

It was Frost's campaign that galvanized Markham to create the Friends of the Ledges, which in the beginning was mainly a self-policing effort to keep her quiet. Signs were posted along the trails and the shoreline to discourage encroachments on the Frosts or other property owners. "Naturism isn't about sex at all," Markham likes to say. ("Nude is not lewd" is another naturist bromide.) Of course, Margaret Frost believed otherwise, and she began conducting occasional patrols, turning up used condoms and condom wrappers, she said, along paths that branched into the woods from the main trail. When the *Deerfield Valley News,* a weekly paper in Wilmington, reported on the controversy, it noted that the Ledges, in addition to being listed in several reference guides to nude beaches, was included on a gay Web site called www.cruisingforsex.com. These and similar awkward facts and allegations were on the table when the Selectboard allowed Frost to have her say. The board members didn't challenge her claims, but they obviously didn't relish the prospect of instituting, much less enforcing, an indecency ordinance, which the chair of the Selectboard, Fred Skwirut, described as a "last resort." And, presumably, they were relieved when the summer wound down and the notion of an indecency ordinance got dwarfed by September 11, which meant that for the time being they didn't have to think about who was or wasn't doing what in the woods.

ON LABOR DAY WEEKEND, I saw the Ledges for the first time. Phil Markham and Joanne Ruppel and I had agreed to meet at one o'clock on Saturday afternoon, a day that proved to be less than ideal for swimming (overcast, sixty degrees, intermittent mist). I parked in an uncrowded cul-de-sac at the trailhead and followed the trail until I came to a sandy shoreline area that fit a description Markham had given me over the phone. At first, I wasn't sure — the place was deserted — but then I spied several man-made rock structures (benches, walls, cairns) that he'd mentioned. I'd brought along an inflatable camping mattress and was making myself comfortable on a granite chaise longue that I would be happy to have in my living room, in an area that I'd gathered was the Temple of Friendship, when two other visitors, fellow middle-aged guys, arrived singly and found spots on the uppermost ledge. I didn't know that Markham's departure from Albany had been delayed because he was busy at his computer, dousing fires on a Ledges Web bulletin board, and I kept expecting him and Ruppel to show up at any minute.

At around two o'clock, a couple who looked to be in their late fifties appeared, carrying aluminum folding chairs. The man had a mustache and glasses and an ample belly. The woman was solidly built, with colossal breasts. Both wore slouch hats, loose-fitting shorts and tops, leather sneakers, and tube socks. No, they weren't Phil Markham and Joanne Ruppel; they were — this became apparent when the man got busy with a camera, taking shots of the rocks and the woods — tourists. After a few minutes, the man approached me with a slightly puzzled look, introduced himself (Tom Cooper, Elmendorf, Texas), and asked a question I'd anticipated: Where were the naked people?

The Ledges, as of three days earlier, was no longer a nude beach, I explained. Then I filled him in on the recent historical developments: between the fall of 2001 and the summer of 2002, Margaret Frost and others managed to revive the debate. In early June, Frost again appeared before the Wilmington Selectboard — this time offering to share incriminating video evidence of nudists invading her space — which had agreed to reexamine the issue. The topic of discussion was whether the self-policing effort had been effective. Frost obviously thought not, and her position was, paradoxically, strengthened by the unwillingness of USGen New England, which was wary of a discrimination lawsuit from naturists, to establish no-trespass boundaries. Another factor in Frost's favor was that, over the winter, there had been murmurings that someone wanted to open a topless bar in Wilmington. Never mind that this was an extremely dubious business proposition in a town with a population of 2,000, too small even to entice a McDonald's; alarmists with hyperactive imaginations suddenly envisioned Wilmington teeming year-round with non-clothing-obsessed strangers. And the result? On June 12, the Selectboard passed a law prohibiting public indecency (sexual intercourse, fondling genitals, etc.) and its no less evil twin, public nudity, which it defined as "the showing of the human male or female genitals, pubic area or buttocks with less than a full opaque covering, or the showing of the female breast with less than a fully opaque covering of any portion of the nipple, or the depiction of covered male genitals in a discernibly turgid state." According to Vermont law, the ordinance could be challenged by a popular vote, provided the requisite signatures were secured within a statutory waiting period, and, on the Tuesday before Labor Day, the vote duly took place. The ordinance was upheld by a narrow margin (289–282), and the new law immediately became enforceable. This meant that, at the Ledges, Labor Day weekend — the unofficial end of summer — would possess, even more than usual, a valedictory, melancholy air. Though I welcomed the prospect of hanging out at a suddenly erstwhile nude beach and gawking at the novelty of the situation, Tom Cooper was dismayed.

He shook his head with a what's-the-world-coming-to weariness. Tom and his wife, Pat, were active, peripatetic members of the Naturist Society, the American Association for Nude Recreation, and an organization of not necessarily nudist recreational-vehicle owners called the Escapees RV Club. They'd been nudists for eight years and full-time RVers for two years, ever since they sold their home in New Jersey, bought a thirty-eight-foot diesel pusher, and established residency at a nudist RV park near San Antonio.

I asked Tom whether they were in the mood for some civil disobedience. "Am I prepared to flout the law?" he said, then arched his eyebrows. "Maybe if it were warmer."

"It is a little cold today," Pat said.

"We're nudists, we're not stupid," Tom said.

"But this is a nice place to come even if you're not nude," Pat added.

Tom paused, plainly still troubled by my account of the new ordinance, then said, "Part of me says, 'If this is a local issue, who am I to come in here and stir up everything?' We're not traveling activists. But I'll tell you, we're seeing this same thing take place all over the country — down in New Jersey, for instance, at Higbee Beach. When they shut down Higbee, they said it was because they wanted to make it more of a 'family place.' A family place? The American Association for Nude Recreation is all about family — family unity, family nudity. That's our motto!"

We walked back to the parking lot, where we discovered that Phil Markham and Joanne Ruppel had arrived and, along with a small contingent of Friends of the Ledges, were preparing a cookout, a preliminary to a traditional end-of-summer gathering that was scheduled for the following afternoon. I introduced myself to Markham, and then introduced the Coopers. Markham, who seemed to be in something of a state, wasted no time before volunteering details of his recent tactical maneuvers, and segued into a dissection of the opposition's dirty tricks: "They took photographs of these condoms in the woods. But you could tell they hadn't been used, they'd been planted there, because they weren't weathered." He was also suspicious of the topless bar threat, which smelled like a red herring: "I could only allege that somebody paid somebody off to put that on the table." Despite Markham's insistence that he was eager to arrive at a "win-win" solution with the town, he had recently sued Wilmington and had posted on the Ledges Web site ad hominem criticisms ("stupid," "official bias and hatred") of Selectboard members. He mentioned the lawsuit to Cooper, who nodded and said, "We're losing beaches all over the world, so — whatever it takes. Losing beaches is killing us. We lost Higbee, and now this one. This kills me."

"This one isn't over yet," Markham said.

THE END-OF-SUMMER potluck picnic the next day was a six-hour affair, and as the sun (behind the clouds) was setting on it Joanne Ruppel asked me, "Have you ever been to a more depressing party?" In fact, I'd had a fine time. About forty people showed up and made themselves comfortable on folding chairs or on the re-arranged glacial rubble that is the permanent furniture of the Temple of Friendship. There was plenty to eat (grilled steaks, roasted corn, appetizers galore) and plenty to drink, and everyone seemed animated and friendly, if not exactly exuberant. The autumnal weather discouraged swimming, but one brave woman did skinny-dip — Ellen, from Massachusetts, who had come with her husband for an anniversary ritual. (They met at the Ledges during Labor Day weekend in 1990 — refuting one of Markham's pet theories, that the Ledges is "the worst place in the world to pick up chicks.")

Not counting the young father with a toddler and a five-year-old or the preadolescent grandchildren of one couple from Rochester, the median age of the crowd was mid-forties to early fifties. Most were summer renters or second home owners, and probably no more than a half dozen were registered to vote in Wilmington. The scuttlebutt at the Ledges that afternoon was that the ordinance was actually "about real estate and homophobia" — the real estate in question being a 122-acre residential subdivision adjacent to the Ledges (and the Frost property). The developer, a local broker and builder named Brian Palmiter, had been selling lots ranging from ten to twenty acres at an average price of $250,000. When I met with Palmiter later in the week, I couldn't make up my mind about him, mainly because he presented two versions of himself. On the one hand, he pointed out that he'd already sold eight of ten parcels, the implication being that he wasn't terribly worried about his investment and didn't need to defend it. On the other hand, he had also paid for a cranky full-page ad in the *Deerfield Valley News*, which urged voters to combat "Flagrant Nudity! Lewd Behavior! Illegal Sexual Activities at the Ledges!" And he'd written letters to the editor, one of which concluded with a rant about the Ledges having become "a haven for largely out-of-state degenerates. . . . 'Stop the rape of the lake!'" (As it happened, Palmiter's customers were affluent out-of-staters who, though perhaps not certifiable degenerates, represented what other letter writers had in mind when they groused about real estate development causing the property around Harriman Reservoir to become "Connecticuttized and Yorkeretted.")

The homophobia factor was a tricky proposition for all parties. Even those who were aligned with Friends of the Ledges didn't have a consistent position. After accusing the ordinance proponents of homophobia, straight Ledges users might, two sentences later, complain that the reckless behavior of promiscuous gays had spoiled the fun for everyone. During the picnic, I heard someone describe having once witnessed "heavy cocksucking" at the far end of the Ledges. (On my first walk to the Ledges, I saw, posted on several trees, flyers encouraging "like-minded guys" to gather in the "cruisy woods" near the Frost cottage. Within a couple of hours, the flyers had been removed.) The issue clearly troubled the Wilmington Selectboard, given that the interlopers who typically strayed closest to the Frost property and to Palmiter's development were gay. "Homosexual trysting" was the delicate term used during Selectboard proceedings to characterize whatever took place along the side trails that disappeared into the birches and maples.

FOR THE PEOPLE of Wilmington, the Ledges controversy has represented a distracting, unwelcome issue that they've felt compelled to take seriously. The exercise of democracy in Wilmington, as in most Vermont towns, is an earnest pursuit. The most recent annual town meeting — a hallowed institution, still worthy of Norman Rockwell — lasted eleven and a half hours. The focus of the discussion was how to cope with a state funding formula for schools, which has made property taxes a frightening burden for many residents. Beneath Wilmington's postcard charms — when you take away the "country lodging" and "fine dining" and the boutiques selling scented candles, homemade fudge, and calico-lined baskets — it's a place where many people work at two jobs because that's what it takes to hold on to their homes. In such an atmosphere, a certain quotient of free-floating nativist backlash should come as no surprise.

The backlash has now been in progress for some time, dating to 2000, after the passage of Vermont's civil union law, which generated a steady influx of gay pilgrims coming to get hitched. The reactionary response was a movement called Take Back Vermont.

Around Wilmington, the person most closely identified with Take Back Vermont was perhaps Donald Towne, an archconservative moral crusader. Predictably, Towne seized on the Ledges dispute as an opportunity to launch a fresh volley of letters to the editor. (His pièce de résistance managed to connect nudity at the Ledges to child kidnappings and to Palestinians dancing in the streets after the September 11 attacks.)

In November, Wilmington's voters will get yet another chance to rethink the ordinance. (The law allows for a new petition campaign and a new vote. Lucky Wilmington!) The prevailing wisdom is that Markham has overplayed his hand, and, unless the right wing blunders by making excessive preelection noise, it seems the vote may not be quite as close this time around. Fred Skwirut, the chair of the Selectboard, summed up the anticarpetbagger sentiment when he said, "We don't need to be told that Vermonters love their freedom." Even Joanne Ruppel, Markham's breadwinning mate, has — rather nakedly — posted musings on the Web bulletin board, which alternate between defensiveness and contrition. "Many, many, many times we have discussed just dropping this whole issue," she wrote recently. "At this point, I wish we had never gotten involved."

Perhaps anticipating another defeat, Markham seems to be gazing toward a more distant horizon. During a phone conversation the other day, he told me, "I've been doing some Web research on the phrase 'turgid state' — you know, that language from the ordinance. You just type in that key phrase and see what happens. All sorts of Web sites come up. You can see how this thing has spread across the country, and the problems it's caused in other towns. There's an outfit called the American Family Association behind a lot of it. And I'm really shocked that such a right-wing thing has made its way to Vermont. People think this indecency ordinance thing started here, but it's going on in Mississippi, Tennessee, all over the place. You should try it yourself. Go ahead: 'turgid state.'"

Meanwhile, there's a new bumper sticker visible on the roads in the land of live-and-let-live. It says, "Take Back Vermont. Again."

★

My prognosis for the outcome of the revote in Wilmington proved inaccurate. Less than three months after the antinudity ordinance went into effect, it again appeared on the ballot, and this time a majority concluded that skinny-dipping was tolerable after all. (The tally was 495–478 — roughly the same margin, percentage-wise, as when the vote had initially gone the other way.) The following summer, Phil Markham and his fellow naturists returned to Harriman Reservoir and were more or less ignored by Wilmington's residents, who had moved on to other public policy preoccupations — chief among them escalating property taxes, a less felicitous way to lose one's shirt.

A YEAR OF TROUBLE

Cincinnati, Ohio
MAY 2002

Late on the night of Friday, April 6, 2001, so late it was already well into Saturday morning, a young man named Timothy Thomas went out for a pack of cigarettes in a near-downtown Cincinnati neighborhood known as Over-the-Rhine. Thomas lived a few miles away, with his mother, stepfather, younger sister, and other members of their extended family, but he spent weekends in Over-the-Rhine because his girlfriend, Monique Wilcox, and their three-month-old son, Tywon, shared a two-bedroom apartment with her mother and her sister on Republic Street, a characteristically dismal-looking block in a once gloriously vibrant part of town. Heading back from the convenience store, Thomas passed a nightclub. One of the club's security guards, an off-duty police officer, recognized him; at the time, Thomas was the object of fourteen arrest warrants, twelve arising from relatively minor traffic offenses and the other two from obstruction of justice misdemeanors (specifically, running from the police). For reasons that remain open to conjecture, he started running again.

During the next few minutes, he covered a lot of ground. He ran east and then south, doubled back, sprinted through a parking lot, scaled two chain-link fences, one topped with barbed wire, and wound up in an L-shaped alley. Several policemen joined the pursuit, and one of them, Stephen Roach, jumped from his cruiser on Republic Street and entered the alley. Roach, who had been on the Cincinnati police force for almost four years, had his nine-millimeter Smith & Wesson drawn and his finger on the trigger. As Thomas turned the corner in the alley, Roach ordered, "Show me your hands!" Before Thomas had a chance to comply, Roach shot him in the chest. When three fellow officers arrived moments later, Roach's explanation for what had happened was "It just went off. It just went off." Under questioning that same day by homicide investigators, Roach offered a different rationale: Thomas had extended a clenched fist, he couldn't see what was in the fist, and he feared for his life. During an interrogation three days later, when confronted with a videotape recorded by another police unit at the scene — the tape revealed that Roach had fired his weapon three and a half seconds after entering the alley — he reverted to a narrative in which the shooting was accidental. The internal investigation report said that Thomas was wounded at 2:16 A.M. An ambulance delivered him to a hospital where, just after three A.M., he was pronounced dead.

Because Timothy Thomas perished in the manner he did — an unarmed African American, shot by a white police officer, the fifteenth black person killed by Cincinnati policemen during a six-year period in which no white suspects died — he has exerted a forceful and resonant influence over subsequent events in that city, something he hardly seemed destined to do while he was alive. Among certain groups of people in certain parts of town, he has been elevated to a celebrity status a few rungs shy of apotheosis. Throughout the metropolitan area, which has a population of almost two million, most people know his name. When his path crossed Officer Roach's, Thomas was a dyslexic nineteen-year-old with a high school general equivalency diploma, an off and on minimum-wage job as a laborer, and nothing in the way of more lucrative employment prospects. As a father, he was not exactly poised to shape for his infant son a future any brighter than his own. He was, in other words, a disheartening archetype — one among the millions of non–upwardly mobile young men whom we, as a nation, have shown far more readiness to arrest and lock up (or, insidiously, to ignore completely) than to welcome into the mainstream of American social and civic experience. In the year or so since he was killed, the citizens of Cincinnati have grappled painfully and earnestly, as well as clumsily and rancorously, with the import and consequences of Thomas's life and death.

The killing ignited protest rallies, civil disobedience, and three days of mayhem in Over-the-Rhine and other neighborhoods — what media reports in Cincinnati and beyond described as riots but what many black people, investing these events with the gravity of a cumulative historic struggle, insist on calling a rebellion or an uprising. The city called it a state of emergency and enforced an eight P.M. curfew. By the time order was restored, sixty-six people had been charged with felonies, eight hundred with misdemeanors. The damage, including police and medical costs, was estimated to be at least $14 million. One police officer was shot but not seriously wounded; remarkably, no one died. Compared with the death and devastation that have accompanied racial unrest in other American cities in recent years — say, the riots in Los Angeles in 1992 after the acquittal of the policemen accused in the Rodney King beating case, which left more than fifty people dead and material losses of a billion dollars — what occurred in Cincinnati might be considered small potatoes. Nevertheless, it made big headlines when it happened, and in a variety of ways the city has paid a steep price ever since. "We were in the wrong place at the wrong time," a member of the City Council told me recently, his point being that the Thomas killing and its aftermath generated unwarranted notoriety. According to this logic, it was

Cincinnati's bad luck to have uncorked a prime-time paroxysm of racial disharmony at a moment when, inconveniently, no other American city happened to be conspicuously doing the same.

WHAT, IF ANYTHING, ailed Cincinnati that set it apart? With hindsight, a lot of people in Cincinnati, black and white, maintain that what happened to Thomas was entirely predictable. Three weeks before he was shot, a civil rights lawsuit was filed in federal court against the city, alleging a pattern of "discrimination in policing": a predilection for treating black people differently from whites, not only by stopping and searching them in disproportionate numbers (racial profiling) but by subjecting them to gratuitously intimidating tactics (dogs, pointed guns, chemical sprays, abusive language). These violations were compounded, the lawsuit maintained, by more than thirty years of politically expedient — but unfulfilled — promises from city officials to reform police practices. The plaintiffs in the suit included the American Civil Liberties Union and an organization called the Cincinnati Black United Front. Appended to the complaint were sworn declarations from thirty individuals who described specific mistreatment at the hands of law enforcement personnel.

Five months before, an African American named Roger Owensby Jr. died in custody, while handcuffed, after being stopped for questioning in connection with a drug investigation. A coroner testified that Owensby had been asphyxiated, possibly by a choke hold, while several officers piled on top of him because, they said, he tried to flee. (Before attempting to handcuff him, they had sprayed a chemical irritant in his face.) In January 2001, two cops were indicted for their role in Owensby's death and removed from duty pending trial. Meanwhile, the City Council passed an ordinance requiring officers to file reports after every traffic stop, a tacit acknowledgment that racial profiling existed. This was the atmosphere in which the Thomas shooting took place.

When court records were scrutinized after Thomas's death, one hard-to-resist inference was that he was very familiar with racial profiling. To hear his mother, Angela Leisure, tell it, Thomas also had experiences that fit the definition of "discrimination in policing." A recent article in *CityBeat*, an alternative weekly, laid out the chronology of traffic offenses that led to the arrest warrants that led to the chase that terminated in the alley off Republic Street. During a sixty-six-day period in early 2000, the police stopped Thomas eleven times and wrote twenty-two citations, only one for a moving violation. Either Thomas was maddeningly obstinate or an unusually slow learner: eleven of the tickets were for driving without a license and six were for not wearing a seat belt. Once he was cited for playing music too loudly, another time for driving a car with illegally tinted windows. The law enforcement rationale for racial profiling of African-American motorists has been that such traffic stops often turn up evidence of criminal behavior — typically, illegal drugs or weapons. In Thomas's case, no such evidence materialized. Was he somehow baiting the cops? If so, it was a time-consuming diversion. He appeared in court nineteen times and spent sixteen days in jail. There is, of course, no way of knowing what Thomas was thinking when the fatal final chase got under way. In any event, if the police were so eager to apprehend him, the simplest approach would have been for a couple of officers to go to his mother's home and knock on the door. He wasn't hard to find.

Angela Leisure migrated to Cincinnati from Chicago in 1997 because she wanted a better life for herself and her children. In Chicago, she had been raising Timothy (her eldest child, born a month before she turned fifteen), a daughter nine years younger, and six other children not her own, in the Robert Taylor Homes, the infamous paragon of how not to design a public-housing project. During a visit to Cincinnati, she was impressed because "I saw children playing outside unattended," she said. "There were no drive-by shootings, no filth, no gang writings on the walls." Once she relocated, however, she discovered other perils. She described for me an episode a year or so before Timothy died. Along with a cousin and a couple of other young men, she said, he was standing one afternoon in front of the building where they lived, in a neighborhood called Evanston, when they were suddenly accosted by policemen. "The police came up and slammed them against the wall," she said. "Then they got them down on the ground. It wasn't like they said, 'Get on the ground' — they literally threw them on the ground. Put the knee in the back, pulled the arms back, put cuffs on them, and searched them. But no one was arrested." A similar encounter occurred a few months later, she said, when Timothy was walking to a corner grocery store and abruptly found himself nose to the pavement, along with five or six other young men. "The police in Evanston have a habit of where they drive up and just jump out. They have this cowboy mentality. But very seldom anybody went to jail."

Thomas would be alive today, presumably, if he hadn't run from the off-duty cop who recognized him. So why did he? "My son had a fear of police officers," Leisure told me. "We had conversations about that. His thing was 'Mom, if they could do this to me in broad daylight with everybody watching, what would they do in the dark?'" Whatever else went through Thomas's and Roach's minds as they faced off in the alley, neither was in the presence of someone he instinctively trusted. Then the only one of them holding a gun fired it.

ONCE THE RIOT or the rebellion or whatever it was subsided, some promising developments occurred. Two days after Thomas's funeral, the mayor, Charlie Luken, announced the formation of a task force on race relations called Cincinnati Community Action Now. He appointed three co-chairmen, among them the Reverend Damon Lynch III, a Baptist minister who was the head of the Black United Front, one of the lead plaintiffs in the lawsuit against the city. The mayor had also formally invited the Department of

Justice to investigate the police division, a politically astute move; better to extend a preemptive welcome to the federal government's lawyers than to have them unilaterally impose new procedures and policies. Over the course of several months, the lawsuit and the federal investigation coalesced into a single mediation process known as the Collaborative. The Collaborative's objective was to produce an agreement that would mandate specific reforms in police procedures and insure police accountability by establishing, for instance, a citizens' complaint-review panel with subpoena and investigative authority.

Notwithstanding the goodwill implicit in the Collaborative, there were ominous countercurrents. Street cops, it appeared, had begun a passive-aggressive job slowdown; arrest rates dropped by fifty percent even as serious-crime rates rose alarmingly in Over-the-Rhine and other predominantly black neighborhoods. In the three months after the Thomas killing, there were fifty-nine shooting incidents with seventy-seven victims, compared with nine shootings and eleven victims during the same period the previous year. All but one of the victims were black. The then head of the police union, Keith Fangman, told the *Times* that officers were "afraid to take enforcement action in black neighborhoods. . . . It's not a physical fear. They are simply hesitant for fear of being labeled a racist, especially if it's a white officer." In other interviews, Fangman emphasized the mitigating circumstances in the deaths of the thirteen black people other than Thomas and Owensby killed by the Cincinnati police. Almost all had been armed; one was an ax-wielding man who had just decapitated a teenager; one had robbed a bank and shot at a teller; another was a driver who dragged a police officer to his death. And, of the last fourteen Cincinnati police officers killed, twelve had been shot by black men. For the time being, however, the police were not winning the public relations battle. Obviously, black Cincinnatians wanted evenhanded law enforcement, not a dearth of law enforcement. Expressing a virtually unanimous sentiment, Fangman said, "The aftermath of the riots has actually been more harmful to the city than the riots themselves."

By midsummer, an alliance of African-American religious groups and activist organizations called for an economic boycott of Cincinnati, urging conventions, tourists, and popular entertainers to stay away. Without a scorecard, it was a challenge to keep straight the groups promoting the boycott. One was the Reverend Lynch's Black United Front and another was the Coalition for a Just Cincinnati, not to be confused with the Coalition of Concerned Citizens for Justice. The boycott advocates had long lists of demands. Their ostensible goals, however, often seemed secondary to the business of jockeying for power or legitimacy in a "community" where the most prevalent attitude toward the boycott has been ambivalence.

For several months, the boycott effort didn't seem to have much impact — September 11 pushed it into the background — but the momentum shifted after a succession of events last fall. First, Stephen Roach, who had been indicted by a Hamilton County grand jury on misdemeanor charges of negligent homicide and obstructing official business, was found not guilty after a nonjury trial. Then the officers indicted in connection with Owensby's death were acquitted of misdemeanor assault charges and a mistrial was declared in the only felony case, an involuntary manslaughter charge. Because the jury had been hung, ten to two, leaning toward acquittal, the county prosecutor announced that he wouldn't retry the case. The Black United Front's reaction was an open letter addressed to "Dear Friends of Justice." The letter reiterated the call for an economic boycott, on the ground that Cincinnati's blacks were "struggling through the highest state of apartheid." It continued, "Police are killing, raping, planting false evidence, and along with the prosecutor and courts are destroying the general sense of self-respect for black citizens." Shortly after the letter became public, Mayor Luken fired the Reverend Lynch from the co-chairmanship of the task force on race relations.

Earlier this year, the boycotters began registering tangible victories. Bill Cosby canceled two appearances at a downtown performing arts center, Whoopi Goldberg backed out of a lecture series, and Wynton Marsalis, Smokey Robinson, the Temptations, and the O'Jays decided not to honor concert dates. The Progressive National Baptist Convention elected to hold its annual 10,000-member gathering elsewhere, as did the Organization of Black Airline Pilots. The most telling measure of the boycott organizers' effectiveness occurred in February, when Mayor Luken referred to them as "economic terrorists."

Today, the widely shared perception is that the boycott isn't going to end any time soon because the realistic means to end it don't exist. The various groups who support the boycott don't have identical demands, and many demands are too broad or unwieldy to lend themselves to swift solutions by local government (improve access to health care for low-income people; create jobs targeted to populations with the highest levels of unemployment). There are, as well, several demands — remove the police chief, Thomas Streicher; grant amnesty to all people arrested and jailed for riot-related crimes — which the boycott leaders know that the city leadership won't agree to. Since the boycott began, opinions about its tactical wisdom have been sharply divided, not least among the black population. One casualty, for example, is this summer's edition of a three-day jazz festival that has been an annual event since 1962. In peak years, the festival attracted 35,000 ticket buyers per night to a stadium along the Ohio River and generated $27 million in revenues. The concertgoers have tended to be black, as have the employees and owners of many service and concession businesses that depend on the festival. When occupancy rates in downtown hotels plummet because convention traffic evaporates, or when restaurant volume declines because tourists stop coming, an inordinate percentage of the workers who lose income or jobs are black. When I mentioned to the Reverend Lynch the plight of an African-American business owner I'd heard about whose limousine company normally employed thirty drivers during the jazz festival, he said, "To miss singing and dancing for a larger cause, I think he would understand that."

THERE'S ALSO the view that a major psychological obstacle to ending the boycott is Cincinnati's odd penchant for self-subversion. (A slightly more generous interpretation might be that the city is afflicted with an urban variety of multiple personality disorder.) Construction has begun on a new museum devoted to the city's history as a nexus of the Underground Railroad, and no one will be surprised if, at some point, boycotters set up a picket line and carry signs referring to — this is one of their favorite rhetorical tropes — Cincinnati's designation as "the eighth most segregated city in America."

At other times, in other ways, conservative impulses have thwarted social and economic progress. For instance, in the early nineteenth century, Cincinnati was the nation's leading cultural and mercantile outpost beyond the Alleghenies; but by mid-century the city fathers, prosperous and satisfied stewards of an economy tied to steamboat transportation, resisted the imperative to adapt to a railroad-based system. (One consequence was that this hastened the meat-packing industry's shift from Cincinnati to Chicago.) More recently, that self-subverting conservatism has manifested itself as a cavalier disregard for the rights of individuals. Cincinnati is where the pornographer Larry Flynt was prevented from selling his magazine *Hustler* for more than twenty years. In 1990, the same bluenose lawman who had hounded Flynt invaded the Contemporary Arts Center, where an exhibition of Robert Mapplethorpe's photographs, including several homoerotic images, was on display, and arrested the museum director for pandering obscenity. In 1992, the city's leading gay rights organization, Stonewall Cincinnati, lobbied the city council to pass a human rights ordinance that included protection against discrimination on the basis of, among other factors, HIV status, sexual orientation, or "Appalachian regional origin." The follow-ing year, this progressive piece of legislation was obliterated when, by a two to one margin, voters approved a charter revision (Article 12) that specifically prohibited the city from enforcing the human rights ordinance on behalf of gays and bisexuals and for-bade the council to pass any future gay rights legislation.

Today, the collateral damage of Cincinnati's racial strife in-cludes, curiously, a deep schism within the gay community. Vet-erans of the fight against Article 12 recall that, though the organ-izers and financial backers of the charter revision were ultra-conservative whites, the campaign's most prominent public face was a black Baptist preacher named K. Z. Smith. The ingenious divide-and-conquer slogan of the Article 12 proponents was "Equal Rights, Not Special Rights," and one frequently aired tele-vision advertising spot featured the Reverend Smith's wife saying, "Some people say that homosexual behavior is the same as being black. Does anyone really believe that? This makes no sense to me. We need to stop this in Cincinnati. I'm voting 'Yes.'" Another unabashed supporter of Article 12 was the Reverend Lynch.

In the current situation, a bit of amnesia, it seems, has proved useful to Stonewall Cincinnati's board of directors, a new slate that was elected late last summer (to be precise, on the evening of September 11). This winter, the board issued a qualified endorse-ment of the boycott, accompanied by a rather tortured explana-tory statement. "Stonewall will stand in solidarity with all groups in search of economic and social justice," the statement said, "whatever the cost." One cost has been the philosophical and fiscal alienation of Stonewall's traditional core constituency, gay white men. Scott Knox, an attorney who served on the Stonewall board for six years and is active in a group called Citizens to Re-store Fairness, which is trying to reverse Article 12, told me, "There are a lot of well-intentioned people on Stonewall's board who have no sense of history. Their actions tell me that they don't have a good sense of what's politically savvy. We've been building bridges with the business community and politicians to try to get rid of Article 12. How can we accomplish that if the leading gay rights organization endorses a boycott that punishes the city and its businesses? The perfect boycott was the Montgomery bus boycott, where you were boycotting the company you wanted to change. The precipitating event here was the Timothy Thomas shooting. And the answer is to boycott hotels?"

THERE WAS a brief respite in mid-April, when, the Collaborative having produced a fourteen-page blueprint for police reforms, John Ashcroft went to Cincinnati for a ceremonial signing of a five-year agreement between the Department of Justice and the police department. "This is a truly historic day for all law enforcement in America," the attorney general proclaimed. "This agreement represents the best opportunity for the city of Cincinnati, its residents, and its police department to move forward." Also present for the occasion was the Reverend Lynch, who posed for photographers with Ashcroft and Mayor Luken and said, "The hard work has ended and the harder work begins." Though the Reverend Lynch refrained from making any reference to the boycott, his subsequent utterances made it clear that only a fraction of the demands had been satisfied.

One public figure in Cincinnati who has declined to express an opinion of the boycott is Angela Leisure. In the year since her son's death, Leisure has become lionized as a spokesperson for nonviolence. "My public role now is a peacemaker," she told me. "I walk around Over-the-Rhine and speak to people on the street. I'm constantly urging them to remain calm, be peaceful. I don't want another rebellion. There's a lot of angry people. I speak in churches, community centers, high schools, on the radio. I'm very adamant because I want to keep the peace here in Cincinnati, because we have to live together."

To anyone who expresses an interest, she's also eager, naturally, to gild the memory of her son. "Tim wasn't dislikable," she said.

"He had a magnetic personality. He was six-four, two hundred twenty pounds. You could see him in a crowd and, the way he carried himself, there was nothing intimidating about him. He could meet you and, an hour later, introduce you to someone else as his friend. Everybody he met was a friend."

Except, I thought, maybe not Officer Roach. But that wasn't really a fair example. After all, things happened awfully quickly that night in the alley. Officer Roach ran in, saw Thomas, and shot him, all in less than four seconds. They never did have a chance to get to know each other.

THE RADON CURE

Boulder, Montana
JULY 2001

For PATRICIA LEWIS's sake, and also for profes-
sional reasons, I wish I'd felt worse last month when I traveled to
Boulder, Montana, where I intended to spend a few days inhaling
radon gas in the company of people who believe that doing so
cures what ails you. During the winter, my right knee began act-
ing as if I'd overextended a ligament, and I also had some lower-
back pain, probably from slouching in my desk chair. By the time I
showed up in Boulder, an unprepossessing town with a population
of 2,000, in the west-central part of the state, midway between
Helena and Butte, these symptoms had inopportunely vanished.
In their absence, it would have been convenient if I'd brought
along a crippled dog — but, well, I hadn't. Nevertheless, I didn't
experience a diminished sense of purpose or a feeling of not fitting
in, mainly because Boulder, an old mining settlement, impressed
me as a place where hopefulness tends to prevail over careful planning or exactitude. Pat Lewis and her husband, Burdette Anderson, seemed a prime example. Seven years ago, they packed up
their lives in Seattle — at the time, she was doing office work for a

shipping company and he was repairing hydraulic pumps on heavy machinery — and moved to Boulder, even though, she told me, "we didn't have a clue what we were getting into." She said this during our first conversation in a tone that sounded both cheerful and mildly bewildered, as if, having somehow boarded the wrong train, she'd decided to ride it wherever it was heading.

What brought Lewis and Anderson to Montana was an erstwhile uranium mine on a gentle granite slope overlooking Boulder, which is situated in a typically Montana-sublime mile-high valley in the Elkhorn Mountains. In 1949, the mine produced its first commercial quantities of uranium ore from one of three claims staked by the Elkhorn Mining Company, whose president and principal owner was a geologist and mining engineer named Wade V. Lewis, Pat's grandfather. Two years later (and two years before she was born), he made an inadvertent and peculiar discovery. According to legend — a legend Wade himself promulgated in *Arthritis and Radioactivity*, a book that he published in 1955 — one day he was giving a tour of the mine to a woman from California who mentioned that she suffered from bursitis, and Wade "facetiously" replied that the radiation inside the mine might alleviate her symptoms. Sure enough, the very next day she was pain-free. Subsequently, another California woman with bursitis, an acquaintance of the first, came to the mine and she, too, got relief. "Thereafter," Lewis wrote, "the stampede started."

During the next few months, hundreds of people, most of them encumbered by arthritis or other rheumatological complaints, some in wheelchairs and some carried on litters, made the journey to what became known as the Free Enterprise Radon Health Mine. So, inevitably, did reporters. A photographer and a correspondent from *Life* came around in June 1952, and by then the Merry Widow mine, in the nearby town of Basin, had also begun welcoming the afflicted. The story in *Life* alerted potential customers as well as potential entrepreneurs, and eventually there were sixteen radon-therapy mines operating within a thirty-mile radius.

In a revised edition of *Arthritis and Radioactivity*, published nine years after the first, Lewis set forth his theory of radon's medicinal application. When inhaled for a prescribed amount of time in the sort of optimal conditions that just happened to exist at the Free Enterprise mine, radon — which is a byproduct of the decay of radium — stimulated the endocrine system to increase the body's natural secretions of hydrocortisone, and this reduced inflammation of the joints. Radon therapy, he maintained, also ameliorated sinusitis, asthma, and eczema. Lewis wasn't a medical doctor or a nuclear physicist, of course, nor did he have tangible medical evidence to corroborate his hypothesis. But he had lots of anecdotal evidence in the form of written testimonials from happy visitors who described how they'd given up their wheelchairs or canes or crutches or pain medications. Not everyone who came to the mine benefited, but the majority apparently did. Lewis couldn't prove that radon therapy worked. On the other hand, anyone who insisted that it didn't work was in the logically awkward position of trying to prove a negative.

Radon is ubiquitous in nature, constantly emanating from the earth's crust and filtering into the atmosphere. It has a half-life of not quite four days, and as it breaks down, or ionizes, it emits electrically charged alpha and beta particles and gamma rays. Epidemiological studies conducted on miners have shown a correlation between prolonged exposure to radon gas — specifically to the heavy alpha particles — and lung cancer. There's less than absolute scientific consensus about radon's effect on humans who don't spend their working lives underground. The majority viewpoint goes: if exposure to a lot of ionizing radiation from radon is bad for you, so too is exposure to a little. This school of thought has predominated since the mid-eighties, when the Environmental Protection Agency launched an aggressive and often hyperbolic public relations campaign to warn of the dangers of radon in the home. The public health consequences of the EPA's efforts across the years are debatable, but one clear economic consequence has been the creation of the estimated $100-million-a-year radon-abatement industry. These are the friendly contractors who charge homeowners disconcerting sums to ventilate their basements.

BECAUSE there's no countervailing economic incentive to promote the salutary effects of low-level ionizing radiation, there's no such thing as an organized pro-radon lobby. One natural constituency would be the owners of Montana's five remaining radon mines and their patrons — a declining population, it turns out. Pat Lewis had warned me that I would be visiting the Free Enterprise during a slow week, and, indeed, as I dropped in and out over a four-day period I encountered only eleven customers and two superannuated dogs. Then I made the rounds of the other mines — Merry Widow, Sunshine, Lone Tree, and Earth Angel — and discovered that, with the exception of the Merry Widow, where the amenities include a campground along the Boulder River, most weeks are slow weeks everywhere.

The unresolved mythology that surrounds radon — terribly bad for you? not really so bad? spooky but beneficial? — probably explains why the Montana state government has shown little inclination to regulate the radon mines or, for that matter, to promote them as a tourist attraction. There's considerable variation in radon levels from one mine to another. One chart I came across showed that the level at the Merry Widow was eighty-five percent higher than at the Free Enterprise and almost six hundred percent higher than at the Sunshine. Nevertheless, more than a decade ago the mine owners agreed to adhere to a standard that limits visitors to thirty-two hours of exposure during a calendar year. In practice, however, anyone who wanted to spend thirty-two hours a year in each of the mines could easily do so undetected. Whether it would make any difference, positive or negative, is another question.

Of all the testimonials that get recited inside radon mines, I'm partial to the canine variety. I heard my first iteration at the Free Enterprise courtesy of Patrick McGowan, a retired iron-worker who, unlike most radon seekers, lives in Boulder and spreads his annual thirty-two hours over several weeks. I met him as he emerged from a therapy session in what a former custodian of the mine — a cousin of Pat Lewis's whom she unaffectionately refers to only as "previous management" — had christened the "Ionization Inhalatorium." (Lewis just calls it the radon room.) This is a ground-level, ten-by-forty-foot space with wall-to-wall carpeting, wood paneling, easy chairs, footrests, a card table, shelves filled with old magazines and *Reader's Digest* condensed books and board games, and, most important, vents that deliver radon-saturated air from the mine. The economics of the Free Enterprise are sufficiently marginal that, in the off-season, Lewis asks patrons to take their treatments in the radon room, which obviates the need to burn electricity inside the mine — where, eighty-five feet down, accessible by elevator, there's a 400-foot-long drift furnished with more chairs, benches, tables, and bookcases.

McGowan had a medley of health problems — arthritic feet, emphysema, diabetes — and a faith in the general curative powers of radon. "I wasn't a true believer until I seen a gal that had one finger crooked as a snake," he said. "They'd all been crooked until she started going in the mine, and then there was one left that was all curled up. And she showed it to me and, just like that, it straightened out. That's what changed my mind." Before that, his imagination had been piqued by a Wade Lewis vintage story about a dog so hobbled with arthritis that it had to be coaxed into the mine backwards. "After three or four days or weeks or whatever," McGowan said, "that dog was running and chasing cats." He repeated this anecdote verbatim the next day when I joined him in the radon room, along with a married couple from Oregon. They were nearing the end of an eight-day sojourn and had brought along a geriatric Shih Tzu. "She's nineteen years old," the woman said. "She's got some sight in one eye and she's deaf. We only bring her in for an hour a day, but she seems to have perked up some. How? Well, she bounces around a little more, she acts younger. You'd never know she was nineteen by how she acts."

I collected more rejuvenated-pooch stories at the Merry Widow, Lone Tree, Earth Angel, and Sunshine mines — always the same basic theme, the only variation being that, instead of cats, the dogs would chase rabbits or chipmunks. The subtext of these testimonials was "Okay, maybe you think it's all in our heads, maybe you think it's all psychosomatic. But are you telling me that when a dog goes lame, comes to the mine, and then gets better, *that's* psychosomatic?"

Actually, I wasn't telling anybody anything; I was busy listening. Most radon mine devotees are pensioners, most are middle-middle-class, and a high percentage come from Canada, where the government has a far less alarmist view of radon. I overheard many conversations about arthritis case histories, cross-country meanderings in recreational vehicles, and memories of the mines themselves. A man at the Merry Widow, who was wearing an "Official Montana Bullshit Cap," rhetorically asked no one in particular, "If this is quackery, why do the same people keep showing up year after year?" And I thought, Because it might be cold and dank inside, but the atmosphere is remarkably convivial, especially if you enjoy canasta and cribbage.

One afternoon at the Merry Widow, I met Ola Veselovsky, a hairdresser in her early seventies, who had driven that day with her husband from their home in Alberta. She'd been coming to the mines for fourteen years and had tried them all. Unlike the Free Enterprise, the Merry Widow is a walk-in mine. And, unlike all the other mines, it has a natural spring and built-in basins where people soak their hands and feet or, if they don't mind forty-degree water, their entire bodies. Veselovsky told me that on her pilgrimages she collects water in gallon jugs and brings it home. Drinking a cup a day throughout the year, she believes, helps deter migraine headaches, and she bathes her eyes with a daily dose in an eyecup. As a child, she was myopic and wore glasses, and when her reading vision began to deteriorate in middle age she needed a prescription to correct for that as well. But since she began washing her eyes with Merry Widow radon water, she said, her vision had soared to twenty-twenty. Or perhaps there was an entirely different explanation. On a bookshelf inside the Merry Widow, along with back issues of *American Hunter*, *Arthritis Today*, *Golf Digest*, *National Geographic*, *Sunset*, and other magazines, I found a copy of *The Merry Widow Mine Cookbook*, a compilation of recipes, contributed by mine guests, for dishes of possibly profound therapeutic value: Porcupine Meatballs, Tuna Cheese Chowder, Hamburger Soup, Iowa Ham Balls, Honey Almond Pork Chops, Hutterite Borscht, Strawberry Pretzel Salad, Unnamed Salad.

THE MERRY WIDOW changed hands this spring, when the longtime owners sold it to Dwayne and Diana Knutzen, a young couple from Washington State. Dwayne, who used to own a garbage-hauling business, has stayed busy lately reading books and articles about radon, many of which Pat Lewis referred him to. In addition to monitoring the growing literature about low-level ionizing radiation, Lewis invites scientists to the Free Enterprise and occasionally travels to scientific conferences out of state. This fall, she's going to Europe to visit radon spas in Czechoslovakia and Germany. The added value of her expertise, she feels, justifies the price at the Free Enterprise — five dollars an hour, versus three dollars and change at the competition (except for the Earth Angel, where the owner, an eccentric octogenarian who calls himself Buffalo Bill, charges only a dollar per day). But there's a tendency among radon mine visitors, who are interested, above all, in a pain-free night's rest, not to want to know any more than they need to know. Lewis, meanwhile, looks at the numbers — last year, the Free Enterprise had taxable income of $11,000 — and wonders how much longer she can stay afloat.

My last day in Boulder, down in the mine at the Free Enterprise, I had a conversation with Art Berg, a retired electrical con-
tractor who had flown in from New York the previous day after
calling Lewis and telling her that he regarded the radon mine as
his "last hope" for relief from arthritis pain. A trim, talkative fellow in his mid-seventies, Berg wore blue slacks, a blue Hawaiian
shirt, and a blue cap from the golf course on Long Island, where,
when he feels up to it, he works as a ranger.

"When I took that trip on the plane yesterday, I thought I
was gonna die," he said. "But I can already feel the difference. I
thought I was gonna feel terrible because of the time zone change,
but I woke up at three in the morning and I could move around in
the bed. I figure it's worth a shot.

"I first heard about these radon mines from a friend. A friend of
his, a guy three years in a wheelchair, came here, nothing happened, and he went home and said what a lot of baloney it was.
Then, three weeks later, he gets out of bed and he can walk. He
walks into the kitchen and grabs his wife around the waist, and she
almost has a coronary because he hadn't been like that in years."

Back at ground level a half hour later, Berg sat outdoors in a
lawn chair and chatted with Lewis. He recalled how, months earlier, he'd checked out the Free Enterprise Web site.

"We're probably 1,389,676 out of eight million radon sites,"
she said. "Most of them about how bad radon is for you."

"Yeah, I read all the negatives," he said. "But, you know, water
can be bad for you, too, if you drink too much of it."

"That's right. You could drown in it."

He wandered off to the housekeeping trailer he'd rented for
the week, and Lewis remained seated, musing about her uncertain
future. "I'd like to ride this thing out to the end," she said. "Because my goal is to try to do everything I can to bring it back. The
science, if we can just turn the tide, with all the knowledge we've
got, and convince people that this is something worth trying as a
first step rather than as a last resort . . ."

"Then what?" I asked.

"I dunno." It was a sunny afternoon in the mid-seventies, a beautiful day to match the view. Five days earlier, it had snowed several inches, but, except for some traces on the Elkhorns across the valley, you'd never know it. "I guess if we decided to move back to Seattle I'd be able to find work there. We figure if we sell the land here — we've got thirty acres — that would pay off our credit card debt. Burdette and I have no heirs. Unless somebody needs a write-off really badly, I'm not gonna dump this on anyone. The problem is, even if you give it away it's a liability. After all, it's got radon."

JUST A LITTLE TOO SWEET

ONE THING that attracted Gary Williams to worm farming was the prospect of watching his investment literally grow — as opposed to the stock market, where, he'd discovered, money had a way of disappearing before you had a chance to get friendly with it. In the fall of 2000, Williams retired from Southwestern Bell, where he'd put in thirty-one years as a telephone technician. He was fifty-three years old and eager to maximize the hours he spent fishing on a lake not far from his home in Weleetka in eastern Oklahoma. Offered the choice of collecting his pension in a lump sum or a monthly payout, he opted for the former, immediately parked the money in mutual funds, and about eleven seconds later noticed that more than half of it had vaporized. Time for Plan B.

The notion of worm farming, or vermiculture, as a retirement occupation had first crossed his mind when a phone customer mentioned that he knew some people who'd been doing it at home and making decent money. Williams lived with his wife, Pam, in a house they'd built in the late seventies. It was made of sandstone that had been quarried nearby, and it sat on a forty-acre plot with a front pasture, where they'd grazed a small herd of Charolais cattle before deciding fifteen years ago that cows weren't worth the trouble. Across the road was a 200-foot cell phone tower, something most people would consider an eyesore but which the Williamses envied for the rental income it generated for the property owner. In the wake of his stock market losses, Williams needed a new revenue source, and he felt encouraged after speaking with a couple of worm growers who lived near Weleetka. Each had signed a contract with a firm called B&B Worm Farms, and they gave it a solid recommendation.

B&B's headquarters were in Meeker, Oklahoma, less than an hour from Weleetka. The company's business plan seemed straightforward. A grower signed a three-year contract with B&B that called for an up-front investment of between $3,000 and $5,000, which paid for a hundred pounds of slimy but promising breeding stock (about 100,000 worms), technical guidance (via a manual and a toll-free number), and, in most cases, a mechanical worm harvester (which sifted worms from the soil). B&B promised to buy back, for seven dollars a pound, as many mature worms as a grower could produce. The contract also included a first-year, money-cheerfully-refunded guarantee — not that anyone was likely to take advantage of that clause, given everyone's understanding, from the start, that worm farming wasn't a get-rich-quick scheme but a long-term, labor-intensive, yet inevitably rewarding endeavor.

According to the B&B people, the market for adult red worms (a.k.a. *Eisenia fetida*, or red wigglers) was essentially unlimited. Every twenty-four hours, a composting worm could consume its weight in food. And — this was the truly beautiful part — what did worms love to eat? Shit! (Or, specifically, composted livestock manure.) All across America, on small farms, medium-size farms, and megafarm agribiz feedlots, cows and hogs and chickens were doing nothing, 24/7, but eating and excreting. Hundreds of mil-

lions of tons of bovine manure, swine manure, and poultry manure were relentlessly accumulating, releasing noxious vapors into
the air, polluting water supplies, wreaking environmental havoc
. . . *unless* you dumped enough red worms on the problem, in
which case they'd just eat that smelly mess right up. Better yet,
worms, like all God's creatures, pooped regularly, and worm manure, or castings, performed splendidly as an organic fertilizer and
soil builder. No wonder B&B's sales pitch boiled down to this:
vermiculture could make you prosperous — and it could help save
the planet, too. All the company needed was an army of cottage-
industry mom-and-pop worm growers.

"Real good, solid, hardworking people" was how another eastern Oklahoma grower I spoke with described B&B's enlistees. For
someone like Gary Williams, rural and blue collar, with an ingrained suspicion of anything that sounded like too good a deal,
the fact that vermiculture required getting your hands more than
a little dirty — that it amounted to what one literalist worm farmer
referred to as "mainly shitwork" — was a reassuring emblem of its
fundamental integrity. When you finally got paid for your harvest,
the abstract and the tangible neatly converged; the agrarian ideal
was rendered tidily functional and profitable. Indeed, cash on the
kitchen table was the ultimate evidence that everything at B&B
was on the up-and-up.

BY THE TIME Williams formally signed on with B&B in early
2002, the minimum price of a three-year contract had risen to
$8,000. (Later, it escalated to $10,000, and then to $12,000.) Some
growers, too bold to start small, loaded up with $40,000 or $50,000
or $60,000 contracts, but Williams wanted to proceed cautiously.
Next to his house were two painted tin storage sheds, one for his
boat and the other for his tools. Before his worms arrived, he
moved the boat out and replaced it with eight wooden boxes; each
was four feet by eight feet and a foot deep and was filled with composted horse manure that he'd bought from B&B, which bagged

and sold it under the label Grower's Pride. (The main source was a racetrack in Sallisaw, Oklahoma.) Three times a week, he watered the worm beds. To keep the worms warm, he installed a propane heater, and to curb their natural predilection for escaping in the dark he added overhead lighting. Four months later, having begun to feel less cautious, he doubled his capacity, clearing out the toolshed to make room for eight more wooden boxes. Half the worms and bedding material went into the new boxes, and he topped everything off with compost. In September 2002, he harvested for the first time: 250 pounds of *Eisenia fetida*. Because he delivered the worms himself to B&B's Oklahoma distribution center two hours away in Cashion, the company paid him an extra dollar a pound. After the $2,000 check from B&B came in the mail, he and his wife agreed to boost their capacity again.

Last November, Williams added a new building to his property: another tin structure, 1,500 square feet, with a concrete floor, drains, propane, fluorescent light fixtures, and twenty worm boxes. By then, his total investment was up to $37,000, $20,000 of which he'd financed with a home equity loan. Along the way, he'd acquired a chipper-shredder (red worms thrive on shredded newsprint in their bedding), a cement mixer (for blending a slurry of compost, newsprint, and peat moss), a utility trailer (for toting manure from Sallisaw), and an emergency generator (Weleetka is situated in prime tornado territory). Appalled by his propane bills, Williams also bought a wood-burning stove. Every couple of months, he harvested again, at two hundred pounds a pop, and hauled those worms to Cashion.

The mechanical harvester, eight feet long and three feet in diameter at its widest point, consisted of two mesh cylinders, one slightly tapered, which were welded together at their bases and mounted horizontally on an aluminum frame. The contents of a worm box would be loaded into the left cylinder and, as the harvester rotated, the castings would sift through. After the remaining material was placed in the right cylinder, where the mesh was of a slightly larger gauge, out would fall baby worms, eggs, and bedding material, all of which would be promptly returned to the box. At the tapered terminus of this cylinder, nothing would remain but mature worms. That the yield represented money didn't mean that the process was necessarily enticing. A clipping I came across from the *Wichita Eagle* quoted a worm farm hired hand: "Once you see them go across the harvester, you don't want spaghetti no more."

Gary Williams had no such squeamishness, and Pam felt equally upbeat about the enterprise, though there had been a few details that had given them pause. For instance, last summer they attended a growers' seminar in Cashion during which Greg Bradley, the president of B&B, spoke. As they listened to Bradley, it occurred to Pam that this heavyset, goateed, forty-year-old smooth talker seemed "just a little too sweet," and Gary thought he had "the air of a big shot." But wasn't Bradley well on his way to becoming a major big shot? He'd started B&B from scratch in 1998, four years later it was a $25 million business, and everything he said indicated that things were only going to get better.

"Greg Bradley stood up there and said, 'I need more growers,'" Gary recalled. "He said, 'I have twenty-five contracts in my briefcase that we can't fulfill because we don't have enough worms.'"

When one grower asked Bradley to identify the end users — the giant hog farms, poultry farms, and feedlots to which B&B was selling those millions of ravenous manure munchers — he replied, "We can't tell you that, because another company might hear about it and underbid us."

That evasiveness bothered the Williamses a bit, but the fact was that B&B had promised to buy all the worms they could produce. Even if six or seven weeks elapsed between delivery and payment, once the check arrived it cleared at the bank. The Williamses saw no reason to worry. If B&B said it needed more worms, they'd gladly grow them.

*   *   *

GREG BRADLEY'S entrée into the world of vermiculture had an altogether different trajectory. In 1998, he and his wife, Lynn, moved from northern California, where he'd worked as an information technology officer for a small college, to Meeker, where his mother, stepfather, and half brother lived. Looking for a business opportunity, he spotted a "Grow Worms at Home — Earn $$$!" come-on in a bargain hunters' tabloid. When he dialed the number listed in the ad, the call was answered in Las Vegas, where a squad of salesmen worked the phones in a boiler room operation. After listening to a high-pressure pitch, Bradley wasn't convinced that he wanted to spend the rest of his life farming worms — but he was convinced that the company had a clever business model. He decided to set up his own worm company, and B&B was born.

Not long ago, when I asked David Desormeau, a Las Vegas accountant who did occasional work for Bradley, to characterize him, he said, "Greg was a we-can-get-this-done type of guy, a we-can-move-this-forward-no-matter-what guy." Just like the Las Vegas company, B&B advertised in *Thrifty Nickel* and similar tabloids; in addition, word of mouth and a Web site got things percolating. But what really made the difference — what enabled B&B, in time, to become the largest earthworm-buyback firm in the country — was Bradley's energy and verbal agility.

He was equally nimble one on one or in front of a large group, and, whatever the context, he didn't restrict his palaver to the confines of truthfulness. At one point, he told farmers that he would buy not only their worms but their worm castings — under terms that he knew, and the growers later figured out, made no economic sense. "Greg was always ready to promise the world to anybody," Desormeau said. "He'd do anything to make a deal. He was a closer."

Eventually, B&B's network spread across the map — 2,400 contractors in forty-three states — with concentrations in regions where traditional farmers were especially eager to diversify. Scattered across the South, for example, were clusters of anxious tobacco growers who were facing a decline in demand and needed to develop alternative crops. Some had explored raising freshwater shrimp, others had bred alpaca, and now worm farming looked like the ticket. B&B's sales momentum was primarily driven, however, by another, more peculiar urgency. The fact that properly nurtured worm populations expand geometrically meant that, for the company to honor its pledge to buy all the worms its growers harvested, cash flow had to increase at a concomitant rate. B&B had to sell worms faster than they came in the door. This imperative wouldn't have posed such a pressing problem if Bradley had succeeded, you might say, in discovering a humongous manure pile at the end of the rainbow. As it was, his shortcomings as a manager eclipsed his capacities as a deal closer.

To bolster his legitimacy, Bradley had created an advisory board of directors. One of his more imaginative appointments was of an organic farmer from Washington State named Kelly Slocum, a high-visibility person in vermiculture circles — mainly among Earth First! types who compost their kitchen scraps, maintain worm bins in their basements, and till the castings into their vegetable gardens. Slocum's Left Coast paradigm didn't really fit the B&B model, but Bradley wooed her with documents that convinced her he had made environmentally responsible agreements with industrial end users — a poultry operation in Ohio, a hog farm in Illinois, a composting facility in Iowa, a racetrack in Louisiana. Another deal was in the works, Bradley said, to export large quantities of worms to Sierra Leone, where, as elsewhere in Africa, there was a premium on organic fertilizers that wouldn't leach harmful chemicals into water supplies. Seduced by Bradley's save-the-planet-through-worm-farming vision, Slocum agreed to join the board. A few months into her tenure, however, she became troubled by B&B's potential obligations to its growers, and she urged Bradley to stop selling new contracts. In the summer of 2001, he assented to her request, but she later discovered that he had "blown right through those limitations." Not that Slocum or other board members had real leverage; they didn't receive compensation, nor did they own stock in the company.

A less skeptical B&B recruit — not a board member but a well-chosen piece of window dressing — was Wes Watkins, a ten-term United States congressman from Oklahoma who had met Bradley during an airplane trip to Washington. Watkins was a farm boy with two degrees in agricultural science, and he too wanted to save the planet, particularly after traveling to Africa and seeing the consequences of pollution, drought, overpopulation, and starvation. Before leaving office (Watkins didn't seek reelection in 2002), he became a consultant for B&B. One of his responsibilities was to lobby for legislative language that would enable vermiculturists to qualify for government-sponsored agricultural loans. He also had a mandate to connect B&B to prodigious end users — say, Tyson Foods, the poultry processor. Another target on Bradley's wish list was Wal-Mart, which he imagined as an outlet for worm castings and Grower's Pride manure.

It turned out that not only was horse shit the main thing, besides worms, that B&B had to offer in the marketplace; it was, figuratively speaking, what Bradley had been peddling for a long while. (Precisely how long remains a debatable question.) Kelly Slocum says she realized during the summer of 2002 that the touted industrial end users — the big deals in Ohio, Illinois, Iowa, Louisiana, and Sierra Leone — were phantasms. In each case, *something* had been there: amorphous infrastructures, props for photo ops, economic development incentive grants predicated on unfulfilled contingencies. Yet in each case, beneath the bluster and the betting-on-the-come, there was no substance. Bradley had been unable to hustle any customers for his worms; the demand simply wasn't there. Ultimately, the only actual purchasers of worms harvested by B&B growers were . . . new B&B growers. B&B, in other words, bore the earmarks of a Ponzi scheme.

Once Slocum reached that conclusion, she resigned from the

board. When Bradley saw this coming, he dispatched a letter to all growers, a preemptive assault that accused her of, among other things, unspecified "unethical business practices."

In a classic Ponzi, of course, the goal of the scammer is to make himself scarce before the victims wise up. Late last January, Bradley, after a fashion, did just that. One tribute to his talents, or perhaps to his muddled motives, was that, even after the suckers figured out that that's what they were, they refused to abandon faith in what he'd been telling them.

A LETTER dated January 29, 2003, which was signed by Lynn M. Bradley, in her capacity as the company president, and sent to all B&B growers, reported "with great sadness" the death of her husband, Greg. Scrutinized in a certain light, its language now seems to alternate enigmatically between specificity and vagueness. It gives the precise time of his demise ("8:46 A.M. on January 26, 2003"), but the cause is nebulous ("a serious infection and complications . . . I have requested an autopsy . . . of course, I will share the results with you"). Death was unexpected ("We had every reason to believe he would make a complete recovery"), yet, five days before it occurred, he had given her "full leadership of B&B Worm Farms, Inc." As for the ceremonial details: "There will not be a burial. Greg requested that he be cremated and his ashes released in Hawaii. When the time is right, that is what I will do."

Less than three weeks later, eight hundred people showed up at a hotel in St. Louis for B&B's national growers' convention. In the past, the purpose of this annual gathering had been as much to rally the troops as to exchange technical information, and this tone again prevailed, underscored by a heavy quotient of valedictories to the fallen leader. One grower who attended, a dump truck driver who lives north of Oklahoma City, told me that the extravagant veneration of Bradley, especially from his widow, "went on so long a lot of people were getting fidgety." Otherwise, Lynn appeared to be self-possessed as she conveyed the message that growers had been hearing from the get-go and didn't mind hearing once more: The company treasury was full (lots of big numbers were cited); send us your worms; long live B&B!

None of the faithful, therefore, was prepared for the alarmingly contrary message that surfaced almost a month later: B&B had stopped paying for worms. Growers who had harvested in mid-January were, by mid-March, still waiting for their checks. When they called the company headquarters, they could never get through to a human being. Calls placed to the regional distributors led nowhere, because the distributors themselves seemed baffled by the situation. (Invariably, the distributors were growers who had been hired by Bradley to do the heavy lifting — i.e., the recycling of worms.) As the growers chatted among themselves, frustration gave way to panic and then to pleas to government authorities to get involved. On March 19, the Oklahoma Department of Securities opened an investigation and began posting details on its Web site. Subsequently, the attorneys general of Kentucky and Mississippi intervened. The authorities in these states charged B&B variously with failing to register properly before offering to sell "business opportunities," making "untrue statements of material facts," misappropriating funds, and perpetrating "false, misleading and/or deceptive" acts.

The bankruptcy lawyers went to work in early April, and immediately they were flooded with calls from distraught growers. A fraud examiner retained by B&B's bankruptcy trustee began to catalogue assets and liabilities, an exercise that raised many provocative questions. Why had an earthworm-trading company diverted funds to an auto-body shop in Arizona that happened to be owned by the brother of the company president? Why had B&B invested in a pair of Las Vegas sports-handicapping parlors? And why had it wasted a million dollars trying but failing to launch, in partnership with an erstwhile exotic dancer named Holly Caputo, a pornographic Web site? This venture, in particular, aroused curiosity about Lynn Bradley's knowledge of her husband's business practices.

The most salient attribute of Greg Bradley's executive style, his associates later reported, was a tendency toward paranoia. "Greg let individuals know only what they had to know," David Desormeau, the accountant, said. "Nobody else knew more than about half the story. He was afraid of losing the company. He used to carry the checkbook in his briefcase." Among its implications, this observation had the ring of self-defense. Did it mean that if only Bradley knew the true scope of the deception then no one else was culpable? Even if Bradley was a scoundrel, didn't his misdeeds depend on the collusion of his victims? Was B&B conceived in fraud, or was the entire fiasco a consequence of grossly inflated optimism? That Bradley was no longer around to answer these questions made them all the more vexing.

ONE MORNING in April, I paid a visit to Gerry Danley, the B&B distributor in Cashion, a half hour northwest of Oklahoma City. His place of business was on the main street, opposite a grain elevator and a pair of silver silos, in leased space that previously housed a grocery store and a laundromat. When I arrived, Danley, a pink-faced, soft-spoken man in his early forties, was watering worms — in boxes (his own) and in windrows (B&B's), about three tons in all — with a fine spray hose. After we sat down in his office, we were joined by Rance Stein, his brother-in-law and partner in the worm-growing trade. Our conversation was abbreviated (a bankruptcy appraiser was due to come by), but Danley had time for a partial inventory of his woes: B&B still hadn't paid him for worms he'd harvested in January; he had no other income; his lease was running out and he saw no reason to renew it, but the bankruptcy trustee wouldn't allow him to stop feeding B&B's worms; and B&B had borrowed almost $100,000 from the Community State Bank of Cashion and he had personally guaranteed the note.

The bank loan had financed a front-loader, a truck, and some trailers, which Danley bought to transport 23 million pounds of horse manure from a racetrack in Oklahoma City, the first phase of a B&B plan to build a second Grower's Pride composting facility, in Cashion. That project was headed nowhere, of course, as was the horse manure — two twenty-foot piles, each the length of a couple of football fields. ("The mountains of Cashion," Rance Stein liked to say. "When it snows, it looks real pretty.") This topographic novelty sat east of town, next to an old airplane hangar, presumably attracting billions of flies and, Danley feared, the attention of environmental regulators. (Sure enough, this spring the piles spontaneously caught fire.)

Danley recalled a strange scene in early January, a couple of weeks before Greg Bradley's death, during a distributors' meeting at a Holiday Inn in Oklahoma City. Though Bradley attended the meeting, in Danley's opinion "he had no business being there, he was too sick, he'd come down with pneumonia." He was in a wheelchair, with an oxygen supply, accompanied by a nurse who seemed to have him on a timer. Periodically, she'd take him back to his room to rest — though en route he'd be seen in the lobby smoking a cigarette. After that encounter, Danley never saw him again. When he heard that Bradley was hospitalized, nobody would say where, and he was discouraged from visiting. As for Lynn Bradley's promise to share the autopsy results, "We still haven't heard back from her on that."

Nor had the thousands of B&B growers, many of whom were inclined to wonder — among other places, in Internet forums — if Bradley's leave-taking wasn't too neatly timed to be believed. The scenario I heard described most frequently had him absconding to the Cayman Islands with fifteen or twenty million bucks. Danley, for one, found it all distasteful. "As far as him not being dead, there's always an outside possibility," he said. "But until it's proven that he's alive I'm not gonna waste my time." The state of Oklahoma had produced a death certificate for Bradley, which stated that he died from a "septic pulmonary abscess." Nevertheless, it was understandable that in the universe of disgruntled worm growers a lot of folks felt that they had paid for the right to speculate about Bradley. If he wasn't in the Caymans, maybe he was in Hawaii — not Greg's ashes, but all of his original molecules. Because the fact was that no matter where Greg had gone, or in what physical condition, their money had vanished with him.

VIRTUALLY ALL the growers I spoke with, never mind what B&B had done to their lives, told me that they still believed in "the vermiculture concept." Greg Bradley might have let people down, either by lying or by dying, but the worms had done what was expected of them. Gary and Pam Williams, when I went to see them in Weleetka, were in mourning for six boxes of worms that he had dumped in the pasture earlier that week.

"There was probably forty or fifty pounds of worms in each bed," Gary said. "At eight dollars a pound. And that's not even talking about the potential that's in there. How'd I feel? I sat down for about thirty minutes thinking, I've worked so hard on this and now I have to dig 'em out and dump 'em in the pasture — maybe I should hold on. Then I said, 'Well, no, I've got to get some of these out of here, because I can't afford to feed 'em.' But I stopped there, because I didn't feel like dumping out any more money in one day."

Pam, a third grade teacher in the Weleetka public schools, had called home around noon that day, and when Gary told her what he'd done she wanted to cry. After work, she went out in the pasture herself with a rake. "There were all these gorgeous worms," she said. "I raked them into the ground and then we covered them with compost. So that's over."

But it wasn't quite. Last fall, after the first check from B&B arrived, she and Gary had talked a lot about their plans for the future. She'd been teaching for thirty years and, if he could retire young, why couldn't she? They had a grown son and a daughter and grandchildren living nearby. She could spend more time with the grandkids, and, while Gary focused on growing the worms, she could concentrate on coming up with a way to turn the castings into a separate little cash crop — by, say, bagging and selling them wholesale to a garden supply store. In March, she had submitted her resignation; a week later came the rumblings that B&B had imploded. As she tried to figure out what to do next, it was probably a blessing that there were still thirty boxes of worms to tend.

Gary was similarly uncertain about his future. "I may have to go back to work," he said. "But Southwestern Bell won't take me. They've been cutting back. I may become a greeter for Wal-Mart."

The next time I spoke with him, a couple of weeks later, he reported that he'd attended some meetings of B&B growers in Oklahoma and Arkansas who were considering joining a co-op to search collectively for a market for their worms. With a critical mass of growers — and without a Greg Bradley manipulating the situation — it might be possible after all to hook up with a legitimate end user. And maybe you really could sell worms and castings to Sierra Leone. Gary had been in touch with a fellow in Ohio who was willing to assume an executive role in organizing the co-op, but he wanted an earnest-money payment of $3,000 from each grower.

"Gary, are you sure that's what you want to do?" I asked.

There was a moment of silence, and then he said, "Well, no, I already told him I'm not prepared to put up that much." Another pause. "I told him I'd have to think about it. I said maybe I could give him a thousand."

Itasca, Texas
JANUARY 2003

Nᴇᴡs ᴛʀᴀᴠᴇʟs quickly in Itasca, Texas, where, co-incidentally, it doesn't have far to go. Itasca has a central Texas location — just off Interstate 35, equally convenient to Fort Worth and Waco — but its 1,600 citizens are accustomed to the rest of the world's not paying much attention, so they pay particular attention to each other. Visitors wandering off the interstate encounter a billboard that says, "Welcome to Itasca, 'The Big Little Town,'" a friendly display of civic pride and becoming modesty. The slogan also appears beneath the front-page logo of the local weekly, the *Paw Print Press*. When I showed up one morning last month, among the first people to greet me were Allison Bailey and Cymbre Weatherly, the newspaper's coeditors. I had no trouble finding their office. I just kept driving — past the billboard, past black-soil wheat and milo fields — until I spotted Itasca High School, the most conspicuous object on the horizon that wasn't a water tower.

Thirteen students at Itasca High ("Home of the Mighty Wampus Cats") make up the staff of the *Paw Print Press*. Five of them are seniors, but only Allison and Cymbre have been at it since their sophomore year, so Barbara Petrash, the paper's adviser, installed them atop the masthead. Mrs. Petrash teaches journalism (also world history), which makes her classroom the paper's newsroom. More to the point, during the past five years the *Paw Print Press* has been Itasca's only newspaper, and Mrs. Petrash's role in the school and the community has expanded in a way that renders it difficult to define her job concisely. The journalism class meets every weekday from eleven A.M. to noon. Newsworthy events, however, have a tendency to occur at any hour. I happened to arrive, for instance, the morning of the annual holiday brunch hosted by the Itasca Chamber of Commerce and the Itasca Garden Club, which was scheduled to begin at nine o'clock. Mrs. Petrash wanted to be certain that Allison and Cymbre and another reporter, Timishia Mayberry, got there before the fun wound down, so she persuaded their physics teacher to excuse them from class, a sacrifice that the girls were willing to make.

"Mainly, I want captions," said Mrs. Petrash, a large woman in her mid-fifties with short light brown hair, pink cheeks, and a bemused air. "Make sure you find out how this year's brunch compares to previous years'. Get some food. Taste all the goodies. And get lots of pictures, so we have some options."

The girls nodded, Mrs. Petrash handed Cymbre a digital camera, and we headed for the parking lot. Before we took off in Allison's burgundy Nissan Altima, she apologized for the mess in the back seat. She stashed her marching band uniform, a blanket, and a Bible in the trunk. It took less than three minutes to reach downtown Itasca — a low-rise gathering of a couple of dozen retail establishments radiating from an intersection punctuated by the only traffic light within several miles. Along the way, as Allison adroitly dodged potholes, I saw mostly wood-frame housing, much of which looked ready for a paint job, and several vacant lots in need of tidying up. We parked in front of a two-story office building owned by Hilco, a rural electrical cooperative and the town's largest private employer. The brunch was being held in a ground-floor meeting room.

About forty people — Hilco employees, city employees, busy retirees, and cowboy-hatted elderly fellows who any other morning would have been down at Jimmy's Corner Store, discussing local and global affairs while drinking their seventh cup of coffee — were seated at long tables, sampling a potluck buffet. It turned out that the person most in command of the facts was Betty Sumner, a retired schoolteacher and the president of the Chamber of Commerce. She greeted Allison with a hug, and Allison, who has long straight black hair and is strikingly pretty, got right to work.

"I need to do some talking to you," she said. "So you-all been going on for an hour?"

"Well, yes," Sumner said. "We're thinking maybe we want to change the time, because we've been starting at nine, and there's talk that maybe we should do this later."

They discussed the historical evolution of the brunch: the Chamber inaugurated it in 1985 and it became a joint venture a few years later; the Garden Club members provide the food, the Chamber members the beverages; a lot of people belong to both groups, so there's always plenty to go around. When I sensed that Allison was running out of questions ("So you say the Chamber arranges for the poinsettia centerpieces — now, wouldn't that be a Garden Glub thing to do?"), I decided to check out the buffet: raw vegetables, mixed nuts, deep-fried olives, little sausages, pimiento cheese spread on crustless whole wheat, a block of cream cheese topped with salsa.

"Do you like hot stuff?" a woman with silver curls asked me.

"Not this early in the morning, usually," I said.

"Well," she said — and when I thought about it later it occurred to me that I had stumbled across a defining metaphor — "there's a lot of mild stuff, too."

*   *   *

THE *Itasca Item*, the predecessor of the *Paw Print Press*, was founded in 1886, a year after the town — which came into existence because the M-K-T Railroad decided it should — was incorporated. A stately-looking broadsheet, the *Item* was produced, for most of its history, by Linotype and hot lead. From 1926 to 1985, it was owned and edited by the McDonald family — first, Donald, then his sons, Donald Jr. and Gordon. During the Second World War, Donald Jr. was a staff reporter and photographer for *Stars & Stripes*, stationed in Italy and North Africa. Only during wartime would the world outside Itasca — and the implicit acknowledgment that a world outside Itasca existed — intrude upon the content of the *Item*. Front page, December 1944: photographs of two Distinguished Flying Cross recipients and an article headlined "PFC. W. L. CHANDLER WOUNDED IN FRANCE" — also "PRESBYTERIANS AND METHODISTS OBSERVE BIBLE READING SUNDAY," "NEWS FROM THE ORPHANS' HOME," and "BOX TAILOR SHOP SELLS; TO BE KNOWN AS ITASCA CLEANERS."

The McDonalds kept it going through the indistinguishable fifties ("ITASCA GIVES $243.26 TO MARCH OF DIMES," "NEGRO HOUSES BURN," "85TH BIRTHDAY PARTY") and sixties ("ROTARY NEWS," "LIONS MEET," "ITASCA STORES TO CLOSE NEW YEAR'S") and beyond, animated by a we-love-our-town-no-matter-what editorial philosophy. One of its quintessential ingredients was the "Locals" chitchat column, which served up such morsels as "Mrs. Alva Underwood visited her daughter, Eula Gene, in Denton last week. Eula Gene accompanied her mother home for the weekend." Donald and Gordon shared the writing, Donald took lots of pictures, and they maintained an upbeat, boosterish tone even after the interstate came through and the downtown merchants got sucked under, one by one, by the shopping malls a dozen miles away in Hillsboro, the county seat. After Gordon died in 1981, Donald sold a controlling interest to Eddie Chiles, an Itasca native and well-known industrialist (and, in his later years, a noisy right-wing populist), who upgraded the printing equipment. As Donald was declining with Alzheimer's in the mid-eighties, Chiles sold the paper. It was sold again a couple of years later, to a not fondly remembered out-of-town couple who, in the fall of 1990, abruptly halted publication and vanished without bothering to refund prepaid subscriptions. Shortly afterward, the *Item* returned, sort of, as a labor of love by Judi Lackey Underwood, a former flight attendant who not quite every week managed to put out a four-page edition. Underwood had admired the McDonalds' devotion, but she chose not to follow their hear-no-evil, speak-no-evil example. At city council meetings, she asked pointed questions about the annual town budget. She criticized the city secretary after the town's wells ran dry. She took pictures of town employees doing work on the mayor's property. That was the point at which she sufficiently irritated the mayor — a businessman with deep pockets — that he started a rival paper, the *Itasca Express News*, to drive her out of business. Not long after he succeeded in May 1994, the *Express News* also disappeared.

IT WAS BETTY SUMNER, the Chamber of Commerce president, who set in motion the process that led to the *Paw Print Press*'s replacing the *Item* as Itasca's newspaper of record. "It upset me no end when the *Item* closed," she told me. "I was on the city council then and I would get calls all the time about things that were just idle gossip. I hate gossip." Gossip, of course, is the lifeblood of any small town — petty stuff (who donated the Victoria's Secret lingerie to the Second Baptist Church rummage sale), middling stuff (who got arrested for DWI in Dallas), scandalous stuff (what married-but-not-to-each-other couple had been caught in flagrante at the Holiday Inn in Hillsboro), vital statistics (who passed away at a nursing home in Houston). The McDonalds, who were instinctively averse to controversy and only too happy to publish, say, six or ten pages of children's letters to Santa Claus because, well, why not, had drawn the line exactly where Itascans wanted it drawn. They understood that in a small town where everyone knows far too much about everyone else's business the imperative is to refrain from printing certain information that who in the hell wants to see in black and white. After the *Item* died, the town lost not only part of its social contract but its primary source of basic information. "We had to rely on the bank sign" — an electronic display outside the First State Bank building — "to get the word out," Sumner said.

Through the Chamber, Sumner had mobilized the Itasca Board of Revitalization, which included representatives of all the major organizations in town, including the government, the churches, and the school system. "In board meetings, I'd give the truth to those people," she said. "I'd tell them, 'Go to your troops and fill them in.' One day, we were meeting in the office of Ray Freeman, the school superintendent, and I said, 'Wouldn't it be wonderful if we had some means for printing news and getting it out?' And Dr. Freeman said, 'Let's get Mrs. Petrash in here and see what we can work out.'" Though Barbara Petrash had been living in Itasca only since 1990, when her husband's employer transferred him to the area, she'd established a reputation for being able to juggle a remarkable number of tasks simultaneously. After marrying at fifteen and raising five children, she received her bachelor's degree at the age of forty-seven, by which time she'd already spent four years working as an aide at Itasca High School. When she began teaching full-time in 1995, the *Paw Print Press* had had a short-lived existence as a dinky monthly newsletter — an after-school project by a handful of students to which no one paid much attention. When the school superintendent proposed that Mrs. Petrash become, in effect, the editor and publisher of Itasca's weekly newspaper, it barely mattered that she had no clue about journalism. No one expected or wanted the *Paw Print Press* to become a source of enterprising, award-winning reporting. What mattered was Mrs.

Petrash's cheerful demeanor, her go-along-to-get-along pliability, and the fact that she knew and was on friendly terms with just about everybody in town.

BACK AT THE HIGH SCHOOL after the Chamber of Commerce–Garden Club brunch, I found a spot in a corner of Mrs. Petrash's classroom as the *Paw Print Press* personnel shuffled in for their daily meeting. She was seated at her desk, reminding staff members of their assignments and frequently answering a cordless phone ("*Paw Print Press* — how can I help you?"). Propped on a shelf behind her was a sign that said, "You Can't Be Fired. Slaves Are Sold." The *Paw Print Press* is composed and laid out on a computer, laser printed, photocopied on eleven-by-seventeen-inch sheets, and hand-folded. On Wednesdays, when the papers are collated, folded, stapled, and labeled, Mrs. Petrash sits with Robin James, a senior and the business manager, and they cross-check a list of out-of-town subscribers. "We go to New York, Oklahoma, Pennsylvania, Florida, Arizona, Minnesota, California," she told me. "We used to have somebody in Alaska. We've never had a subscriber in Hawaii, though. I don't know why." All this is done on a $3,000 budget (half of which is earmarked for the service contract on the photocopier). There's no charge for advertisements, but donations are welcome; that income gets deposited in a college scholarship fund for graduating staff members.

This was a Monday, and plenty of work remained to be done for the issues leading up to and spanning the Christmas break. As the students got busy (or, in a couple of cases, benignly goofed off), Mrs. Petrash recited for my benefit their strengths and weaknesses, with an emphasis on the former. Eric Covington, who is in charge of sports coverage, blushed when she said, "Eric may be one of the best writers I've ever seen. He can throw together an article in about ten minutes that needs very little editing. He's also an athlete, so he's a member of the teams he's writing about. The only thing Eric can't do is take photographs while he's playing in a game." Of Cymbre Weatherly, she said, "She reports, she writes a column, she keeps people in line. The kids say it's her job to be mean to them. She pretty well takes over when I'm gone."

Last summer, while recovering from knee surgery, Mrs. Petrash relied on Cymbre and a recent graduate to help her put out the paper. "The first couple of issues each summer are awards-heavy," Mrs. Petrash explained, "so we can plan those ahead of time. Except for the big barbecue cook-off in July, there's not a lot of news in Itasca in the summertime, especially with the schools closed. We do always try to have the police report, but there's not much crime. The bank was robbed in 1991."

Mrs. Petrash is a one-handed typist and a straightforward, just-the-facts writer who reserves certain assignments for herself. That afternoon, after school had been dismissed, she was at her computer, filing an account of a recent city council meeting. The Board of Revitalization had been campaigning to have several unsightly vacant lots cleaned up, city employees had done the work, and a public discussion ensued about why taxpayers should have to foot the bill. "We have a city secretary who's sort of full of himself," Mrs. Petrash explained. "When the question came up about why bills hadn't gone out to the property owners, he said something about how these were just lots that had to be cleaned up because 'the old women' had complained. Well, the old women were the Board of Revitalization, which I happen to be a member of. He looked at me and said, 'I suppose you're going to quote me that way in the paper.' And I said, 'Yes, I am.'

"My kids are still intimidated by the police and city officials a little bit. I keep trying to explain to them that they're the press. There's another city council meeting tonight. It starts at seven o'clock. We just elected a new mayor and a couple of new council members. Things are a little turmoily — the usual reasons: small-town politics, everybody knows everybody, everybody knows everything. I'm sending Cymbre, but I'm going, too."

* * *

AT THE city council meeting that evening — City Hall is a double storefront on Hill Street, a block north of Itasca's traffic light — I sat in the same row as Mrs. Petrash and Cymbre, who was wearing her police department–issued press credentials around her neck and her *Paw Print Press* T-shirt, which had printed on the back "If You Don't Like The Way The World Is, Change It." Cymbre is slender and demure and has long honey blond hair. Two years ago, the *Paw Print Press* featured a photograph of her after she'd cut her hair and donated it to an organization that made wigs for children with cancer. Her column, "Inspiration Corner for Teens," runs on page two of almost every issue, and one of its consistent themes is the spiritual uplift that derives from doing good deeds. Typically, Cymbre opens with a quotation from scripture and proceeds to deliver a proselytizing sermonette. Itasca is one of those places where no one rushes to make a fuss about the doctrine of church-state separation. Before the city council got down to business, a local pastor offered a prayer, which he concluded with "in the name of our Lord, Jesus Christ."

For almost fifteen minutes, the audience of a dozen or so citizens sat quietly as the mayor and five council members reviewed the town's finances. Next on the agenda was a complaint from the owners of a convenience store, who felt that they were being harassed by a member of the police force. The police chief, G. A. Couldron, was present and explained, in the manner of someone apologizing for a dog whose howling wakes up the neighbors, that he'd spoken with the officer in question and would do so again. Betty Sumner, representing the Board of Revitalization, addressed the vacant lots issue as well as the matter of Itasca's ubiquitously potholed streets. Unexpectedly, the mayor announced that the council was going into executive session to discuss personnel matters, which meant that the public, press included, had to vacate the premises. Cymbre decided to head home and I decided to head to dinner, each of us knowing that we'd get the low-down the following day from Mrs. Petrash, who spent the next hour and a half waiting outside the locked front door of City Hall, with her bum knee killing her. At a certain point, the police chief reappeared, wearing his house slippers. Inside, the city council gave him the choice of retiring or being fired and he chose the former. The officer who had been the object of the complaint from the convenience store owners was fired, and another officer was named interim police chief. This was by far the most eventful city council session Itasca (and the *Paw Print Press*) had witnessed in several years.

At school the next morning, when I heard this news from Mrs. Petrash, she said, "As of today, Geoff Couldron, the police chief, is retiring. I've already gotten two phone calls from him. He says he turned sixty in May, he's been in law enforcement for thirty-six years uninterrupted, including nine years as chief. And his quote is 'It's time to get out of the business and enjoy my family.' Now, was this provoked by anything? Yes, but that's not what we're going to report. They gave him the option of retiring and that will be our story. I'm going to redo the city council report I was typing yesterday. Basically, I'll just add this news to the bottom of that."

And that was, indeed, how the *Paw Print Press* played the police chief's abrupt departure that week: in twenty words, uninflected, unencumbered by analysis or, in the weeks that followed, op-ed thumb-sucking (though the paper plans to publish interviews with both Chief Couldron and his successor). None of which, of course, distinguishes the *Paw Print Press* as an exemplar of small-town-weekly journalism. The paper doesn't deliver much in the way of trenchant reporting or imaginative feature writing. Nor, with the exception of a successful campaign in 1997 to adopt a new stray-dog ordinance, has it earned a reputation for bold editorials. But for the past five years the *Paw Print Press* has restored a cohesiveness that Itasca lacked when the town was newspaperless, and each week it accomplishes one truly remarkable thing: it appears in mailboxes and next to cash registers throughout Itasca. Then it gets read. It provides a text, and readers go about the grat-ifying business of excavating the unwritten subtext. Whatever the naked truth was about the police chief, no one in Itasca was likely to object to the etiquette of having a cut-and-dried newspaper narrative running parallel to the more baroque narrative that would get chewed over for the next several days at Jimmy's Corner Store and Janet's Beauty Barn.

THURSDAY MORNING, when I walked into the classroom, Mrs. Petrash was giving Eric Covington and Cory Bourland instruc-tions before they went to the First State Bank to photograph em-ployees posing with an all-poinsettia Christmas tree. "You know who looks good and you know what to do as to who's short, who's tall, whatever," she said. "Remember, you're the photographer, they want their picture made. You're the boss." Most of the rest of the staff was out and about — Robin James and Holly Faulkner were driving around town distributing copies to merchants, and a few other people were canvassing the elementary, middle, and high schools, selling copies discounted from a quarter to a dime — so the ambience was more subdued than usual. Though Mrs. Petrash had plenty to do for the upcoming issue, she was still reflecting upon the city council meeting. "We've never had a shakeup like that. It kind of makes me wonder who's running the town," she said. "I had a call at home last night after nine-thirty from a councilman wanting to know what we had in the paper about the City Hall meeting. He couldn't wait. I said, 'I just wrote down what you-all said.'"

All week, I'd been looking forward to immersing myself in the *Paw Print Press* archives, the five years' worth of back issues that were stored in a couple of file cabinets in the corner of the room. Mrs. Petrash led me there now and began pulling them out for my perusal. There was no shortage of Wampus Cats sports coverage.

Also: a new flagpole at the cemetery, a skunk trapped in a garbage can on school property, a front-page feature about an Itasca High grad who had become a "top dog debater" at Southwest Texas State University, news from the local nursing home, Cinco de Mayo celebration updates, a visit to Itasca by Fox's play-by-play football announcer Pat Summerall, an increase in security at the Dollar General Store.

"Here's one I like," Mrs. Petrash said. "They were digging the foundation for the technology center here at the school, and it started raining. It rained many days, so we ran a picture and a caption that said you could sign up for the swim team. And we had students coming in to sign up. We had to tell them, 'Hey, it's a joke.'

"We used to have a feature called 'Yard of the Week.' We'd run a photograph of a house in town and write a nice caption. We dropped it. I guess we ran out of yards to brag about. Anyway, this is a 'Yard of the Week' that I remember very well. These people got a divorce, and the father came to me and wanted a copy of the paper. He wanted to show what a good father he was, and the proof was he put in a little playhouse for his children.

"Look here. This was written by the superintendent's daughter. She wanted to write a golf column, so we had a golf column. And we don't even have a golf course. Well, you have to be innovative.

"Some of the summer issues we put out are a little skimpy. We've been so desperate we've run stories on grasshoppers. I have one in here where I took this grasshopper, put him on my dining room table, and took his picture. The caption said, 'Wanted for Mass Destruction: Dead or in a Jar.' They'd been eating crops. It's a matter of, anything we've got in the summertime, we'll put it on the front page.

"Oh, okay, here's what I was looking for. We had a fire four years ago that destroyed a half block of historic buildings downtown. And a couple of restaurant owners prepared free meals for volunteers at the scene. Well, one Itasca resident went down there and got six to-go plates and took them home to his family. Believe it or not, it was a minister. We thought it was awful, so we ran an editorial about it. After that, he didn't last long. We didn't name names, but we didn't need to. Everyone knew."

ON THE ROAD AGAIN

WITHOUT PREJUDICE, I passed up the chance last month to buy a five-dollar copy of a panoramic photograph inscribed "Northern California Gypsy Tour, Bolado Park, Hollister, California, 1937." It depicted three hundred or so peaceable-looking citizens (motorcyclists, most of them minus their machines), plus several children — a clean-cut bunch, lounging on the grass, attired as if about to head off for some tennis. A charming enough artifact, I thought, but not one that offered any insight into what makes the present-day Hollister economy go ka-boom every Fourth of July weekend, when between 80,000 and 100,000 bikers and gawkers descend on the place.

Ten years after that photograph was taken, a far more memorable and consequential portrait was snapped, this time on San Benito Street, Hollister's main drag, in front of Johnny's Bar & Grill. That photograph is still the centerpiece of the behind-the-counter decor at Johnny's, framed along with the cover logo from the July 21, 1947, issue of *Life*, in which it was first published. It shows a heavyset fellow in a motoring cap, khakis, and leather boots straddling a motorcycle while clutching a beer bottle, with several empties lying in the foreground. A headline and subhead say, "CYCLISTS' HOLIDAY: HE AND FRIENDS TERRORIZE A TOWN," and a one-paragraph caption describes a Fourth of July debauch — how "4,000 members of a motorcycle club roared into Hollister . . . quickly tired of ordinary motorcycle thrills and turned to more exciting stunts." Traffic laws were flouted, vehicles were "rammed into restaurants and bars, breaking furniture and mirrors. . . . Police arrested many for drunkenness and indecent exposure but could not restore order."

No one in Hollister today minds — nor, it seems, did anyone protest in 1947 — that this journalistic account was based on a mostly fictitious premise. What actually materialized that Fourth of July was the equivalent of a couple of frat parties on steroids — an unseemly exhibition of drunken, uncouth behavior, perpetrated by a gathering of out-of-town motorcyclists who temporarily had the constabularies overmatched but who in the end paid their traffic fines and did their brief time in the pokey. The celebrated photograph was staged the day after the noise subsided. Instead of a terrorist invader, the loutish-looking beer guzzler was a photographer's prop — a poseur in a tableau that was lifelike up to a point, but above all *Life*-like, and basically bogus. Nevertheless, the episode proved, in the long run, to be extremely good for business.

In 1996, a year shy of the fiftieth anniversary of the *Life* photograph and whatever had led up to it, some biker-friendly Hollister boosters began envisioning the first Hollister Independence Rally. "A group got together and approached the city," Ellen Brown, the current executive director of the rally, told me. "But the city-government people were not holding their arms open. They didn't want a reenactment of 1947, as they understood it. They weren't looking forward to raping and pillaging." The group persevered, however, and the necessary permits were granted. Though many businesses boarded up for the weekend, the 1997 event proceeded without serious complications. "By the third year," Brown said, "we had won most people over."

Nowadays, the local establishment proudly proclaims Hollister "the birthplace of the American biker," mindful, no doubt, that the image commonly evoked by the term "American biker" is not the weekend hobbyist — the Orange County accountant or the San Fernando Valley dermatologist who gets his jollies riding his Harley-Davidson Road King to the golf course — but the hairy prole in greasy Levi's, the lineal descendant of the cowboy who has skipped several consecutive Saturday-night baths, the creature who would just as soon dismantle a small California town as overhaul an engine. Which is to say that Hollister has deliberately embraced a cliché whose provenance can be traced to Marlon Brando's performance as the alienated antihero of Stanley Kramer's 1954 movie *The Wild One*. For some reason, most bikers have been willing to overlook that *The Wild One*, in addition to being the first biker picture, was the first laughably awful biker picture. Hollister, in particular, has a proprietary fondness for the movie, a fondness rooted in the fact that *The Wild One* was Hollywood's lame imagining of Hollister's mythical invasion of 1947.

MOTORCYCLISTS have been gravitating to Hollister (population 35,000, seat of San Benito County) at least since the 1920s, attracted by an oval dirt racetrack near downtown as well as by hills that offer ideal terrain for climbing competitions. Until the Hollister Independence Rally came along, the local economy was mainly dependent on agriculture (apricots, cherries, apples, lettuce, peppers, onions), although the southern outskirts of Silicon Valley are within commuting distance. I arrived in Hollister a couple of days before the crowds gathered for this year's proceedings, and my first stop was the rally headquarters. As I chatted with Ellen Brown, a friendly, efficient woman in her early forties, a caller delivered the news that a banner that had been strung between utility poles on San Benito Street was welcoming visitors to, oops, the 2001 instead of the 2002 rally. "It's hard to find good free help," Brown said. "But if that's the biggest problem we have this week, we're doing pretty well." This was a not very oblique reference to the very real apprehension that this year something truly frightful might happen in Hollister.

Last April, during a motorcycle rally in Laughlin, Nevada, an early-morning gun battle and knife fight inside a casino left three people dead and a dozen wounded. Hours later and eighty miles away, on the shoulder of an interstate highway in California, police discovered the corpse of a biker with several bullet holes in his back. Three of the dead belonged to the Hell's Angels and the fourth was a member of the Mongols, a motorcycle clan that has grown rapidly in Southern California in recent years, largely by recruiting new members from Hispanic street gangs. A contingent of Hell's Angels were staying at the same hotel as the Mongols, and the result was the bloodiest installment yet in a feud provoked by the Mongols' attempts to expand into the Angels' traditional territory in northern California.

Law enforcement people who specialize in monitoring biker bad behavior said that they weren't surprised by the lethal jousting in Laughlin. Part of it was explainable in terms of a demographic shift: many of the older Angels are, well, old — Sonny Barger, for decades the Angels' equivalent of a *capo di tutti capi*, is now in his mid-sixties — and, until relatively recently, most local chapters haven't pushed aggressively to rejuvenate their ranks. Because the Fourth of July spectacle in Hollister was the next major event on the West Coast motorcycle-rally calendar, and because the Hell's Angels have always made a conspicuous showing there, speculation immediately turned to whether the Mongols would come around for more action. As it happened, a couple of deputies from the San Benito County Sheriff's Department had been inside the casino in Laughlin, on an intelligence-gathering mission, but had gone to bed about an hour before they would have had to duck for cover. In the aftermath, Curtis Hill, the sheriff, told the *San Jose*

Mercury News, "It's flat-out war. It will be interesting to see how many people die between now and when they call a peace to this thing."

When I left the rally headquarters and stopped by Sheriff Hill's office, he wasn't in, but his second in command, Lieutenant Mike Covell, was doing a fine job serving up meaty sound bites. "If there is violence, what's the nature of it going to be?" he said. "Is it gonna be knives, ball-peen hammers, guns? In Canada, they use rocket launchers."

The Hollister Police Department had enlisted forty extra cops for the weekend, and the FBI, the Bureau of Alcohol, Tobacco, and Firearms, and four separate California state law enforcement agencies would be represented, in uniform and undercover. A sizable contingent of media folk were also standing by, ready to wring their hands in the event of bloodshed. I deeply empathized with the anxieties of my fellow Fourth Estaters, who, I suspected, feared an anticlimax even more than they did an outburst of fresh violence.

WHEN I MENTIONED to one of my teenage sons that I would be attending a big motorcycle rally, he pleaded, "Dad, promise me that if you're going to be hanging with the Hell's Angels you won't be wearing your usual polo shirt and chinos." He had a point, but, knowing that I'd be cruising into town behind the wheel of a Chevy Malibu or an Oldsmobile Alero from Avis, I couldn't see the advantage of investing in a leather vest, chaps, boots, gloves, skullcap, and $300 sunglasses. So most days in Hollister I wore Levi's, sandals, and a commemorative T-shirt from the Dan Quayle Center and Museum. (Bikers tend to lean politically to the right.) I calculated that after I had been sufficiently exposed to ninety-degree heat and the shirt had accumulated stains from deep-fried cuisine, it would get sufficiently gamy to enhance my street credibility. Another option — riding, say, a Harley Fat Boy with custom stretch handlebars, chrome Thunderstar wheels, shotgun exhaust pipes, and bullet-hole decals on the gas tank — wasn't really an option. For one thing, I don't have a motorcycle license. And one reason I don't is that the only time in my life I attempted to operate a two-wheeled motorized vehicle — a Vespa, slightly larger than a child's stroller — I was less than five seconds into a test drive, wearing shorts, when I crashed into two parked cars, an experience I relive every time I admire the conversation-piece scar on my right thigh. Anyway, I'd have no time for carefree recreation. I had a job to do: scoping out one-percenters and urging them to share their thoughts and feelings.

The term "one-percenter" derives from the American Motorcycle Association's defensive claim, during the 1950s, that only one percent of the bikes on the road belonged to criminally inclined social misfits. The Hell's Angels and many other motorcycle clubs embraced the designation as a badge of pride — literally, by sewing "1%" patches on their vests. Sergeant Mike Rodrigues of the San Benito County Sheriff's Department told me to assume that all the one-percenters who made appearances in Hollister — he mentioned the Red Devils, Hellbent, Molochs, Ghost Mountain Riders, Ancient Iron, Devil Dolls, Tophatters, Lonesome Fugitives, Solo Angels, Vagos, and Skeleton Crew motorcycle clubs — were allied with the twelve Hell's Angels chapters on hand. (Rodrigues also said that there was a lone Mongol living in Hollister and a Mongol chapter with at least eighteen members in San Jose, less than an hour away. Conventional wisdom held that any Mongols who dared to show up wouldn't be dumb enough to wear their colors.)

A hundred and fifty or so non-one-percenter clubs were represented, in varying numbers, and it didn't take long for all of them to blend together in my eyes and brainpan, like very, very loud wallpaper. Biker fashion, male and female, never mind age or club or gang color distinctions, has such a narrow range of permutations — leather, metal, wraparound shades, bandannas or skull-caps, German infantry–style helmets, Harley-Davidson logos, tattoos — that from half a block away an aggregation of bikers milling on the street, self-consciously checking one another out, looks no less like a unified army than a regiment of uniformed soldiers does. Up close, virtually every bike, proudly polished to an impeccable gleam, struck me as beautiful, especially when parked. But even then there were so many to see that it was almost impossible to focus. Some ninety percent were Harley-Davidsons; the rest were Indians, BMWs, BMC Choppers, Yamahas, Suzukis, American Iron Horses, and a miscellany of customized hybrids. More than 150 venders had rented booths, from which they were flogging every conceivable sort of motorcycle accessory and personal gear, along with such optional merchandise as leather thongs, toe rings, Pig Snot Biker Wax, insulated bodysuits, knives, tank tops ("These Tits Are Real"), legal services, and in-your-face helmet and gas tank stickers ("I Had a Wife Once but Her Husband Came and Got Her"; "Unless You Are Totally Nude Don't Lean on This Bike"; "The Beatings Will Continue Until Morale Improves"; "You're the Reason Our Kids Are Ugly"). The average rider had $25,000 invested in his or her machine. The ambience was nothing if not aspirational. For the right price, presumably, everything in town was for sale, which raised — or perhaps rendered moot — the metaphysical question of who (or what) was the genuine article and who was a wannabe.

On San Benito Street one afternoon, before the festivities hit full stride, I came across a bunch of credibly menacing-looking dudes hanging out in front of Johnny's Bar & Grill. These were members of the Boozefighters Motorcycle Club, the crew who, according to legend, caused all the ruckus in 1947. The Boozefighters regard Johnny's as hallowed ground for its historical significance and because the ashes of Wino Willie Forkner, one of the founding members, who died in 1997, six days before the inaugural Hollister Independence Rally, are displayed inside.

I had a cordial conversation with Carl (Big Daddy) Spotts, who owns a motorcycle repair shop near Lake Tahoe. Spotts was tall and hefty, with a flowing gray beard, and he wore a leather vest, jeans, a wide belt with an oval Boozefighters buckle, and a green cap that identified him as the club's West Coast national representative. "I also belong to the Elks," he said, pointing to a membership pin on the cap. "And the Moose." He had a flaming-wheel tattoo on his right biceps and, on his left, a Boozefighters logo that was a work in progress. "That's a coverup," he said. "Originally, I had a skunk put on there when I was fifteen."

The standard Boozefighters regalia also included a vest patch that said "GB."

"There's disagreement as to what the 'GB' stands for," Potts told me, "whether it's 'gag box' or 'gag bucket.' Either you had to bring a joke to each meeting or you partied till you puked."

I asked why they had come to Hollister in advance of the main event.

"It gets pretty rough," Spotts said. "You can hardly walk into the bar, it's so crowded."

He continued, "Some of our original forefathers are here tonight and tomorrow, so we came to party with them. There'll be about fifty or a hundred of us. Then we plan to drive up north of San Francisco about a hundred miles to visit Wino Willie's widow."

Three self-anointed Boozefighters had come from Norway, provoking an internecine debate about their legitimacy. "We're working on that," Spotts said. "They just have to join the national. Norway's a long ways from here. We'll straighten it out. They're good guys. We just can't afford to have guys who aren't Boozefighters running around with our badge on. If they get in trouble, it reflects on us. We try to keep our image clean."

A passing Harley Electra Glide backfired loudly, and Spotts clutched his chest. "I'm on heart medication already," he said. "I don't need that."

*   *   *

LATER, I wondered what nutritional advice Spotts might have received from his doctors, given that the staples of a rally diet are corn dogs, nachos, funnel cakes, Polish sausages, onion rings, and beer. That, at any rate, was what sustained me as I waited for a bloody biker battle to break out. In the absence of hand-to-hand combat, I decided that the prudent journalistic strategy was to studiously witness, and thus be in a position to capitalize on the dramatic potential of, the tattoo contest, the beauty pageant, the arm-wrestling tournament, and the "bike games," which would feature such tests of skill as the weenie bite — in which teams made up of a male biker and his female rider pass through a wood-frame portal from which a thickly mustarded hot dog dangles vertically, at eye level, on a string. (Big trophy to whoever — no hands allowed — snatches the biggest bite with her teeth.) "At other rallies, they have outhouse races, where the gal sits on the can, which is on skids, while her partner pulls her with his bike," Ellen Brown told me. "But we don't go in for that sort of thing. No wet T-shirt contests, either. We favor family-oriented competitions."

At four in the afternoon on the Fourth of July, ten adventurous women and a modest crowd of witnesses and moral supporters gathered at Hollister's only bowling alley for a preliminary round of the Hollister Independence Rally pageant. Similar sessions had been held a few weeks earlier in two neighboring towns, yielding six finalists, and Niessa Bauder-Guaracha, a clothing designer, who had volunteered to be the pageant coordinator, was hoping to come up with four more. The proceedings were late getting started, so I went outside and surveyed the venders in the bowling alley parking lot. In one booth, a guy in his thirties with straw-colored hair and a handlebar mustache, accompanied by his eleven-year-old son, an up-and-comer who wore Oakley shades and a camouflage bandanna, was trying to decide which sew-on American flag to display on the back of his black leather vest. He was tempted to buy one that included the message "Try Burnin' This One . . . Asshole!"

"You definitely want the 'asshole' on there," the vender said.

"You're right. Matter of fact, make that a double 'asshole'!"

Back inside, the pageant candidates, who had been instructed to wear biker gear, were lining up to pose with a Harley-Davidson Softail Springer that was doing double duty: it was also the first prize in a raffle. "Biker gear" evidently was a synonym for "not very much." Bauder-Guaracha had told me that the judges would evaluate physical appearance, personality and poise, and marketability. It took me no time to spot a potential winner. She had long straight brunet hair and long blue fingernails, and she wore a leather unitard cut so that it gave maximum exposure to her long, tanned, fat-free legs. She also wore lace-up black vinyl and leather boots with three-inch platform soles and stiletto heels, as well as amber-tinted wraparounds. Her name, I sensed, was also Amber, but in fact it turned out to be Melissa Crowley.

"You seemed so relaxed posing on that bike," I told her. "What kind of motorcycle do you ride?"

"I'm not a biker," she said. "What's holding me back? I need a bike. Or somebody to drive it, maybe."

Before I had a chance to reconsider my deep misgivings about riding a hog, Melissa introduced me to her husband, Ryan, who explained that he'd never owned one himself, because his father, back in Boston, was a nurse who warned him, "Before you get a motorcycle, you've got to come to the hospital and see all the guys in traction." Melissa and Ryan, who were in their early thirties, had moved to California five years earlier; he worked in advertising, she was an assistant manager at a health club, and she'd entered the pageant more or less for the hell of it. The prize money — $1,000 for first place, and merchandise prizes to the first two runners-up — wasn't really on their minds, even though Ryan did mention, in passing, his mortgage. "I told Melissa two weeks ago, 'If you're gonna take this seriously, you're not doing it,'" he said.

"First place will go to some twenty-one-year-old. Second will go to the niece of someone on the committee. The best we can do is third."

It soon became apparent that Melissa would indeed be advancing. An official came over and handed her four patches bearing the logos of Miller Lite and Harley-Davidson, along with instructions to display them on her bathing suit. "I don't know how that's going to work," Ryan said. "There's more material there than there is on your bikini."

I WAS ACCURATELY forewarned that the crowd would peak on Saturday, and I had to park my car half a mile from the center of the action. This inconvenience generated an immediate dividend: as I walked past the headquarters of the San Benito County Sheriff's Department, Sheriff Hill happened to be standing out front. I introduced myself and he invited me inside. "We arrested five Hell's Angels last night," he said, as we sat in his office. "Two on illegal weapons charges — a knife and a loaded revolver. Another guy was flanking the cops while they were dealing with the first two guys, they told him to back off and he didn't, so he was arrested, too.

"Today, I'm hearing information that this is the day when something's supposed to happen — all completely unsubstantiated, but I've got a number of people chasing that down. And you've got these one-percenters out there surveilling and countersurveilling each other. That creates a tremendous amount of tension. The Angels are barely paying attention to the police, because we're not the big threat. They're actively looking for something downtown. You see that look. There's all this posturing. It's a big dance being choreographed by all the one-percenters."

Half an hour later, on San Benito Street, caught in a crowd that reminded me of Rockefeller Center during Christmas tree–gazing time, I met three Angels from Merced, California. They seemed to be staring intently at the passing parade, so I decided to test Sheriff Hill's theory that they were doing surveillance. "I see you guys looking around," I said. "What are you looking for?"

"What are we lookin' at? Just lookin'."

"Looking for pussy. Check it out. This is the time of year to look, when they're not wearing much."

Around the corner, milling next to a booth that the Daly City chapter had rented for the weekend, was a contingent of about forty Angels — Budweiser-drinking, bear-hugging, NFL line-backer–size specimens. The Sonoma County chapter president wore what looked like clean, pressed Levi's, but there was no one whom I felt eager to introduce to my mother or to interrogate about the status of the war with the Mongols.

A block away, at the booth operated by the Devil Dolls Motor-cycle Club — adjacent to one stocked with Sonny Barger trade-mark merchandise — a woman named Mickey was pushing Devil Dolls pinup calendars. Barger was in town to promote his most recent book, *Ridin' High, Livin' Free*, Mickey said, and I could probably find him at the factory showroom of Corbin, a manufac-turer of motorcycle seats and accessories. She called him on her cell phone, and he agreed to speak with me.

It took me fifteen minutes to get there, for an interview that lasted about ninety seconds. Barger, who made his name in Oak-land but now lives near Phoenix, was seated behind a table piled with books, accompanied by comrades from the Cave Creek, Ari-zona, chapter. Before we got started, his cell phone rang and who-ever was calling immediately irritated him. "I'll tell you why we've got a problem," he was saying. "Because you keep fucking with me. And if you don't stop fucking with me it's gonna be a bigger problem." For someone whose speech was impeded by a hole in his throat — he lost his vocal cords to cancer twenty years ago — Barger articulated quite well. I wanted to discuss the Mongols, of course, and thought I'd ease into it by explaining that I felt that the media's general approach to the subject had been . . . I was go-ing to say "hysterical," but he beat me to the punch with "like vultures." I mentioned that I already owned a copy of *Ridin' High, Livin' Free* and was sorry that I'd left it in my hotel room. But it was too late; gravity had taken hold.

"I can see where you're coming from," Barger said. "The interview's over." His Cave Creek colleagues rose from their chairs to emphasize the point.

Recalling the closing pages of Hunter Thompson's classic *Hell's Angels* — specifically, the scene in which the hardworking journalist is suddenly set upon, severely beaten, and stomped — I figured why push it. Besides, I'd already had a brush with possible bodily harm that morning, during breakfast in my hotel. I had approached the coffee urn at the same moment as a burly, gray-bearded biker with a long ponytail. "Go ahead," I said, deferentially.

"Goathead!" he said. "Why you callin' me Goathead?"

"No. I said, 'Go ahead.'"

"I thought I heard 'Goathead.'"

"Believe me, I wouldn't call you Goathead," I assured him. Then, when his back was turned, I heard myself whisper, "But somebody else might."

MY PRINTED SCHEDULE promised a Sunday-morning service at the Hollister United Methodist Church, led by members of the evangelical Christian Motorcycle Association. Walking to the church, I heard birds chirping in the magnolias, an experience that hadn't been available for days. I wandered past the spot where the day before I'd witnessed the large gathering of Hell's Angels and saw that during the night they had dismantled their booth. Wisely, the Mongols had been no-shows, and it now seemed clear that the threat of violence, however real it had been, had passed.

As the day progressed, I experienced an odd sensation of community (not to be mistaken for a sense of belonging). I'd hung around long enough for certain faces to become familiar, certain vectors to intersect. In church, I recognized Bobby Bible (né Robert Engel, a.k.a. Bobby Biblestein), a refinery worker from Los Angeles whom I'd seen a couple of days earlier at the tattoo contest, where he was showing off a crucifix on his chest. After the service, I discovered that we had had comparable face time with Sonny Barger. Bible had been in Laughlin and had run across Barger a few hours before the casino shoot-out.

"I saw him at the Flamingo Hotel," he said. "Sonny was signing books. So I felt led by the Holy Spirit to go up to him. I leaned over the table, looked him right in the eye. I said, 'Sonny, I'm gonna ask you one question. Do you believe in Jesus Christ as your personal savior?' He said, 'No, I don't.' Not angrily, just matter-of-factly. I said, 'Sonny, you know, you're gonna go to Hell when you die. Okay?' He looked back at me with that biker look, that get-out-of-my-face you're-pissing-me-off look. So I picked up on that right away. All of his buddies were standing there. And I exited left."

The previous afternoon, at the Hollister Independence Rally pageant finals, caught in a crush of several hundred hooting and hollering guys (and a much smaller number of gals, none of whom appeared to be exercising absolute free will), I found myself standing next to Dallas Roberts from San Diego. I'd also met Roberts at the tattoo contest, where he won first prize in the "flaming" category. He had red hair under a red bandanna, a sunburned face, and a few days of stubble, and he wore a T-shirt promoting a microbrew called Arrogant Bastard Ale, which he'd got Sonny Barger to autograph during a visit to the Corbin showroom. The pageant itself was a repudiation of my powers of prognostication; Melissa Crowley finished out of the money. The winner, as Ryan Crowley had predicted, was a twenty-one-year-old blond surfer-girl type named Tara Rice. During Tara's first stroll down the runway, I realized I'd seen her several times already — at the California Glamour Girls booth, where, for nine or twelve or fifteen dollars a pop, anyone could pose for a Polaroid portrait with one or two or three young women wearing blossom-print pink bikinis and fixed smiles.

I even had a return engagement of sorts with Goathead. I didn't feel like sticking around for all the bike games, but I did catch the weenie bite, where the winners were an oddly matched couple named Sandy Williams and Russ Wood. Sandy was a slender grandmother who told me she'd already started training her two-year-old granddaughter for the weenie bite. Russ, who was about the size of a telephone booth, had such masterly control of his Harley-Davidson Softail that this was his and Sandy's fourth weenie-bite first place in the past three years, one of forty trophies that they'd collected overall. Clearly, justice had been served — though not the weenies themselves; those got spit out — and I knew that it was time to rev up my Chevy Malibu and bid Hollister farewell. I drove out of town, rolling past the apricot and apple orchards for a couple of miles, until I came to a stop sign at an intersection. Four motorcyclists pulled up next to me, and the leader of the pack, hulking over his Harley Dyna Low Rider, was Goathead himself. I thought about giving him a fellow biker's wave, but that wouldn't have been appropriate. I also considered giving him the finger, just to keep things interesting. But I nodded and smiled instead, and, gratifyingly, Goathead did the same. Then we both headed west, into the sunset, or some other destination.

ACKNOWLEDGMENTS

After thirty years at *The New Yorker*, I'm still astonished by the devotion to excellence of the collective enterprise. In a multitude of ways, the following colleagues helped to make the stories in this book more readable: David Remnick, Bill Buford, Daniel Zalewski, Dorothy Wickenden, Cressida Leyshon, Ann Goldstein, Elizabeth Pearson-Griffiths, Mary Norris, Carol Anderson, Lauren Porcaro, Field Maloney, Carin Besser, Peter Canby, Anne String-field, Nandi Rodrigo, Dan Kaufman, Ben McGrath, Sylvia Sellers-Garcia, Julie Tate, Jacob Lewis, Amy Davidson, and Bruce Diones.

Sylvia Plachy took the photographs that accompanied most of my "U.S. Journal" dispatches when they appeared in *The New Yorker*. Besides being a consistently cheerful traveling companion, she routinely alerted me to details I might have overlooked.

My thanks to Jane Rosenman and Erin Edmison of Houghton Mifflin. (And to Pat Strachan, who invited me to Houghton Mifflin in the first place.)

For wise counsel: Andrew Wylie and Jeff Posternak.

For obvious reasons, my sons Jeb, Reid, Timothy, and Paul.

Caroline Mailhot: *Pourquoi? Parce que.*

To Dr. Stephen Paget, my gratitude and admiration — likewise to my lifelong pal, Jeffrey Brown, who, conveniently, also happens to be a remarkably good doctor.